What should students have learnt in art by the end of secondary school?

Aspects of this book have been put together during several evenings of discussion, between some of the contributing PGCE Art & Design students, Freelands Foundation's Creative Director, the designer, and Art & Design tutors at UCL Institute of Education.

The discussions, often centering around the possibilities and difficulties of being an art practitioner teaching in a secondary school, began with the group repeating a survey originally conducted by French pedagogue Célestin Freinet in the 1950s.

In one of the few books of Freinet's writing that has been translated into English, there is a section listing the things that parents thought their children should have learnt by the time they had finished their schooling.

Freinet had been injured in WWI and couldn't use the accepted teaching approach of the time: 'standing in front of the class all day, shouting orders and dictating lessons'. This led him to develop other learning activities based around the child as author, eventually setting up his own schools in rural France.

His techniques included bringing local craftspeople into the school, to show the pupils skills he could not; pupils learning how to put together and print their own newsletters, through which they could correspond with other schools; displaying and reviewing each other's schoolwork, and so on. While the Freinet list includes expected academic targets, relating to numeracy and literacy, it also stresses their relation to other varied general skills, helpful for the students' lives ahead:

> 'The ability to plan a long trip, grease a bicycle, apply splints to a broken limb, understand a pay slip, ask for information without feeling shy, to not be slave to tradition, to understand the cinema, to know how much an item costs, a knowledge of the history of workers struggles, a willingness to help, and an acceptance of responsibility'.

From an emerging art teacher's – rather than parent's – perspective, our group recreated this list. We then tried to explore how we could practically bring some of these values into our classrooms (the diagrams on following pages), challenging what is deemed important to learn, teach, and be taught.

The contributors to this publication are at the beginning of their careers as teachers of art. They are on the verge of something, a transitional moment. They are, quite literally, on the brink of their careers. But 'brink' also feels as though it accurately describes where we are in art education in the United Kingdom at this moment in time: Teetering on the edge of a cliff.

1   To explain what art is, and what it isn't (for them, and for society?)

2   To debate, politely and respectfully, peer's opinions

3   How advertising hoardings on private housing developments are made

4   The ability to read visual images and discuss them

5   To use basic Photoshop and other editing programs

6   What bricks are good for

7   The confidence to try working with new materials

8   How to dress with characteristics, showing personality

9   To be able to determine whether a strike or riot might be a more effective response to a disliked situation

10   How to draw a nose

11   To refuse to conform, challenge orthodoxies

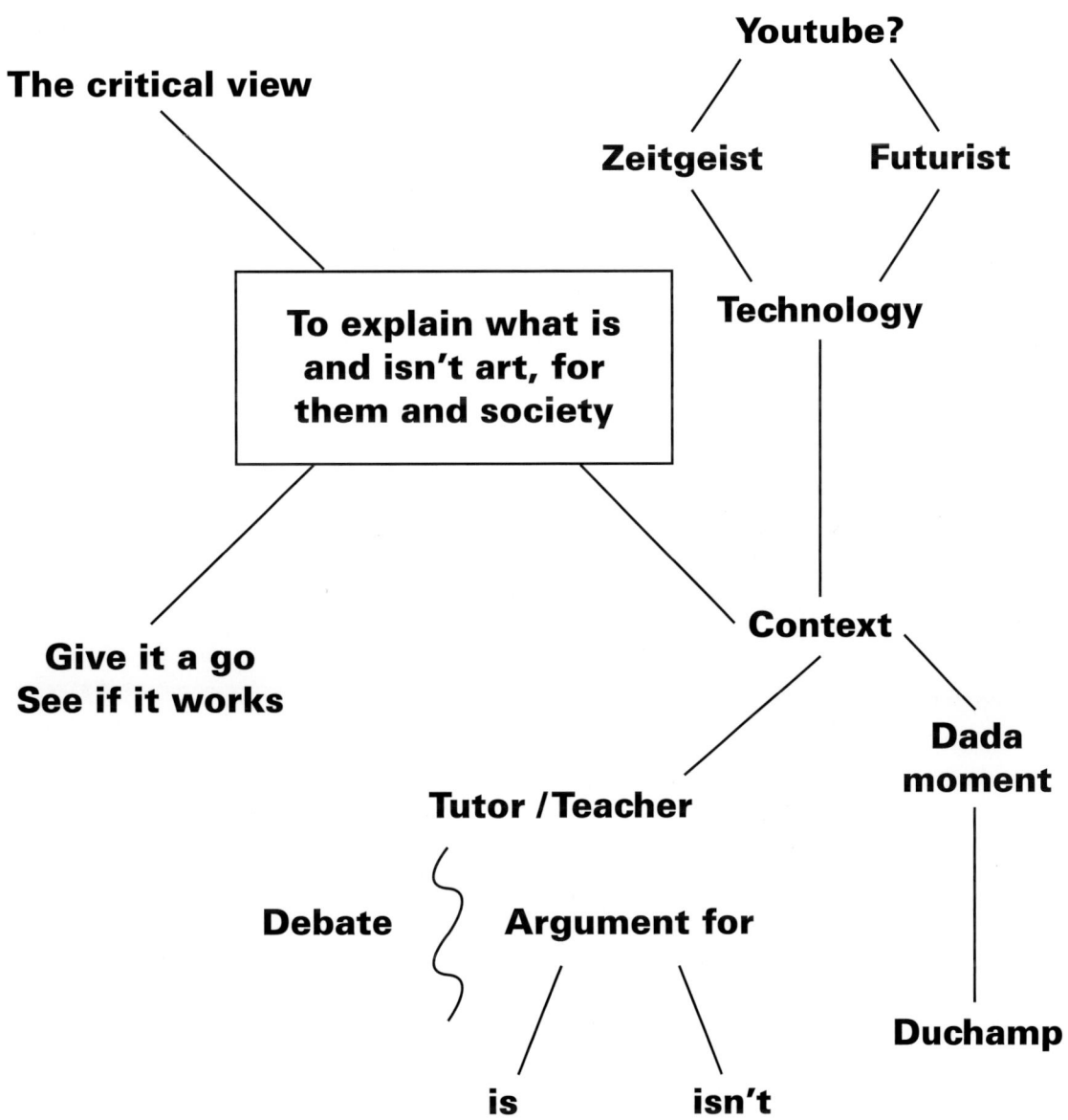

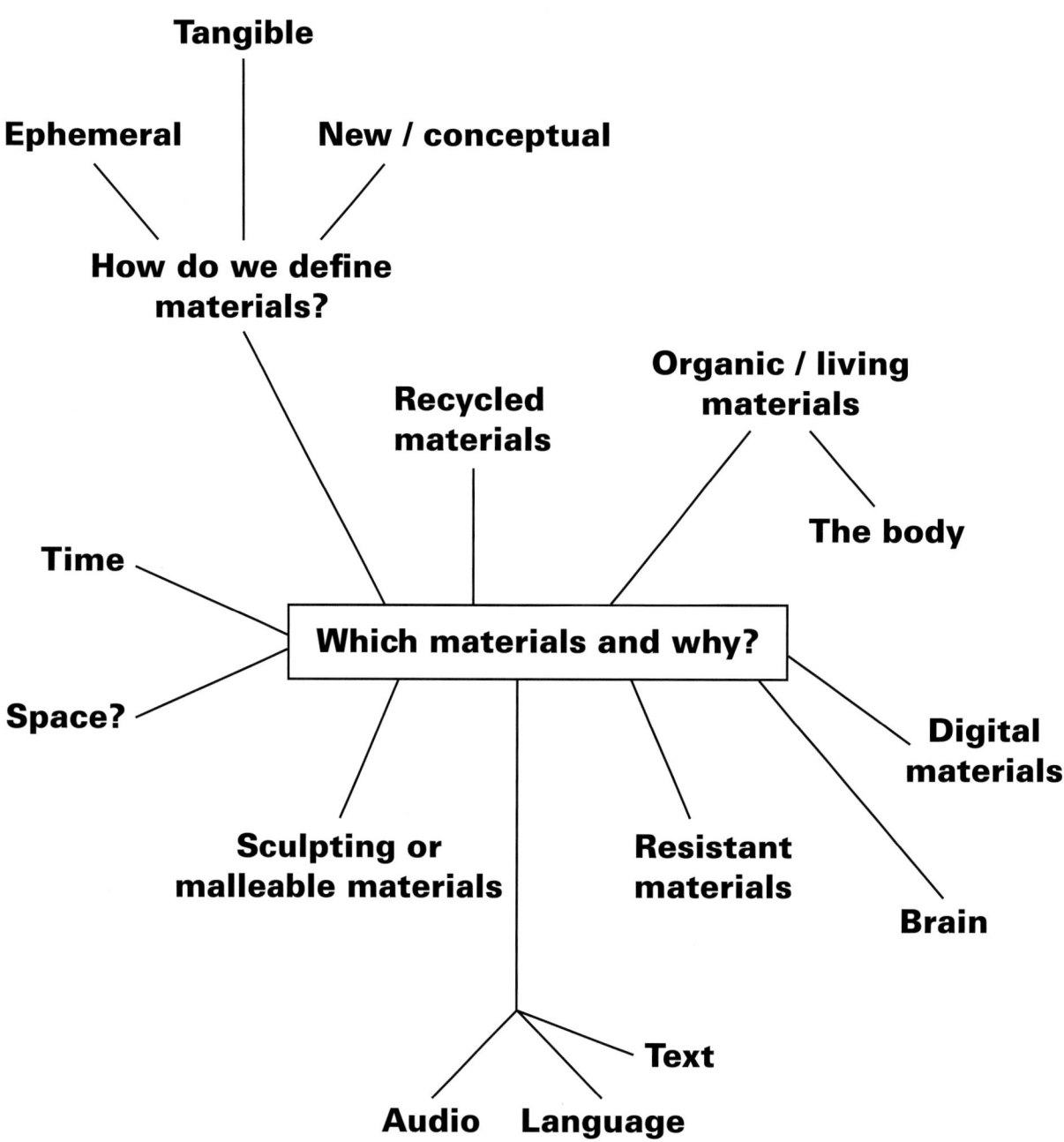

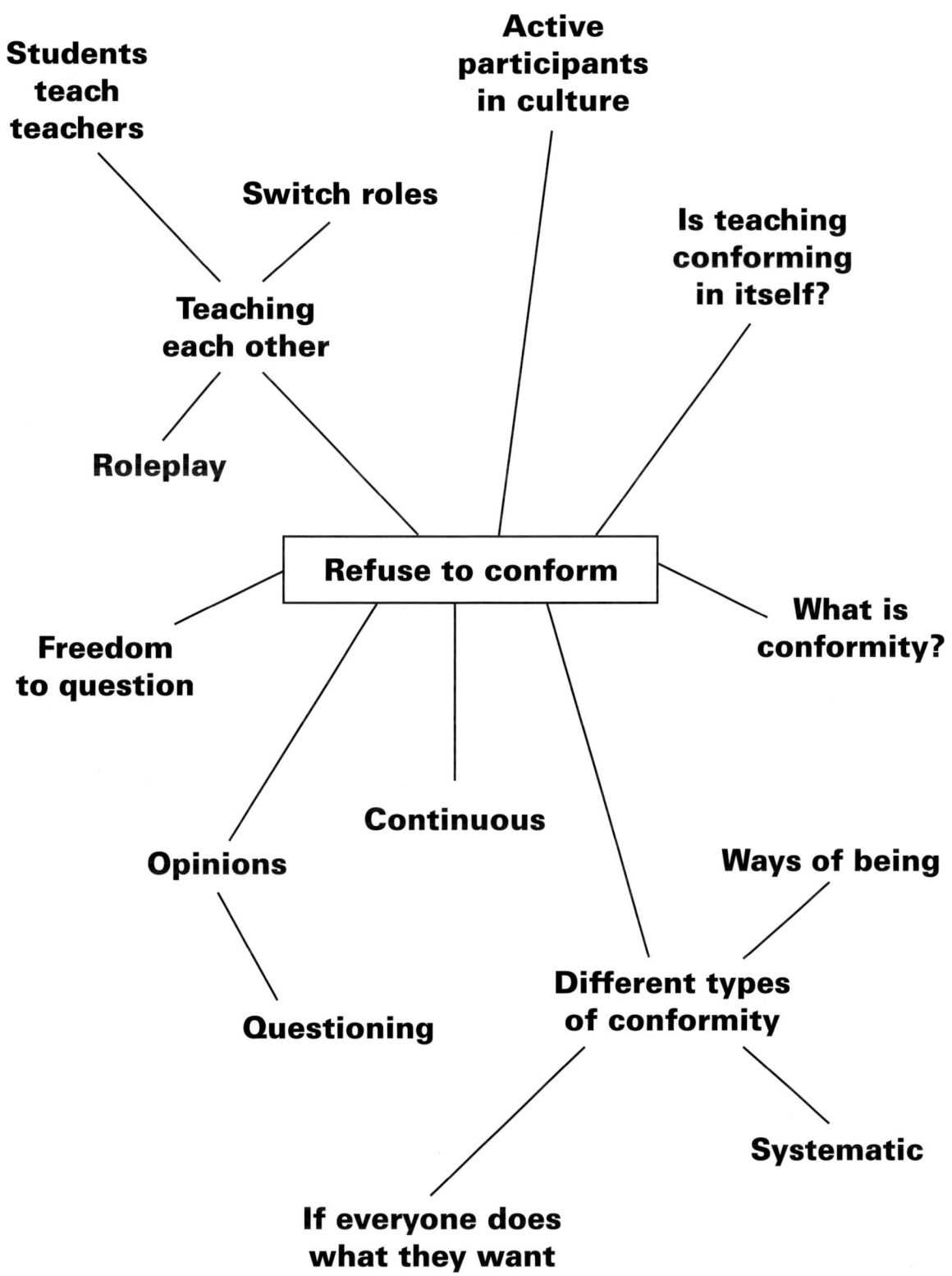

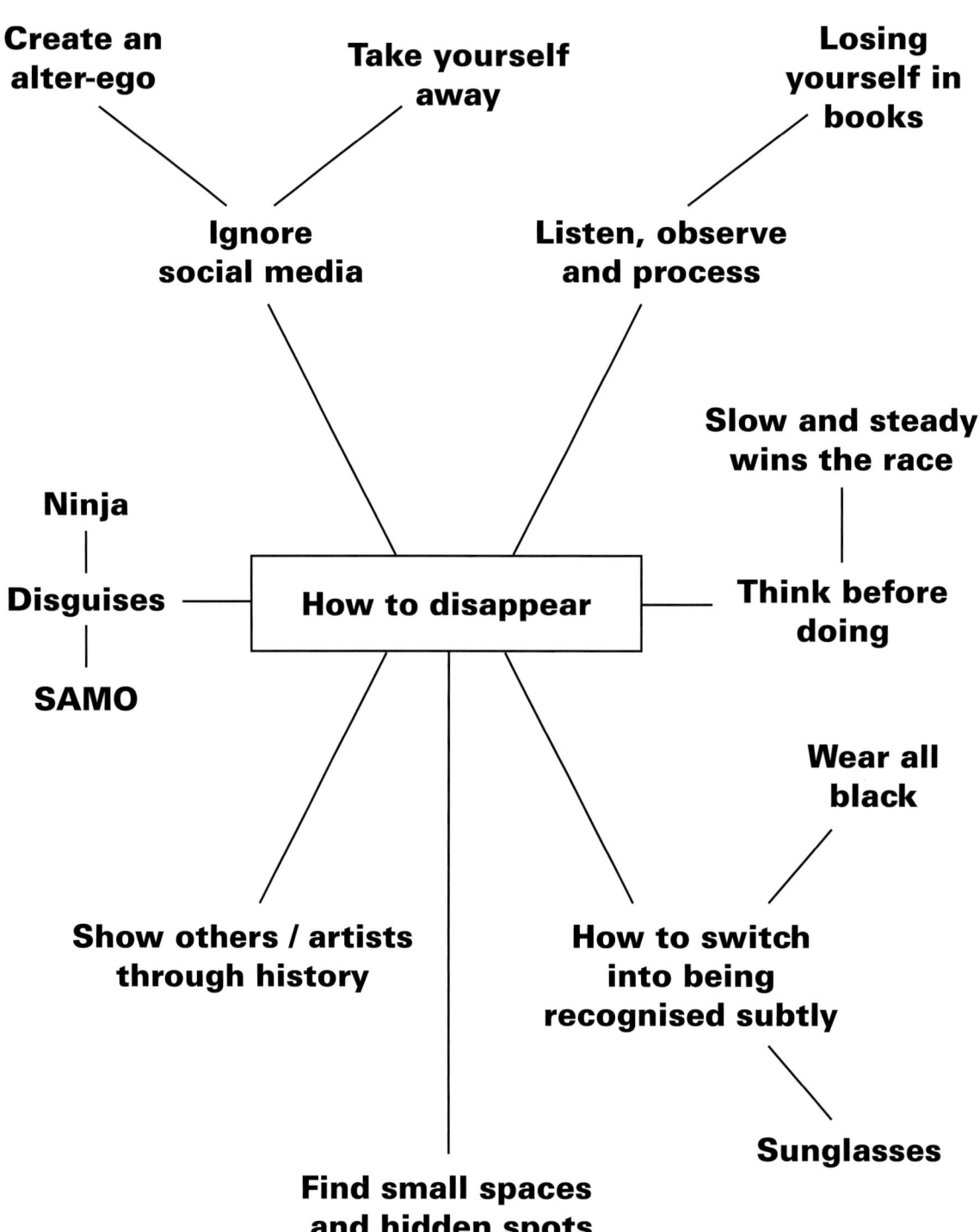

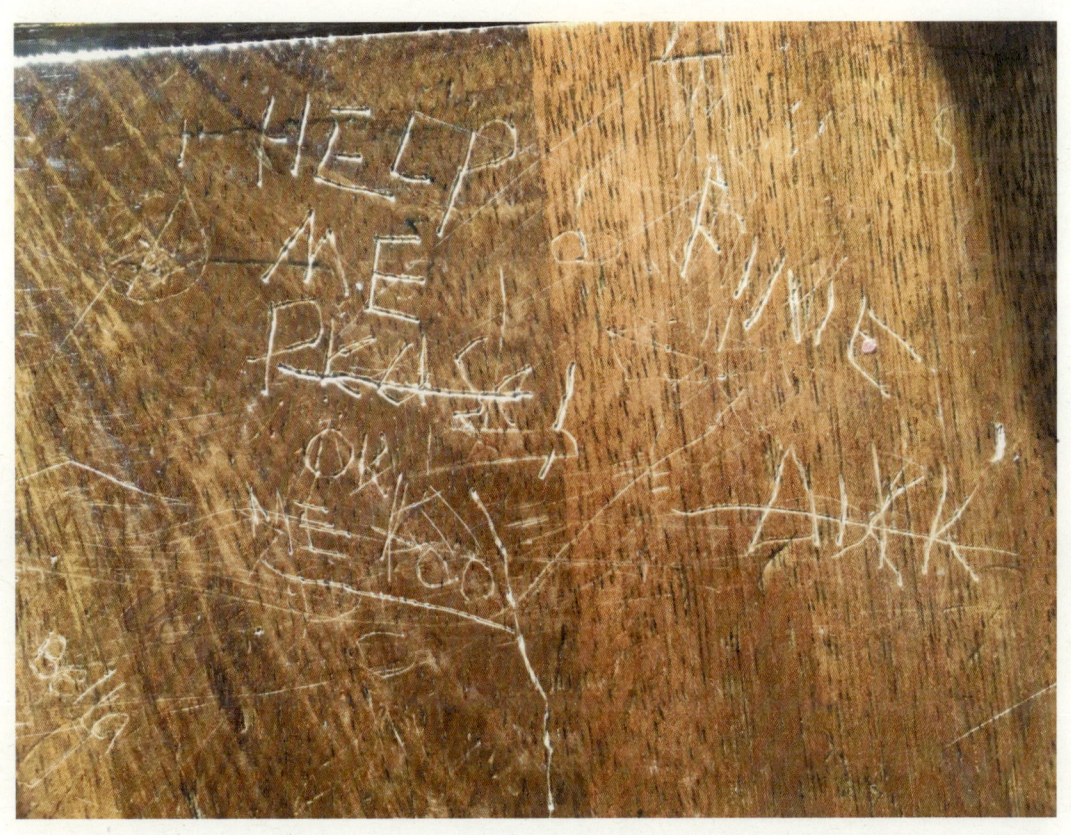

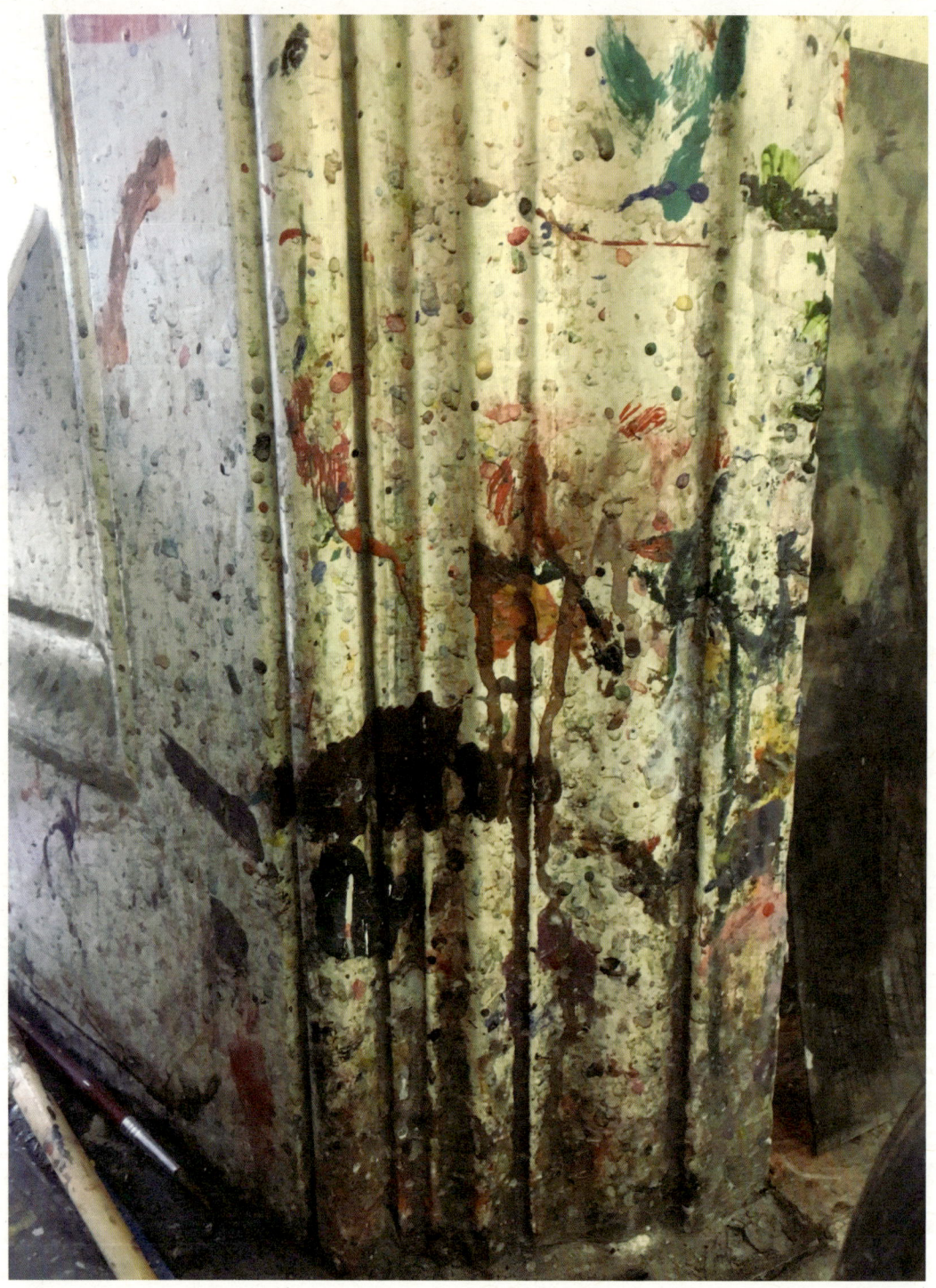

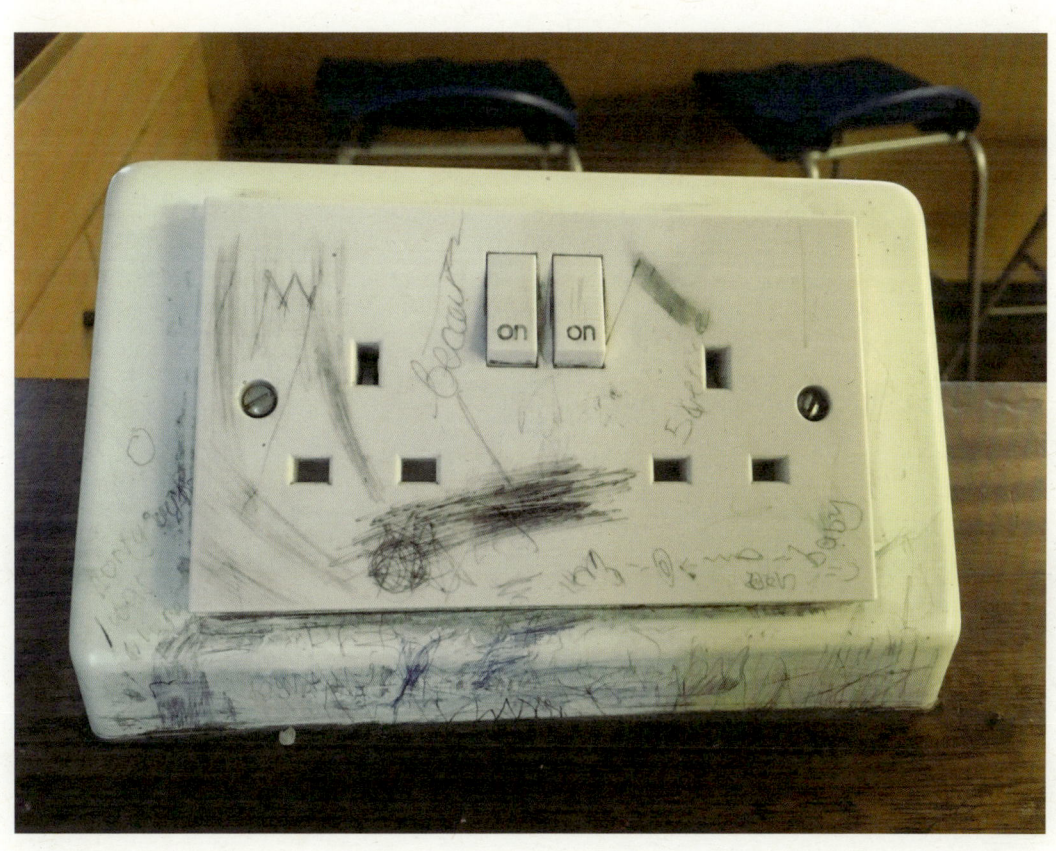

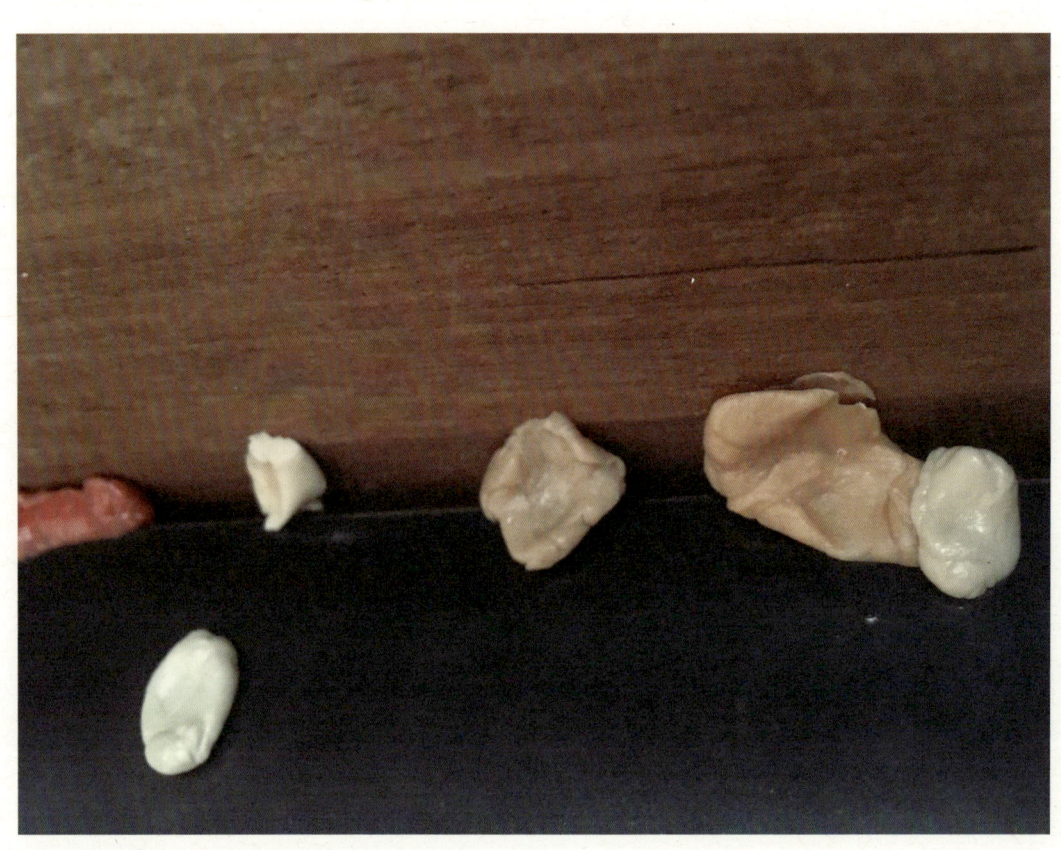

4

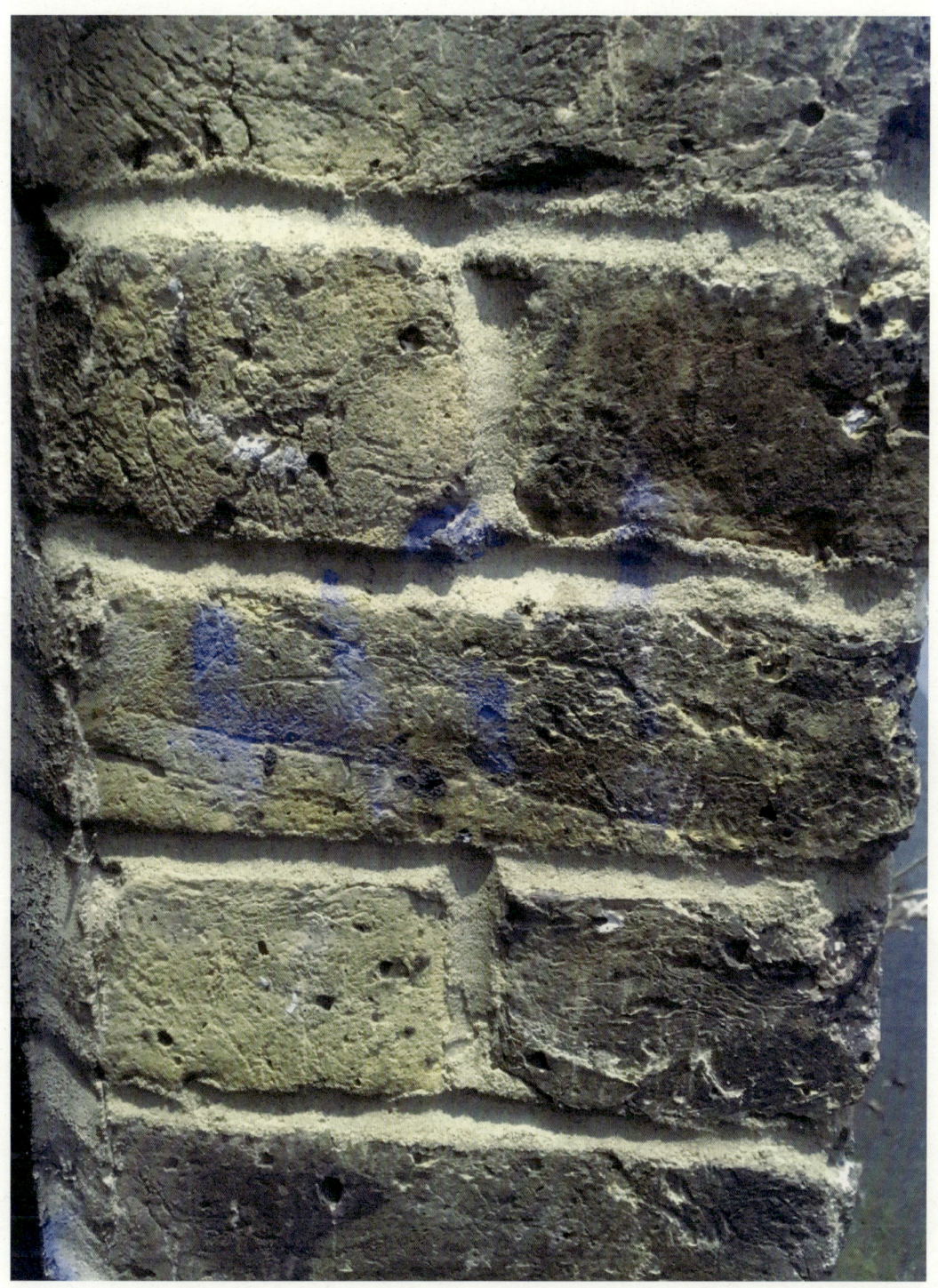

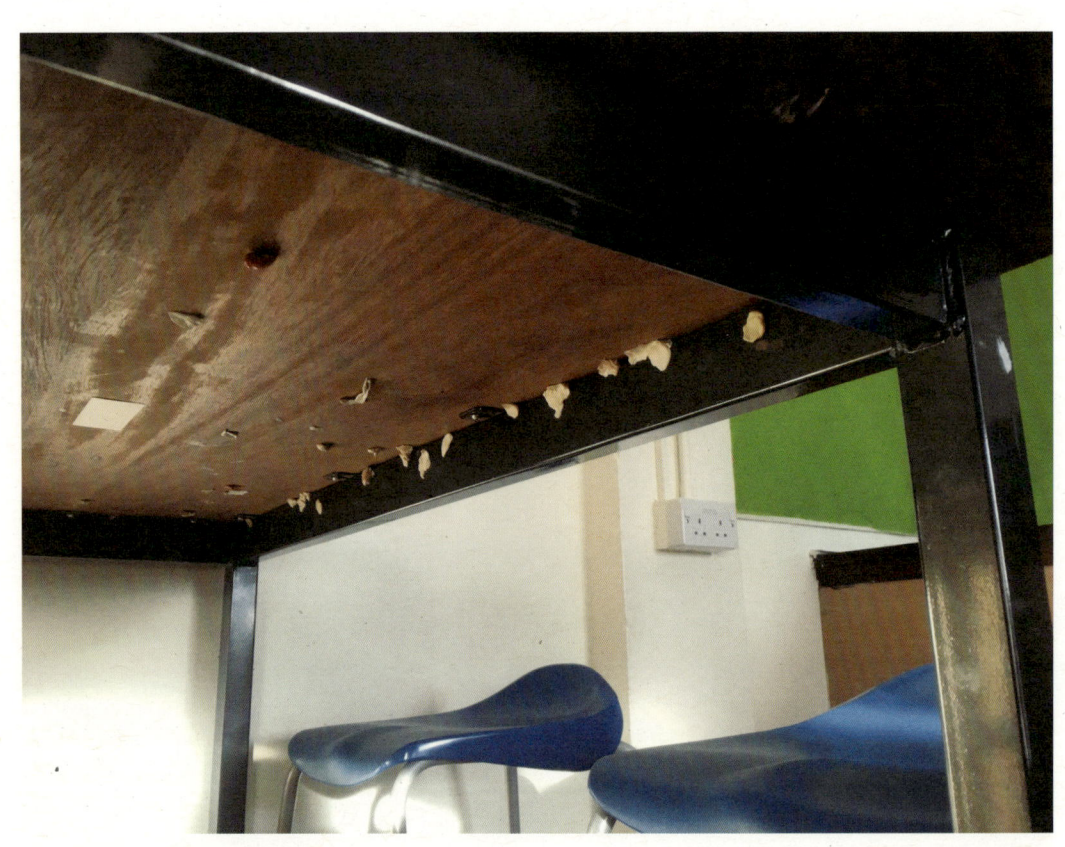

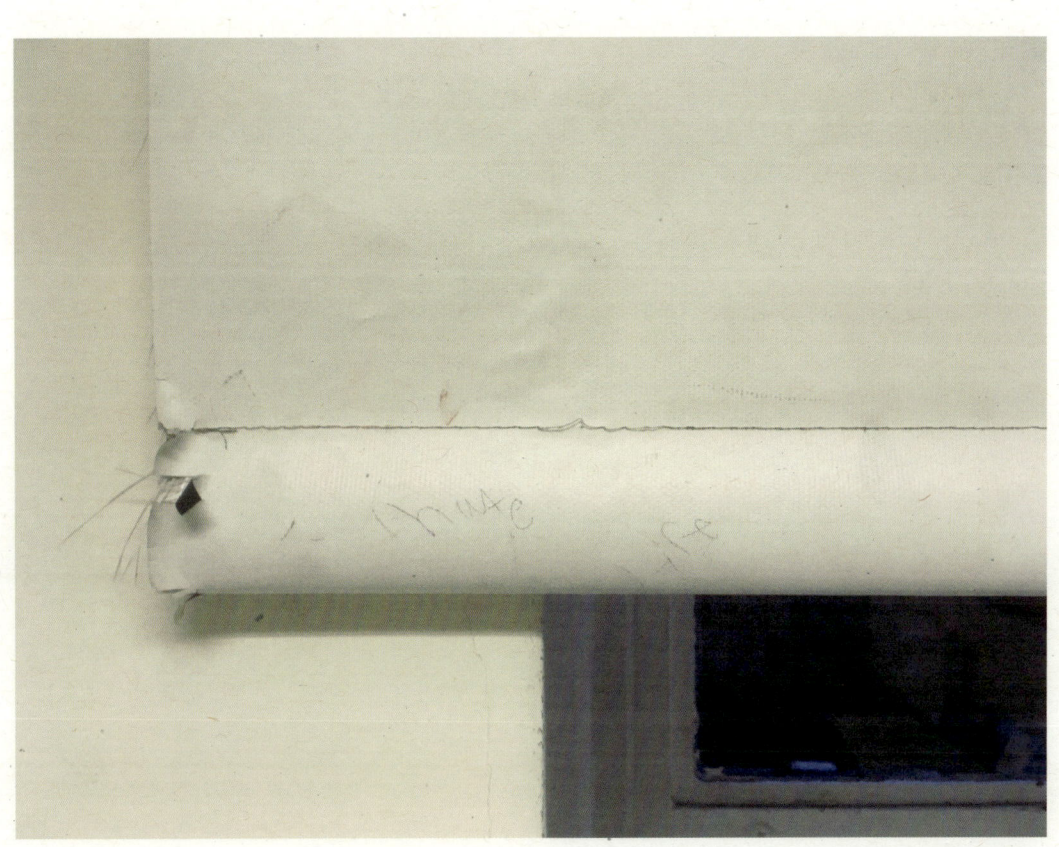

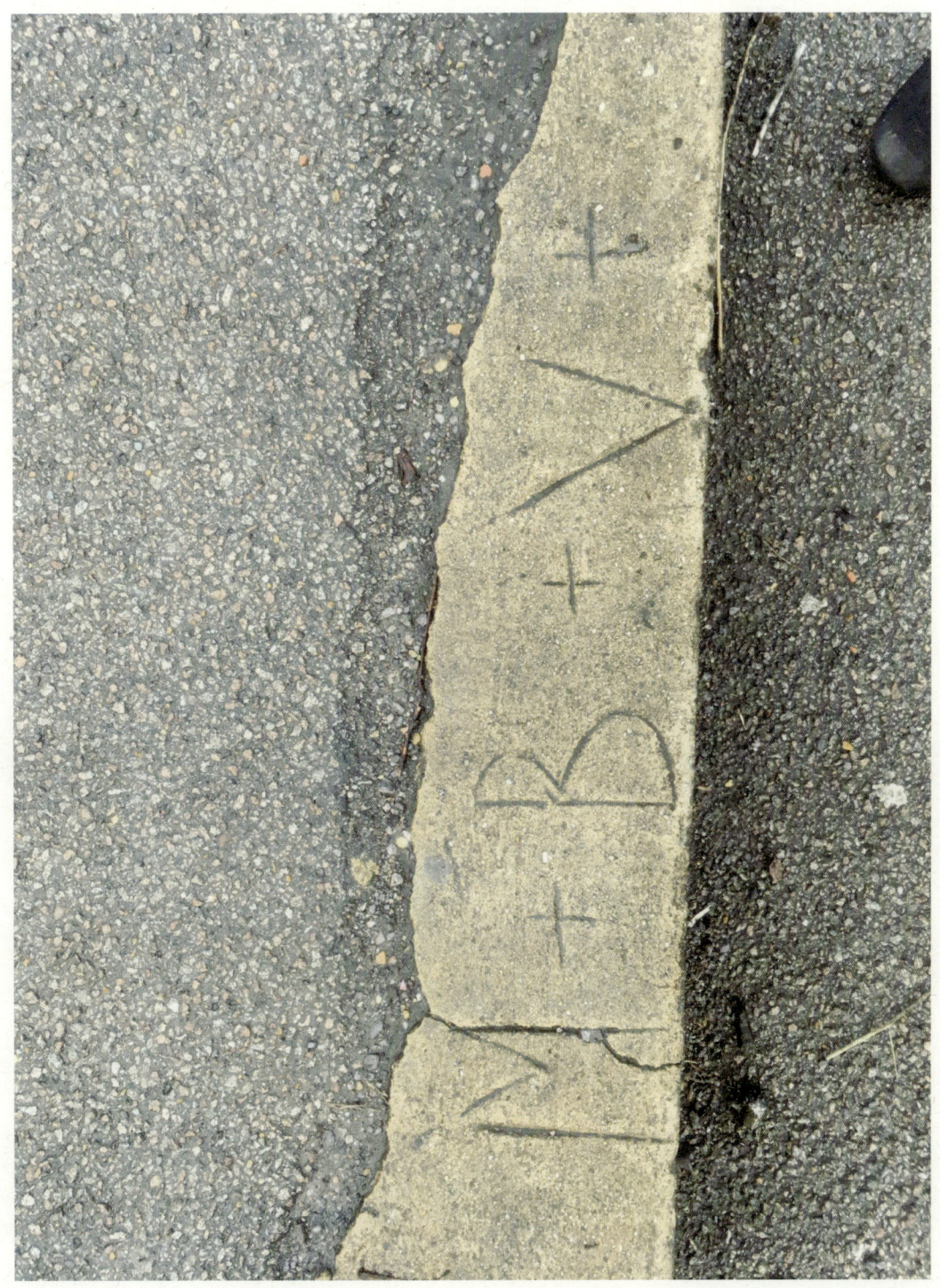

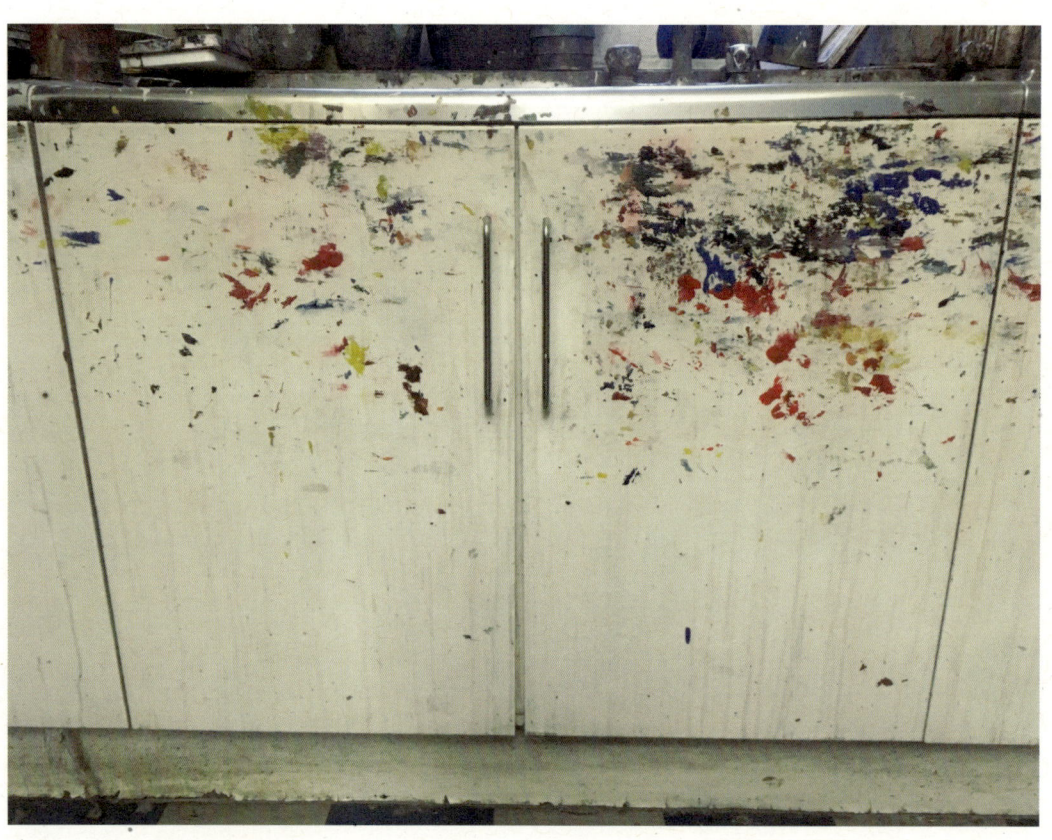

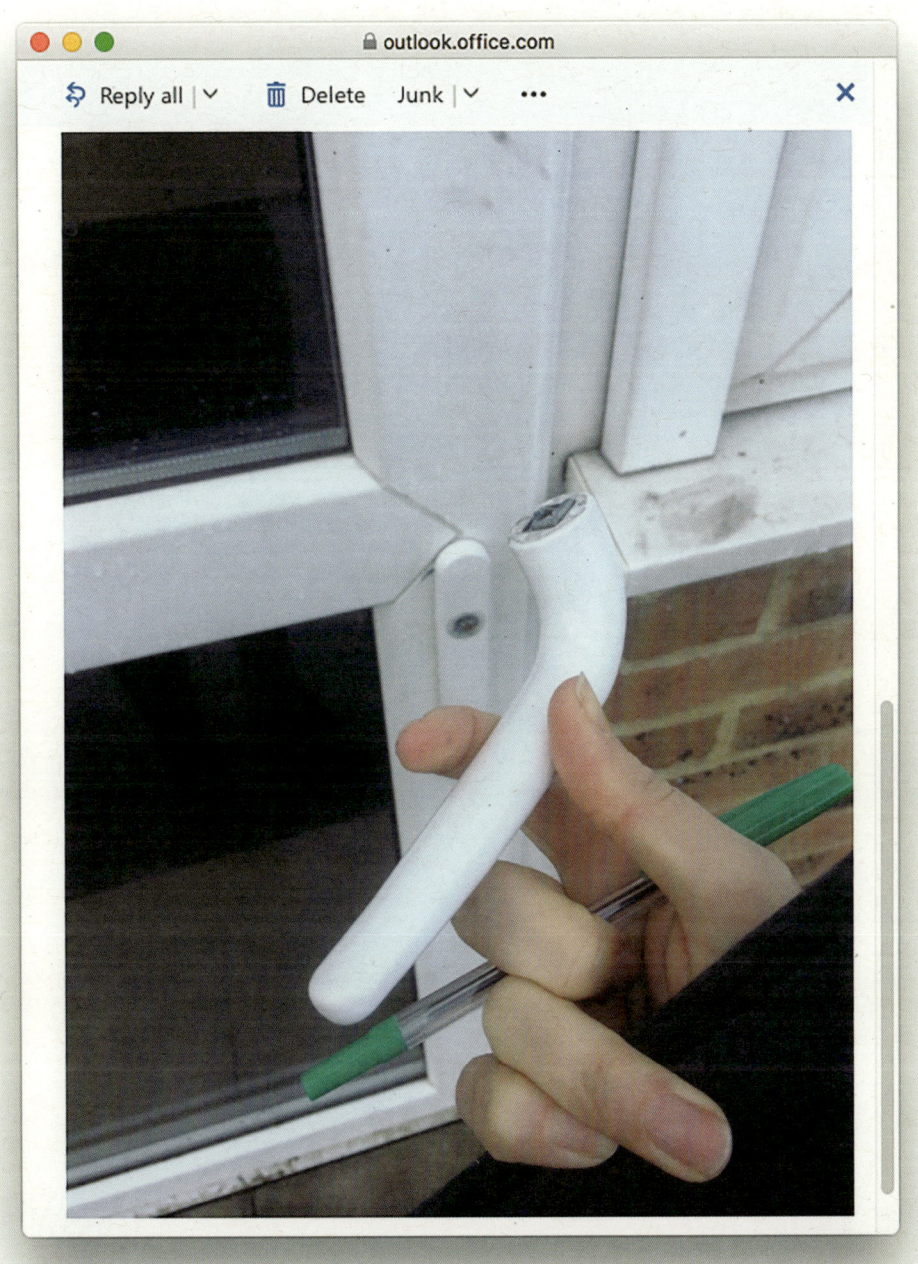

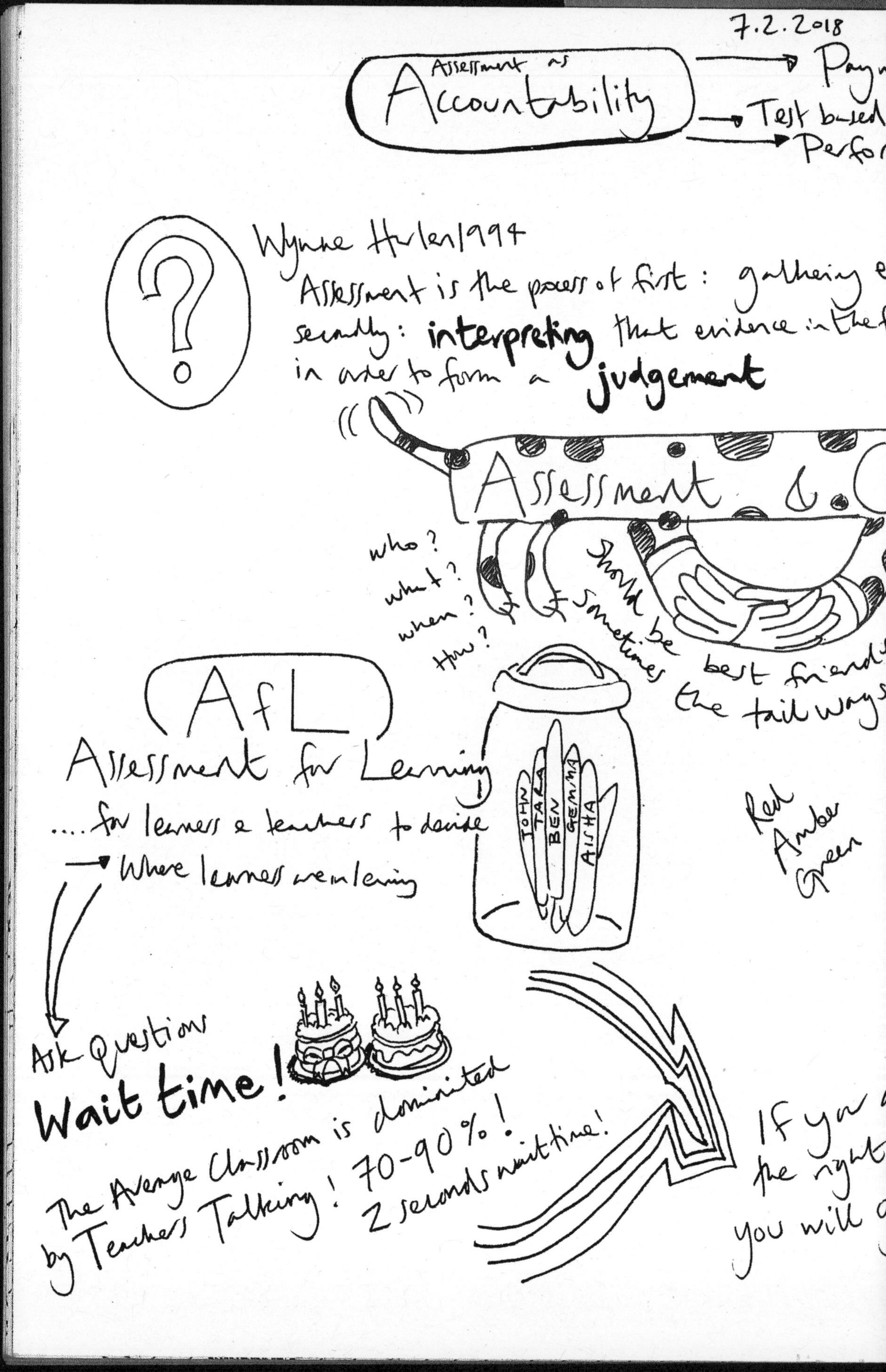

7.2.2018

Assessment as
Accountability

→ Pay...
→ Test based
→ Perfo...

?

Wynne Harlen 1994
Assessment is the process of first: gathering e...
secondly: **interpreting** that evidence in the...
in order to form a **judgement**

Assessment & ...

who?
what?
when?
how?

Should be
sometimes best friend...
the tail wags...

AfL

Assessment for Learning
.... for learners & teachers to decide
→ Where learners are in learning

John
Tara
Ben
Gemma
Aisha

Red
Amber
Green

Ask Questions
Wait time!
The Average Classroom is dominated
by Teachers Talking! 70-90%!
2 seconds wait time!

If you...
the right...
you will...

Results (not direct in UK but Academy / Free Schools / Independent
stability   here is indirect payment
Tables

2

some defined criteria

Competence
Control   Competition
                Content

How are students understand what the **success criteria** are

be crystal clear!

What they're learning & what they're doing!

less you've got the big picture in mind

Having the LO on the board is it necessary!!

negotiation
Exemplus
Modelling
Guided Practice

Feedback

Strategies

what the student aid well
How they could do it better

link with in explain
success criteria

The answer is 20!
Came up with
20 questions...

the task & not the learner
"good job" not "good boy"

Spelling & Grammar!
do it subtley
5 mads SPAG GCSE

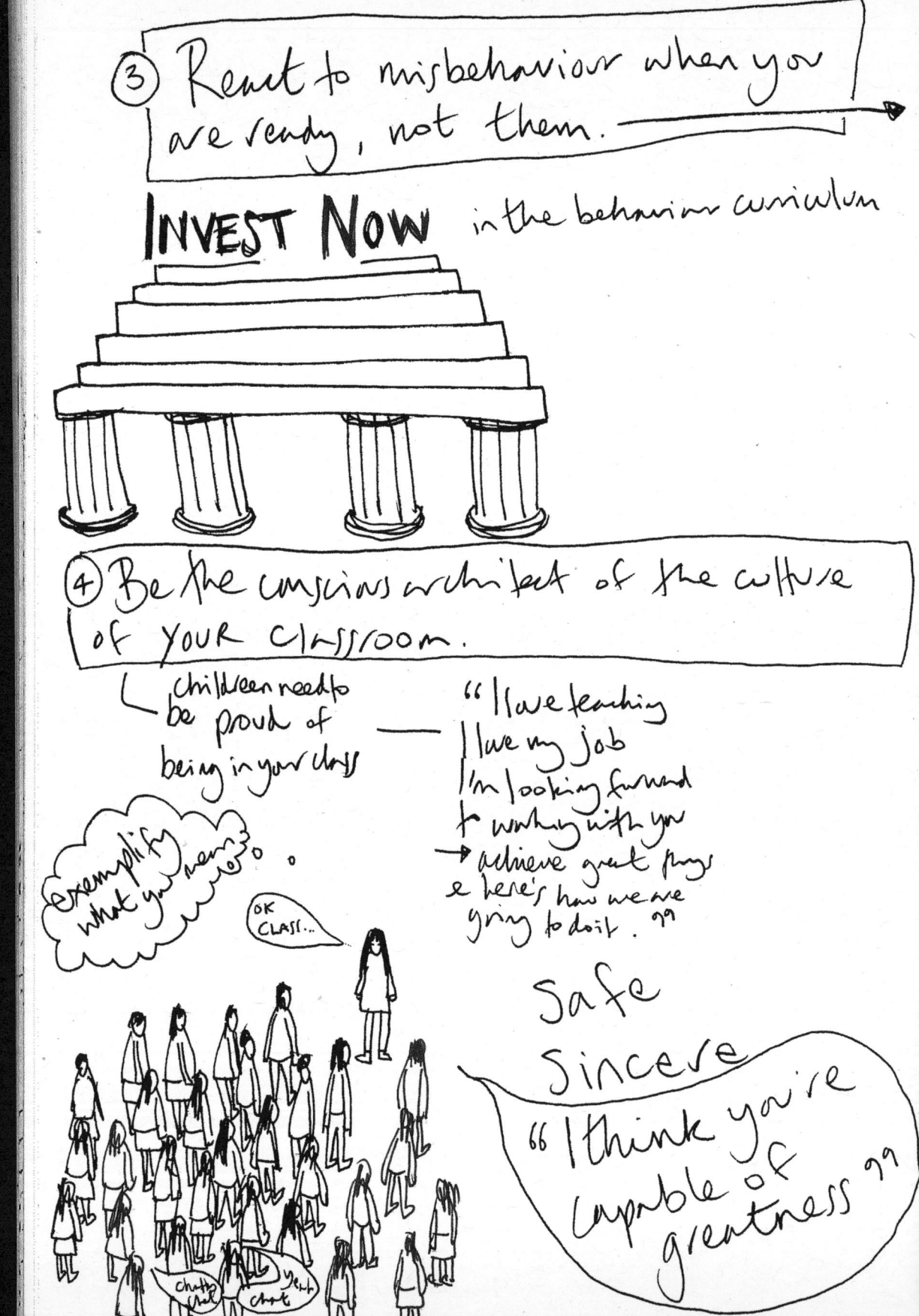

③ React to misbehaviour when you are ready, not them. ⟶

INVEST NOW in the behaviour curriculum

④ Be the conscious architect of the culture of your classroom.

children need to be proud of being in your class —

exemplify what you mean...

OK CLASS...

" I love teaching
I love my job
I'm looking forward
to working with you
→ achieve great things
& here's how we are
going to do it. "

Safe
Sincere
" I think you're
capable of
greatness "

chatty chat / yeah chat

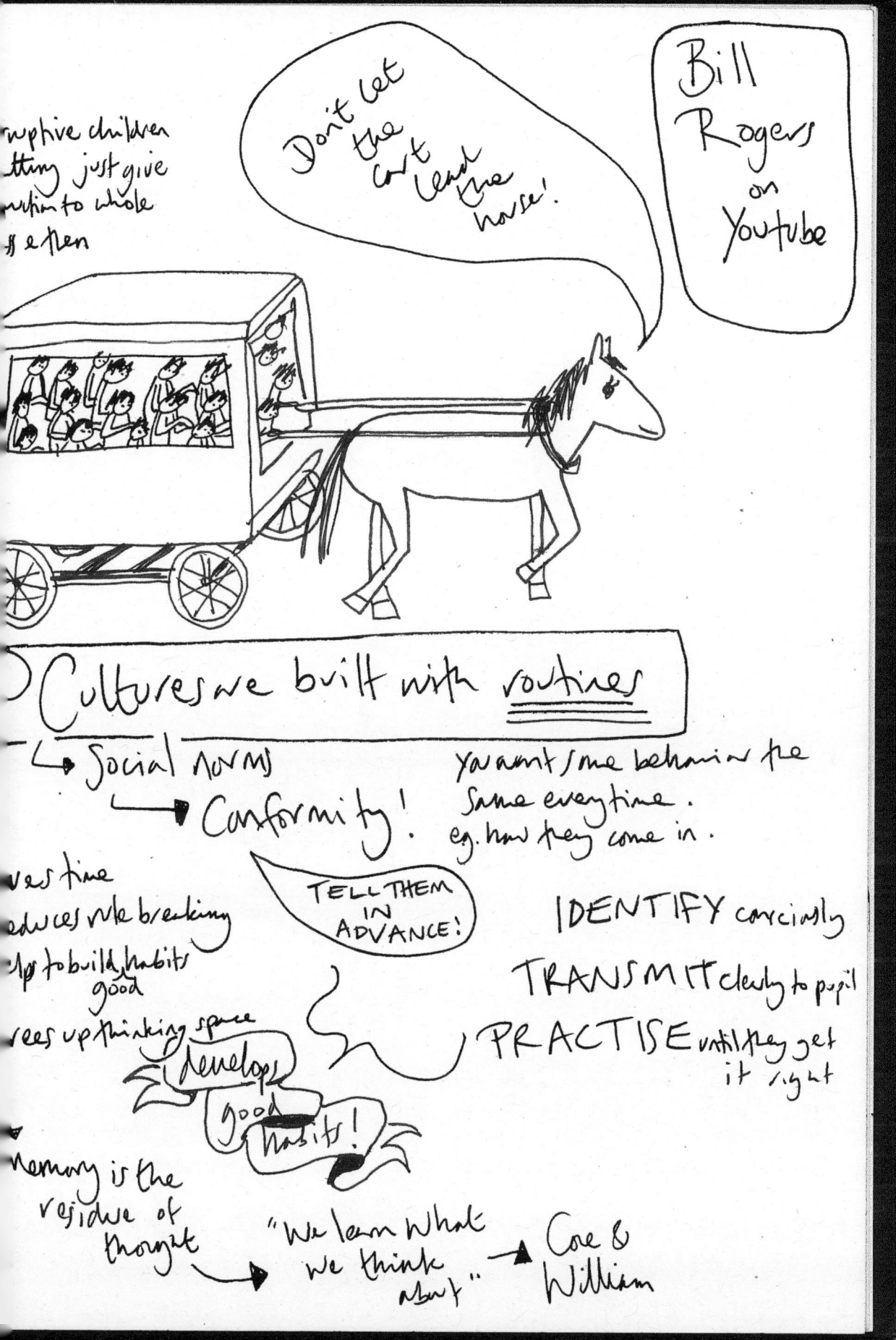

...ptive children ...tting just give ...ution to whole ...e then

Don't let the cart lead the horse!

Bill Rogers on Youtube

Culture is built with routines

→ Social norms
→ Conformity!

You want some behaviour the same everytime. e.g. how they come in.

TELL THEM IN ADVANCE!

IDENTIFY conciously
TRANSMIT clearly to pupil
PRACTISE until they get it right

...ves time
...educes rule breaking
...lp to build habits good
...rees up thinking space

develops good habits!

Memory is the residue of thought → "We learn what we think about" → Coe & William

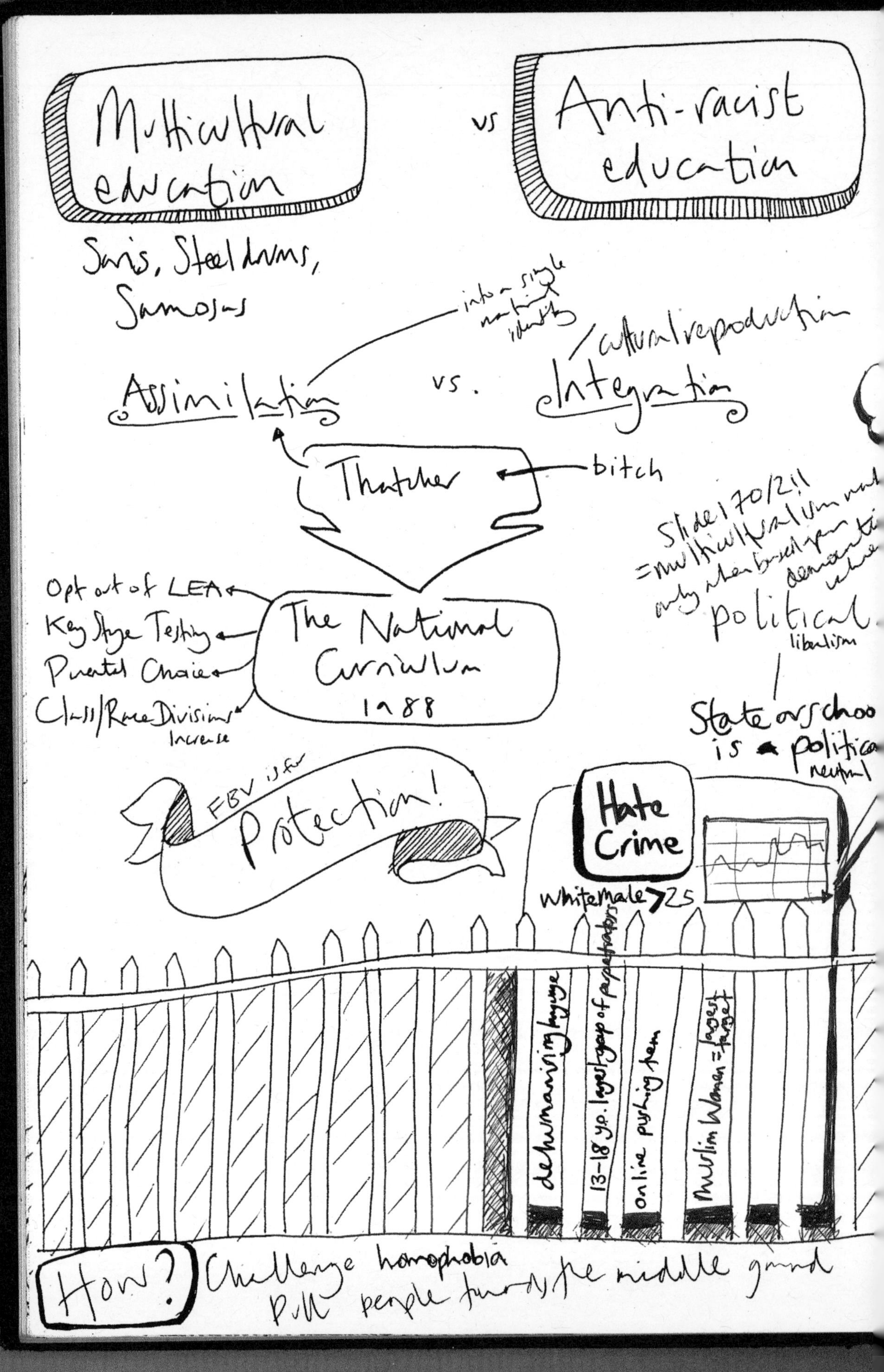

Multicultural education   vs   Anti-racist education

Saris, Steel drums, Samosas

Assimilation → into a single national identity

vs.

Integration / cultural reproduction

Thatcher ← bitch

Slide 170/211
= multiculturalism only when based upon democratic values political liberalism

Opt out of LEA →
Key Stage Testing →
Parental Choice →
Class/Race Divisions Increase →

The National Curriculum 1988

State or school is a political neutral

FBV is for Protection!

Hate Crime

white male >25

[graph]

dehumanising language

13-18 y.o. largest gap of perpetrators reported

online pushing them

Muslim Woman = largest target

How? Challenge homophobia Pull people toward the middle ground

Paulo Friere

There's no such thing as a neutral education process. Education either functions as an instrument which is used to facilitate the integration of the younger generation into the logic of the present system and bring about conformity to it

OR it becomes the practice of freedom - the means by which men and women deal critically and creatively with reality & discover how to participate in the transformation of their world 1971

Burbules et al 2005
multiculturalism only works if you have shared values grounded in rule of law

liberalism

Comprehensive liberalism
School holds that individual liberalism is a good thing

the state needs to protect the child's right to an open future. Feinberg places emphasis on a liberal, open society

UCL Careers
application advice appointment
individualised interview feedback & support

while working class

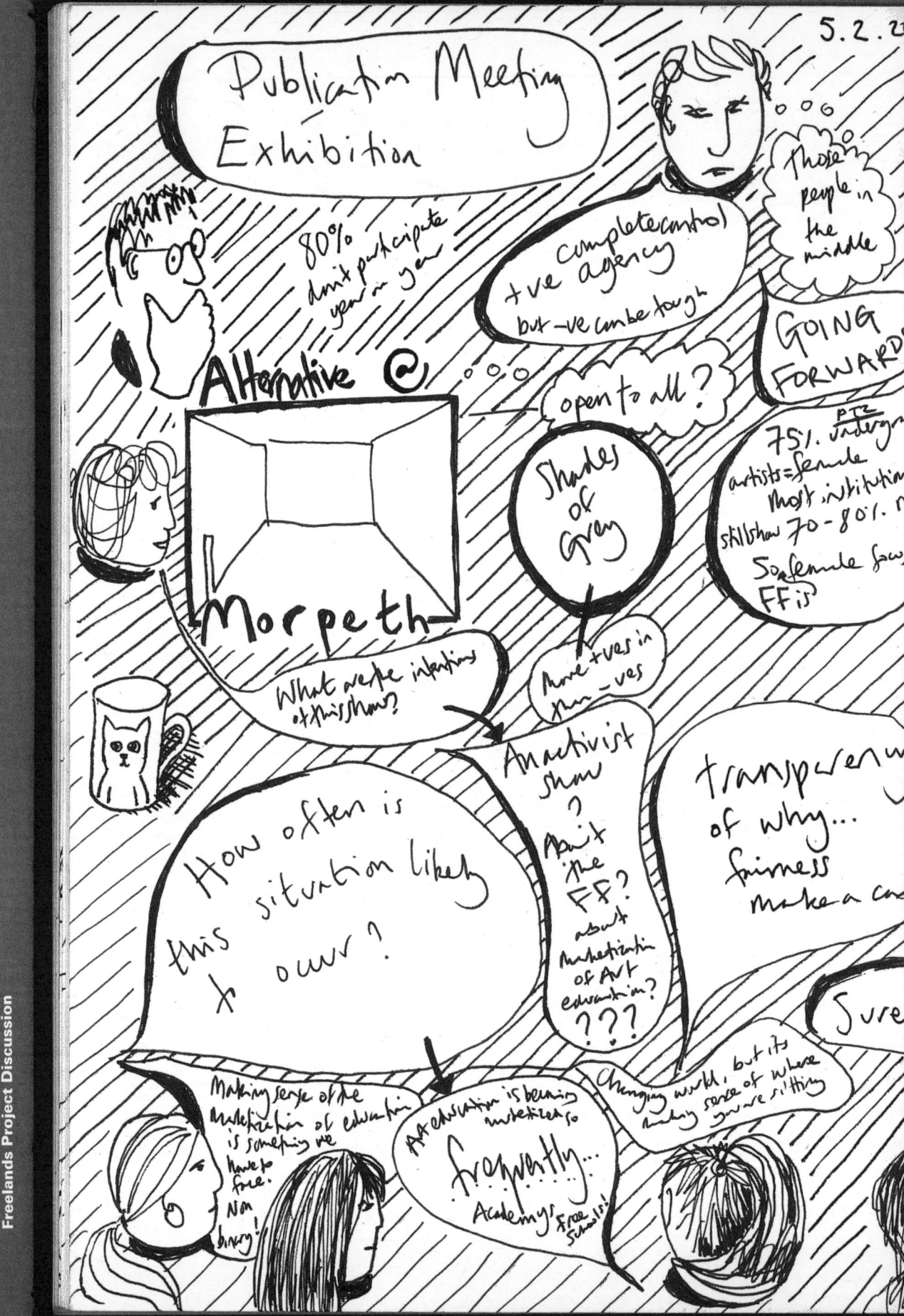

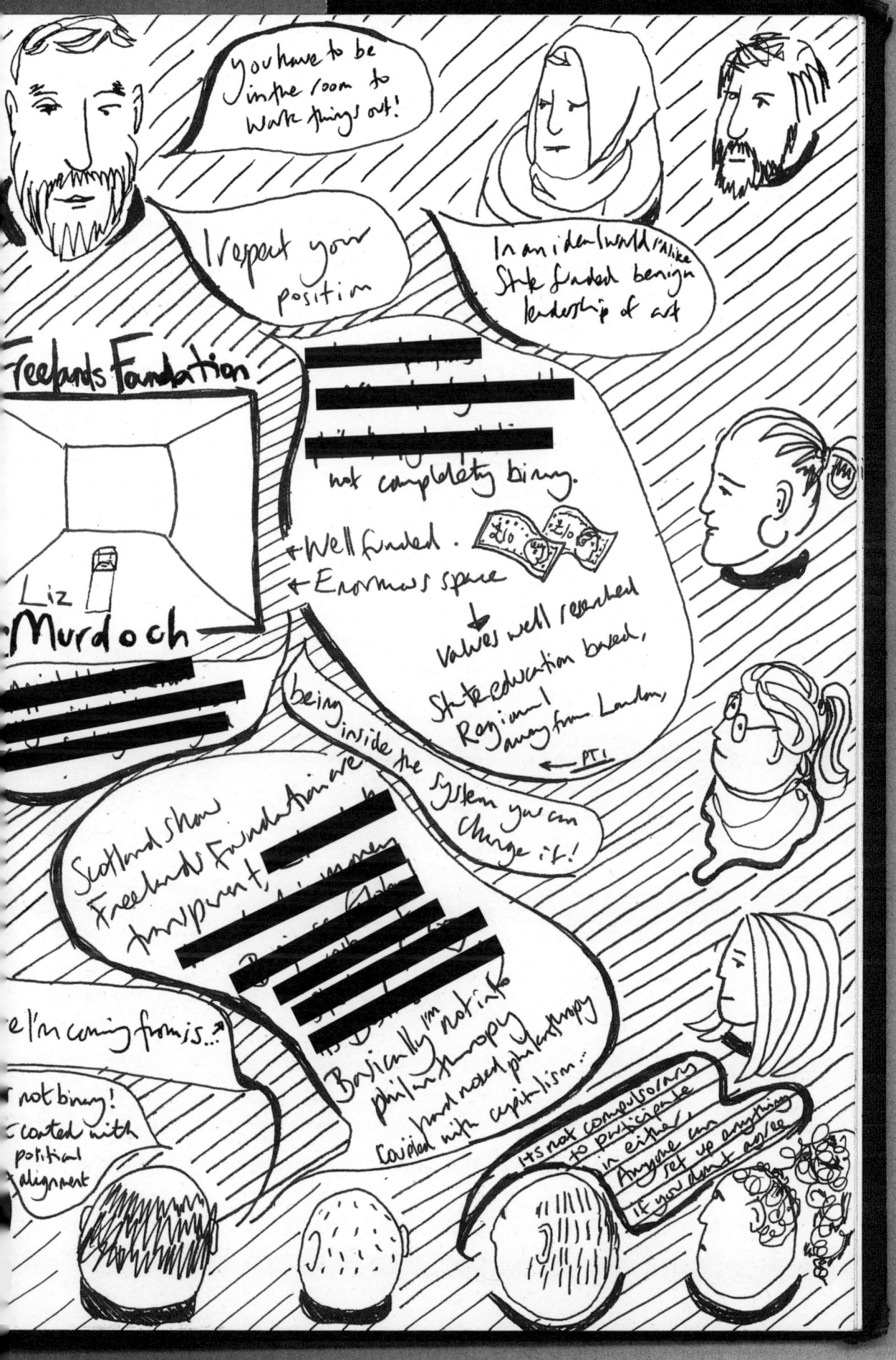

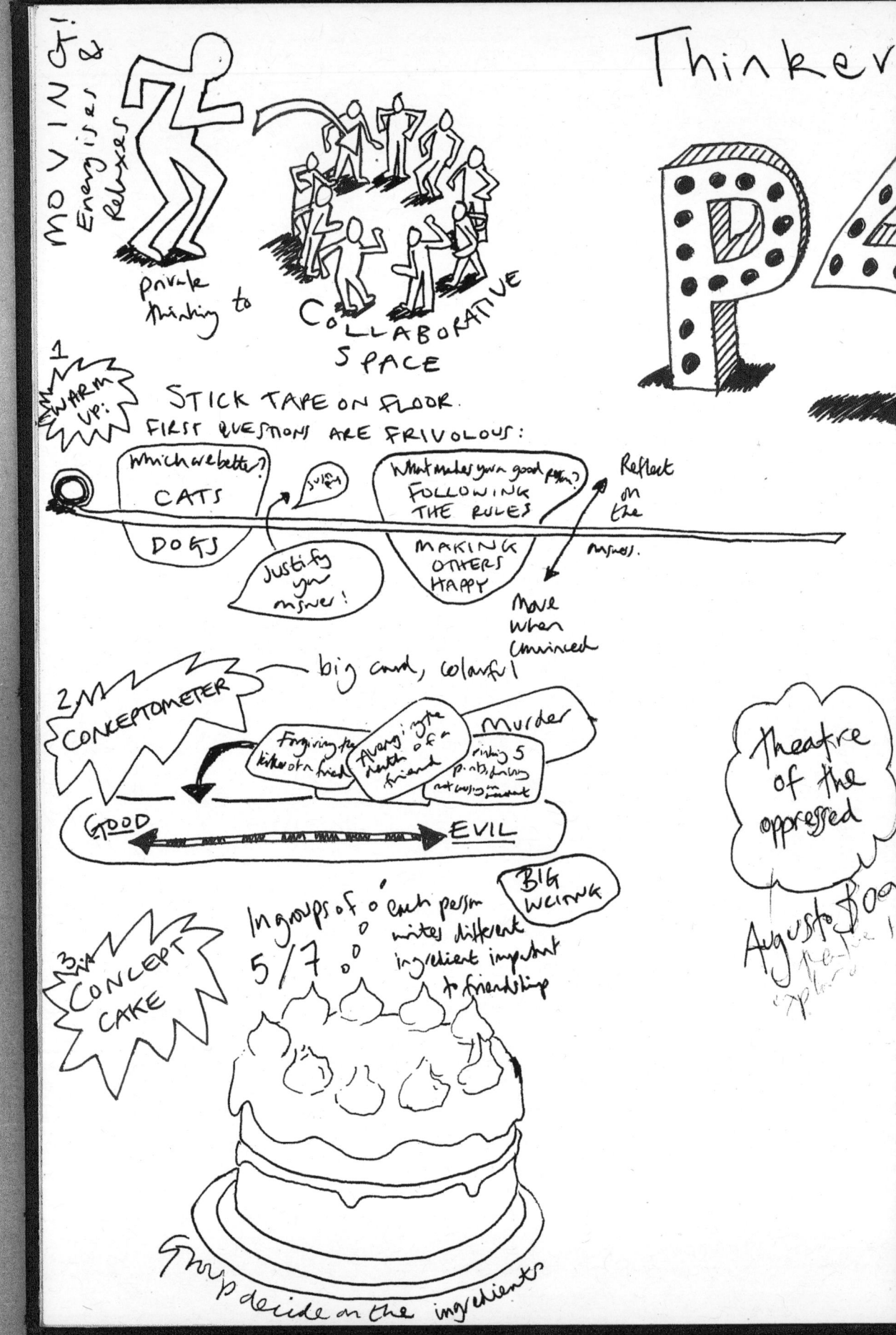

MOVING! Energises & Relaxes

private thinking to

COLLABORATIVE SPACE

P4C

1 WARM UP:

STICK TAPE ON FLOOR.
FIRST QUESTIONS ARE FRIVOLOUS:

Which are better?
CATS
DOGS

Justify your answer!

What makes you a good person?
FOLLOWING THE RULES
MAKING OTHERS HAPPY

Reflect on the answers.

Move when convinced

2 CONCEPTOMETER

big card, colourful

Forgiving the killer of a friend

Avenging the death of a friend

Murder
risking 5 points, doing not caring in judgement

GOOD ⟷ EVIL

3 CONCEPT CAKE

In groups of 5/7 each person writes different ingredient important to friendship

BIG WEINK

Group decide on the ingredients

Theatre of the oppressed

Augusto Boal
Theatre of the oppressed

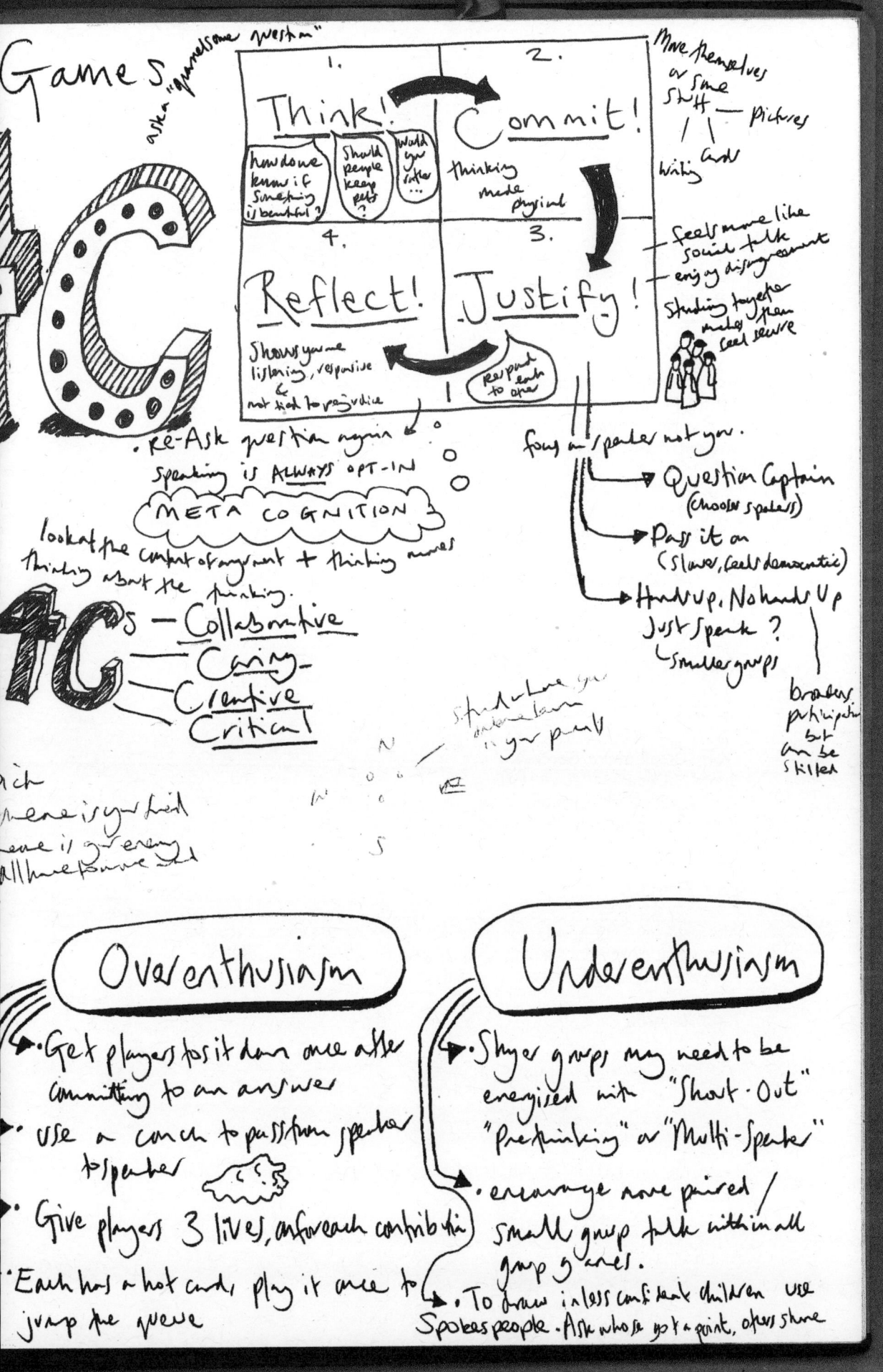

Games

ask a "quarrelsome question"

4C

1. Think! how do we know if something is beautiful? · Should people keep pets? · Would you rather...	**2.** Commit! thinking made physical · Move themselves or some stuff — pictures · writing, cards
4. Reflect! Shows you are listening, responsive & not tied to prejudice	**3.** Justify! feels more like social talk, enjoy disagreement · Standing together makes them feel secure · Respond to each other

- Re-Ask question again
- Speaking is ALWAYS OPT-IN

META COGNITION

look at the content of argument + thinking moves, thinking about the thinking

4Cs — Collaborative / Caring / Creative / Critical

focus on speaker not you.
- Question Captain (chooses speakers)
- Pass it on (slower, feels democratic)
- Hands Up, No hands Up Just Speak? (smaller groups)

broader principle but can be skilled

Overenthusiasm

- Get players to sit down once after committing to an answer
- use a conch to pass from speaker to speaker
- Give players 3 lives, one for each contribution
- Each has a hot card, play it once to jump the queue

Underenthusiasm

- Shyer groups may need to be energised with "Shout-Out" "Pre-thinking" or "Multi-Speak"
- encourage more paired / small group talk within all group games.
- To draw in less confident children use Spokespeople. Ask whose got a point, offer share

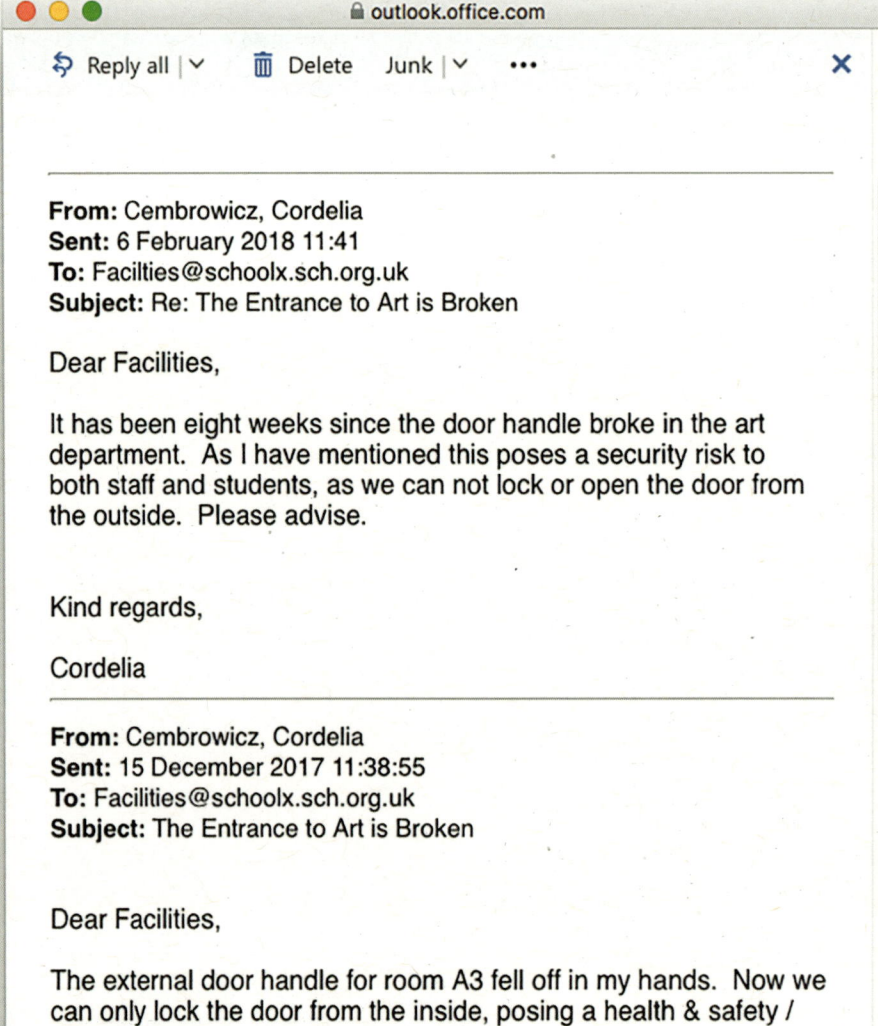

From: Cembrowicz, Cordelia
Sent: 6 February 2018 11:41
To: Facilties@schoolx.sch.org.uk
Subject: Re: The Entrance to Art is Broken

Dear Facilities,

It has been eight weeks since the door handle broke in the art department. As I have mentioned this poses a security risk to both staff and students, as we can not lock or open the door from the outside. Please advise.

Kind regards,

Cordelia

From: Cembrowicz, Cordelia
Sent: 15 December 2017 11:38:55
To: Facilities@schoolx.sch.org.uk
Subject: The Entrance to Art is Broken

Dear Facilities,

The external door handle for room A3 fell off in my hands. Now we can only lock the door from the inside, posing a health & safety / security problem. Please can you fix it.

Kind Regards,

Cordelia

Everyone has heard of yarn bombing right? It's mainstream, like London Kaye who travels on the L train in NYC and crochets around the poles. I thought it would be great to have an after school club, to have the students knit and crochet and wrap some of the trees in the quad, creating an installation to brighten up an otherwise grey and uninspiring outdoor space.

I ran the idea past the art teachers. Check. I spoke to the deputy head as to where we could put the installation. Check. I printed out flyers and distributed them to form tutors. Check.

The first afternoon, five Year 7s turned up and by the end of the hour, four had learnt to knit. Check.

The next week, three Year 7s turned up. They seemed confused when I told them they could not take the work home. We are making an installation for the school. 'But what happens if it rains?', one asked. 'Knitting is grannyish', said another. The third week, two girls turned up, the next, one, and the following …

The girls were disappointed they weren't going to create anything tangible to take home and thought knitting was 'not cool'.

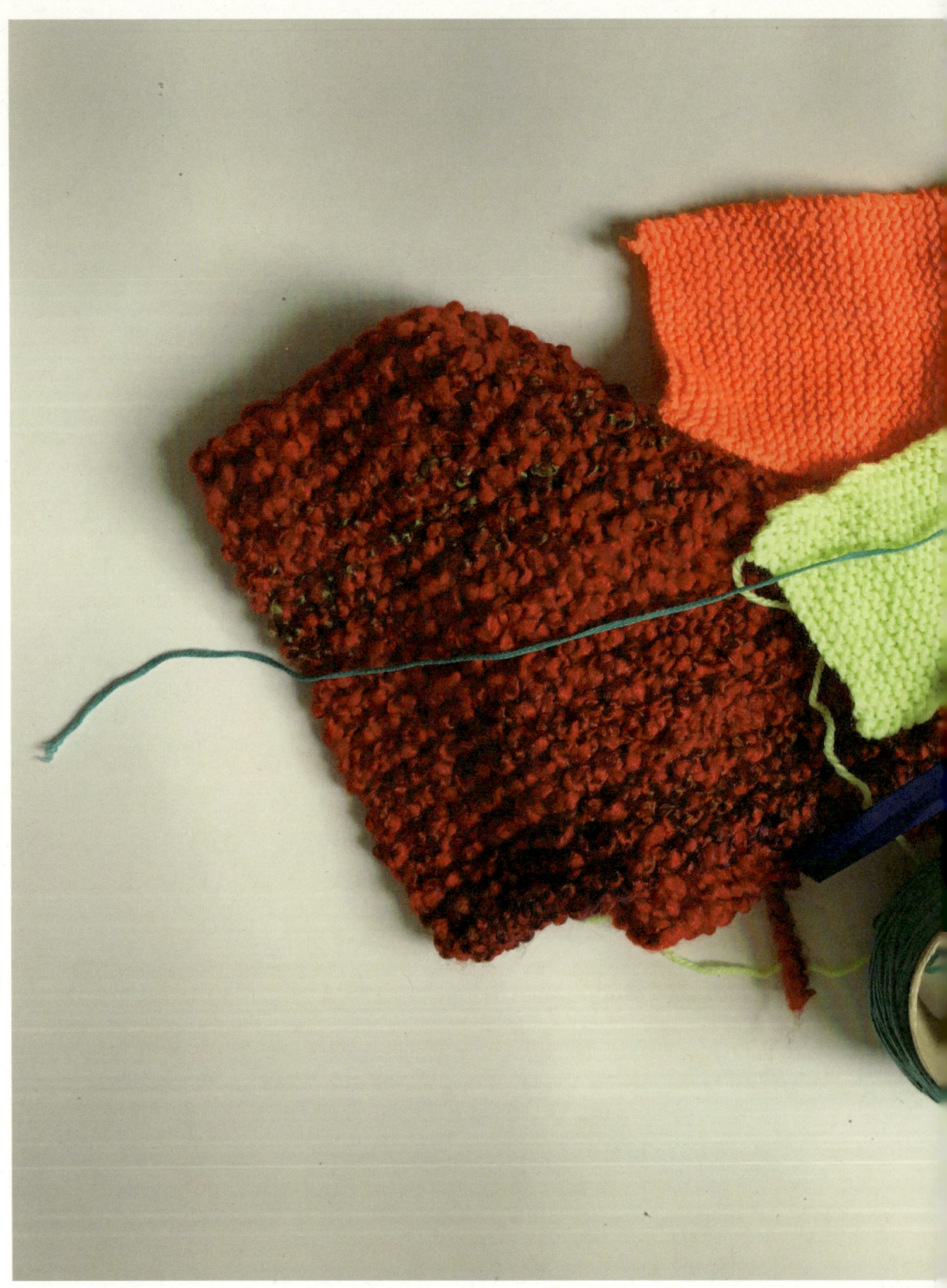

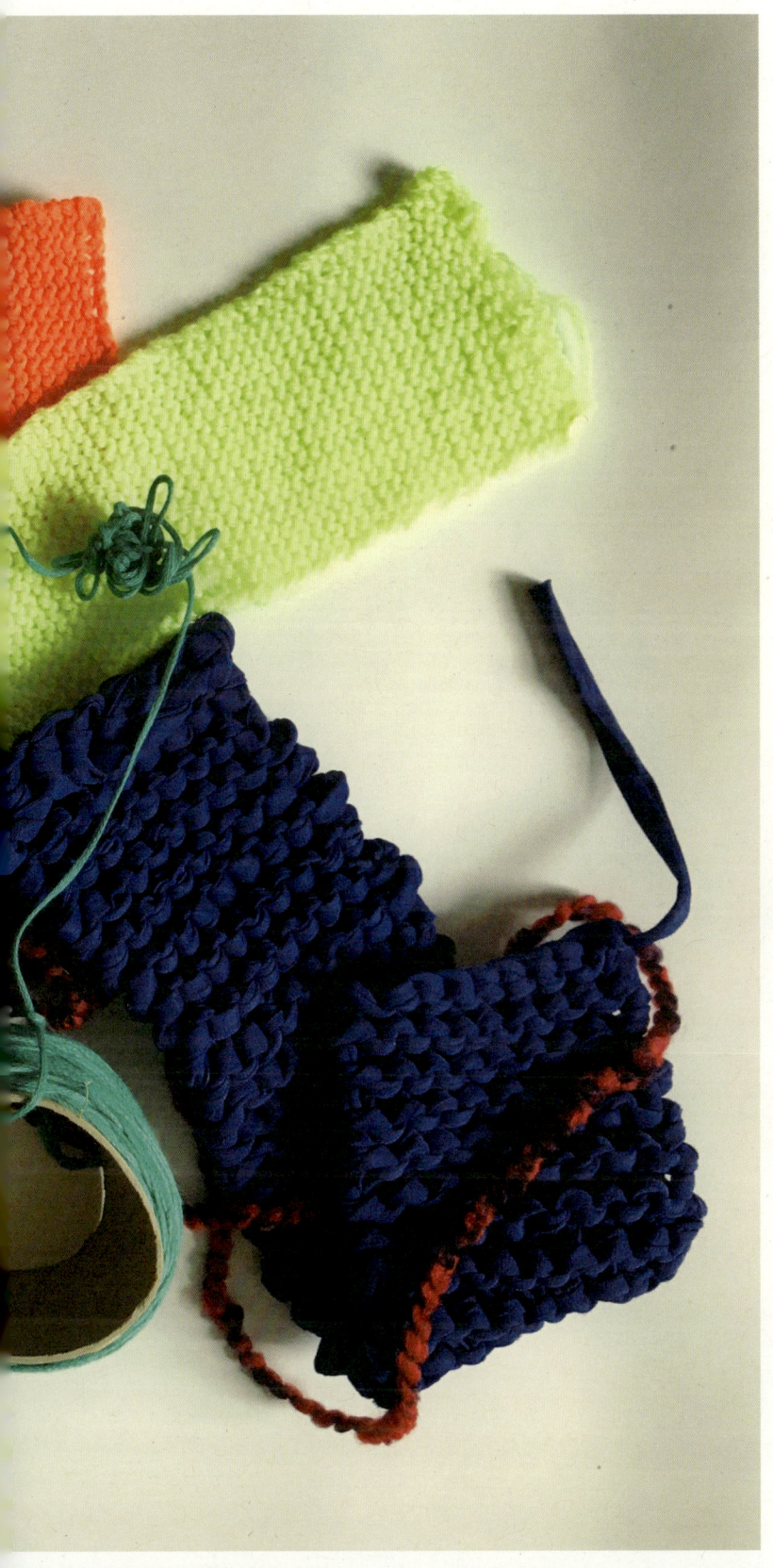

YARN BOMBING

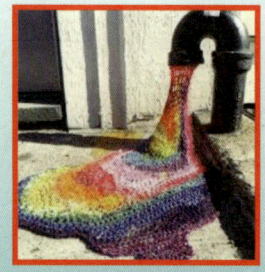
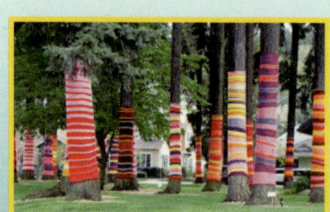
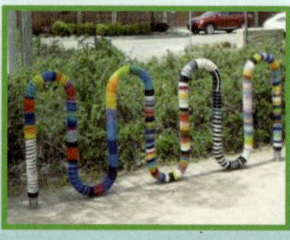
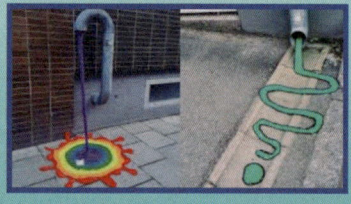
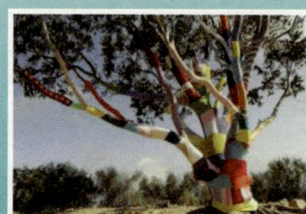
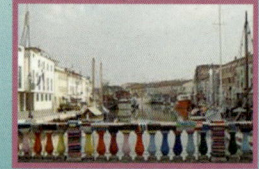

https://www.youtube.com/watch?v=FB_KGZaR9dl

I know this because I left school with pretty much nothing other than an art qualification.

Art education gave me the opportunity to be the best of myself. Art education gave me ambition and passion. Art was the only subject at school where I was able to achieve. I left school with two GCSEs in English and most importantly ART.

When I was at secondary school my head of year called me into her office and said, 'We want to send you to college one day a week, to train in either hairdressing or beauty, because that's what girls like you do, girls who find learning hard at school, go to college after their exams and do that sort of thing'. I remember being absolutely bewildered, I wasn't even traditionally girly, and sometimes I would even go to school without brushing my hair.

Exam results day came and the future didn't look particularly bright. I enrolled at a FE college. This was where I had my turning point, I studied art full time and was finally statemented with dyslexia.

A few exceptional artist teachers took me under their wing and gave me the support I needed to top up my qualifications and make some decent art work. At college surrounded by artist teachers I wasn't in the bottom set, I wasn't stupid or slow, I wasn't a girl without a bright future. I was just an artist.

Three intense and amazing years flew by and I was off on my way to a top art school.

I am the first female in my family to have attended university. At school, I didn't have anyone who believed in me or noticed my talent. Always in the bottom set, miserable and disengaged.

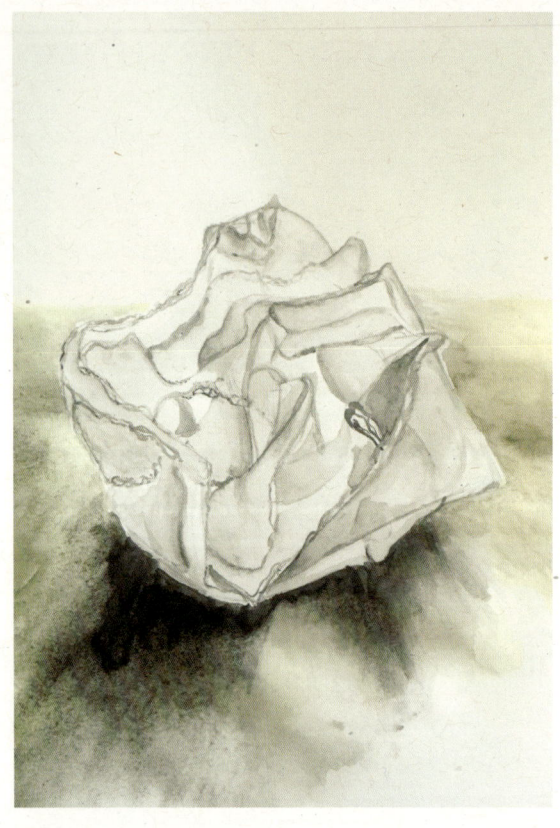

My only comfort my CD Walkman and my sketchbook. The day I received my unconditional offer to study Fine Art at university I couldn't quite believe it. Mum hugged me while I cried. I was so overwhelmed, I had achieved what I had always wanted, I had accomplished what I been told by so many I couldn't.

Art education gave me a love of literature, culture and history. Art education made me inquisitive and a desire to always keep learning.

Art education made me believe in myself. Art education taught me to be myself.

Art gave me a home. It's the place where I fit in and participate confidently. Art means everything to me. I think about it more than most things.

All my accomplishments are down to my art education and some inspiring teachers who helped me along the way. After a few years in the industry, I am now a student artist teacher. If you were to have told me this would be my current vocation a couple of years ago I probably wouldn't have believed you.

So, as the title suggests, Art Education is Important.

ELI SAMUELS

Radio

Sensation Station

Know More Live Better. Your weekly human-interest show with music, chat and discussions on topical news stories. Miss Samuels, who will be sitting in for DJ JabberJones, will host this week's episode on *hard work*. Miss Samuels will be speaking to an

independent boys school, interviewing some of their bright, ambitious students and discussing why hard work is so important and where their drive and determination is rooted. Is a parent at home their source of inspiration? Or is it an inner confidence they gained from their primary education? Perhaps it is something else entirely and their

parents have paid no role in their learning? Whatever it may be, we will be finding out in todays show, so tune in to hear first-hand from the students themselves.

This will be followed by a question and answer session with Miss Samuels, so whether you have a burning question or a contribution yourself,

text in during or following the show (T&Cs below). And as always, this show will be interspersed with a selection of tunes so keep the requests flying in. The word of this week is: *work*.

(Texts cost 50p each plus standard message rate. You must be 16 or over)

G2 | The Guardian | 15

Art and Music cross-curricular collaboration: Pans to Pens

AMY BROCKLESBY

When I first encountered the Year 9 steel pans band at my placement school I was awestruck. I was aware that this school had a particular talent for this prior to working there, but to hear and see them live for the first time was quite incredible. What was also fascinating, was that some of this particular cohort were not always the most focused in my art lessons. To see them playing the pans made me recognise a completely different amazing quality in them and I wanted to capture that energy and talent – as well as the therapeutic effect of their drumming – in a piece of synaesthetic artwork.

The music technician and I made the sound recording during one of the Friday rehearsals, held in the temporary unit by the staff car park – the sound is raw and captures the environment exactly as it was. The following week, I took the students and their drumming teacher over to the art room where their pans had been replaced with paper and their sticks for pens. With intrigue at being asked to undertake this unusual task, they all enthusiastically and passionately played along to the sound recording – every beat of their pens, absolutely and without fault, in sync with their part in the music. They were excited to be creating art in this way and, as a viewer, the process was mesmerising and magical to watch.

The resulting collaborative piece: beautiful pages and pages of colourful mark making, recording every pulse and movement of the music.

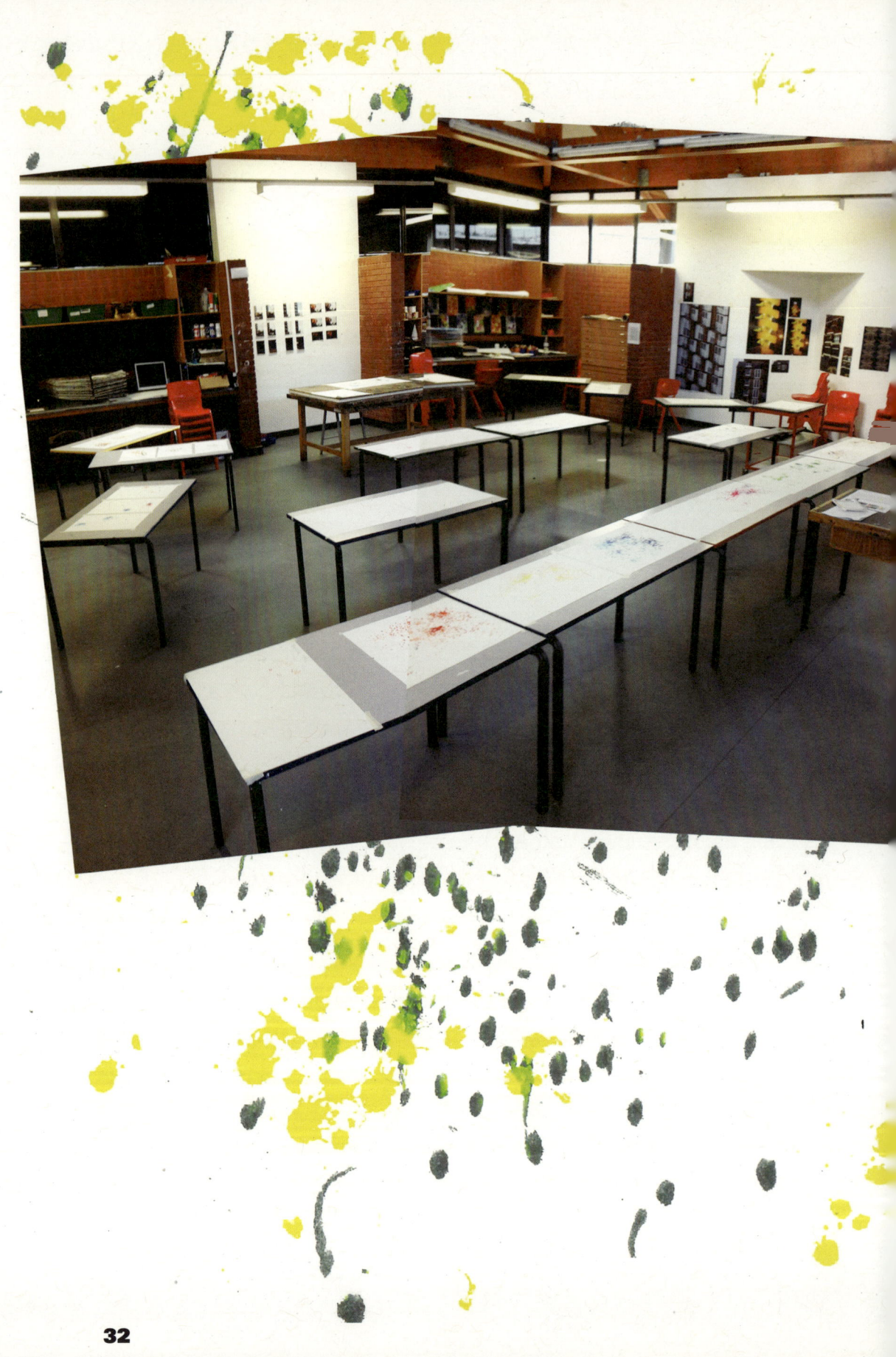

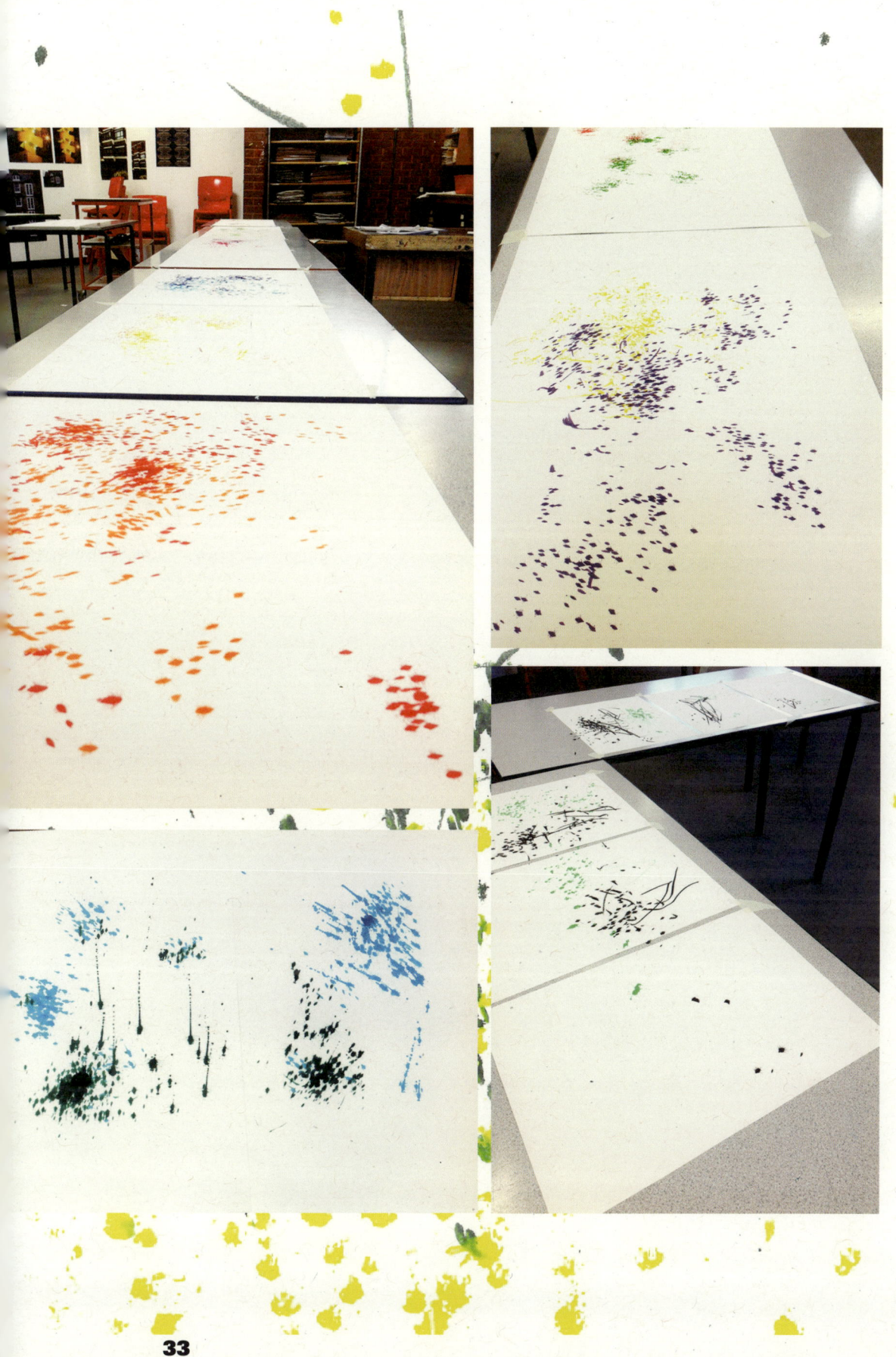

Equipment
Fragments of sentences from
children's stories
A5 paper
Glue sticks
KS3 students with vivid imaginations

Activity
Poem 1: Choose, at random, one
fragment at a time and stick it to the
paper to create a poem.
Continue until your poem is complete.

Poem 2: Take a handful of fragments.
Arrange them into a poem, being
selective, then stick them down.

Read poems aloud
very
seriously.

'But tell me first

the filling-station of a deep secret "I wonder how
looked closer still (enormous great solid

it wasn' here

'Bless my soul, what this

the water! of the cloud,

36

CLOVER BUTTERFLY

and a careless

and

in there

looked

It wasn't raindrops

lake or a whole

silent. I was

and extraordinarily

We'll probably need

the door

,THE GUPPY

'One is Coke,   to lift us.

                                           to its back

with
                                                    THE

bristly black whiskers.   enormous

                                 old breakfasts

in a funny   Danny,'

even bother   the Centipede

He is too old   Of course

    working   frightened

as they   a taxi

once   I shouldn't think"

at this point that   able to imagine

It's the

38

DID YOU KNOW

They'll be bound longer?
What time We're going
once again, waving   very awkwardly
shortage of
a taxi,
give someone funny-shaped
more lifting lift an
she heard the squeezed
and when I moved   They all raised
It's like down in   power   to be like
on the smooth bald head
'Then how dangerous,. . I shall bear it!
If only another –'
'Good morning its face

as though an enormous torches shaped about pits,
There it is again!'

we *didn't*

Three seconds later,

to explore to move.

'Madness!'

'Catasterous!'

a long silence.

yellows, a face that withering look.

a deep, maggoty

' He handed me one

fizzing upwards?

go upward?'

upward,

a step or two

Danny. is thinking,' AROUND making balloon.
dark-green island in the KING mouth
seconds later sharp hairs
into one of those mother gently walking
with her to big job,'

VANILLA FUDGE was covered specks
like, 'How

the keeper

feel,

a result

the King of Arabia Earthworm

with no upstairs

seen

I developed a project which saw Year 12 students create a piece of conceptual art based on the artist's apron. I decided to work with an apron in order to use my six years experience as a womenswear designer to instruct and facilitate students in using a sewing machine and help them to build confidence in handling and experimenting with textiles. The artist's apron is symbolic of an artists' life and can reflect their practice in many ways.

All of the students received an apron and were instructed to manipulate, deconstruct, add to, or alter their apron to reflect their own practice as an artist. The main aim was to encourage students to think conceptually, and the first session introduced them to a number of conceptual artists, followed by discussions about the ideas and theories behind various works of conceptual art.

The experience of teaching students about conceptual art opened up personal anxieties in explaining such works and sharing my own theories with the students. Prior to the project I researched many conceptual artists and attended exhibitions to view a variety of conceptual art, yet I still felt slightly apprehensive and unprepared to answer the questions that the students might pose. Art from this movement can trigger so many different responses, and can be at times difficult to analyse, yet what I came to understand was that all ideas were valid, and the purpose of the movement was to generate discussion and widen an observer's understanding of 'art'.

My priority was to alter the way students thought about and created their own art work. In being given such freedom, many students struggled to form their own concepts, but in sharing ideas and seeing how their peers developed over the sessions all students began to progress and produce different outcomes which were meaningful to them and reflected their own views and practises as young artists.

Student's explanations behind their work:

Joseph Watchorn
(p.49, top left)
'My apron breaks the barriers between what people truly find attractive and how people are engulfed by brand experience. The deliberate messy presentation of logos combined with their re-arrangement, emphasises the way a brand can blur our senses whilst blocking true beauty from seeping through. The tension created by the tape provides an atmosphere of strain and unease at the thought of being stripped of the precious logo which enables us to slot into society. Also, the pocket filled with emotions rubs salt into the wound. The emotions epitomise the power brands have, and their ability to disrupt our train of thought.'

Léa Watson
(p.49, top right)
'My aprons represent the journey from childhood to adulthood. Children are known for thinking outside the box. Their creativity and imagination are what makes them unique. This is what I was trying to show with the smallest apron. The explosion of colours and shapes is a way of representing the originality of a child. This changes, however. As you grow older, some people start trying to fit in with others and society. Peer pressure can also lead to this, hence the eyes on the second apron. The third apron is the final stage of the "process" of growing up. On the last apron, I have hand-stitched on bits of fabric demonstrating how various things (such as books, films, characters and people) can shape your personality. The pieces of fabric also make a brick wall, signifying how as you grow older you start to bottle up your feelings more. The pages which can be seen on the apron are pages from my favourite books, suggesting that nobody knows the full story of the fights and struggles people are wrestling with on the inside. There are holes in two of the

aprons. The smaller apron has been cut out from the medium-sized one and the medium-sized one has been cut out from the bigger one. This is meant to show how your personality changes throughout your life and how younger selves are lost in the past.'

Blythe Walker Sibthorp
(p.49, bottom left)
'My apron design represents the eating disorder anorexia. It displays a very thin body, my intention was to make it an illusion for the person wearing it, portraying them as thin. An apron is usually made to protect a person from damage and mess, almost concealing them from something. However, having an apron displaying anorexia contrasts this idea, as it is not hiding and protecting the body, but making it very vulnerable. I also wanted to include irony as a theme when making this apron as the main idea behind an apron is making food and this is the last thing an anorexic would want to be associated with.'

Chloe Beroud
(p.49, bottom right)
'This "apron" aims to openly compare the illustrious excess often exercised in designing *haut couture* compared with the harsh, cruel and unglamorous mass labour that sits at the heart of fast fashion. The white, pure material cascades down the figure, only partially covering the milky white bones underneath, creating an angelic and sinister reminder that the truth is rarely as beautiful as the surface illusion. Artists wear aprons to protect themselves, almost as a uniform, and the focus on the fashion industry this garment has, reminds the artist that no matter how beautiful the final piece, the process and ideas that precede it shouldn't be forgotten.'

Adam Cady
(p.50)
'This apron derives inspiration from an often-outcast group: street artists. This secretive, but largely recognised form of art, often requires two things. Firstly, spray cans – the grafitti artist's weapon of choice – and secondly,

a hidden identity to escape the watchful eye of CCTV and the law enforcement authorities. My apron has taken these two factors as a necessity, so it has a lot of pockets shaped perfectly for storing spray cans. It also has a hood that can be zipped up with eye holes to avoid detection when in a tricky situation. Another key element of street art is to be unique and make your work stand out from all the others' covering the walls of the city. This apron can give anyone an identity beyond their real one and give them freedom to become a symbol and carry out their work.'

Kjellon Morris
(p.51, top left)
'This apron captures my personal love of music, comparing my thought process to the progression of the music industry as a whole. I used canvas paper to add the notes to a tune I had made in pen and pencil; the notes escape from the page, representing the idea that music is ever-expanding and has no set way of being created. However, such ways can also be too complex, as represented in a spiralling tornado. Often it's best to go with simple chords.

The gap in the apron describes my mind blanks, leaving me uninspired. It also represents how modern music is often samey, comprised of just remixes of older, more memorable classics. However, that does not necessarily mean that said mixes aren't unique – within that blank area, ideas can be re-formed into a style that's both revolutionary, even arguably better – as represented by the various colours of cotton wool at the bottom.'

Finlay Higgins
(p.51, top right)
'Whilst exploring the idea of conceptual art I designed an apron interpreting the idea of both openness and closeness of the self. For this I chose to use transparent material, creating the basic shape of my apron representing what the wearer is willing to share to the world. This material is stiff and thus sits on the subject quite rigid representing that the subject may be uncomfortable displaying this openness. The dark blue pocket on the front of the apron combined with the strands of material

display the things in which the subject is not willing to share to the world and is personal and private to them. However, there are different levels of closeness represented through the strands of red.'

Abigail Bateman
(p.51, bottom left)
'I have designed my apron in the way that I have to represent the effect of expectations and stereotypes "pulling" on us, especially women. The design is similar to that of a traditional, vintage women's apron /dress; a bow can be tied up on the back of the dress and the skirt billows out and drops down to the feet. Additionally, the skirt can be pushed up as I have woven three pieces of string through it; the skirt gathers into itself which reveals the underneath and gets rid of the "trapped" nature that the skirt has which covers "reality".'

Fintan O'Connor
(p.51, bottom right)
'Every trade has their staple, their trademark. For artists it is the apron. Continuing from this concept, I wanted to explore the relationship between the artist and the apron. Aprons are used as protection but I wanted to show the underlying creativity of the artist and explore what would happen if you could display this inner experience of creating a piece of art on the outside of the apron. Following on from this I decided to use the base colour of black for the majority of the apron as I didn't want to distract from the main part, which were the bursts of colour showing from under the folds of the black material.'

Gabriel Kuti
(p.52)
'For my garment, I wanted to deconstruct the traditional apron design. I chose to use a plastic art folder material (similar to PVC); the transparency juxtaposes the function of the traditional apron to cover you, by having a translucent material the body is not completely covered and reveals what is underneath. The plastic, being see-through, also symbolises the superficiality often seen and exploited in the fashion industry. Along with staying true to the apron shape so that my design didn't lack any reminiscence to

an actual apron (my idea was to deconstruct the idea behind an apron and not to completely deviate from its design). I followed the shape of the apron and when I had cut it out in the plastic I ripped apart strands of my original blue apron to sew onto it. The unruly rips of fabric challenge the clinical, unembellished nature of the plastic apron design by creating dissonance in the composition and contrasting the ideas behind having a see-through conventional apron base.'

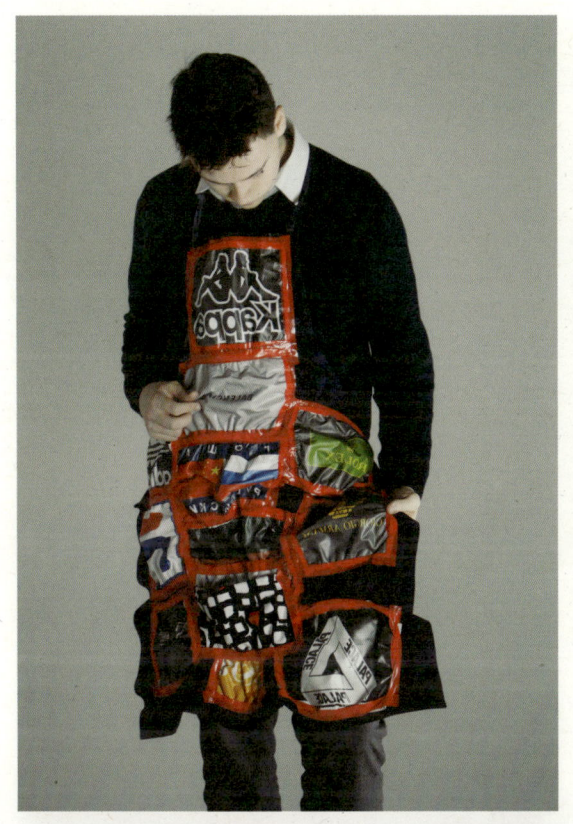
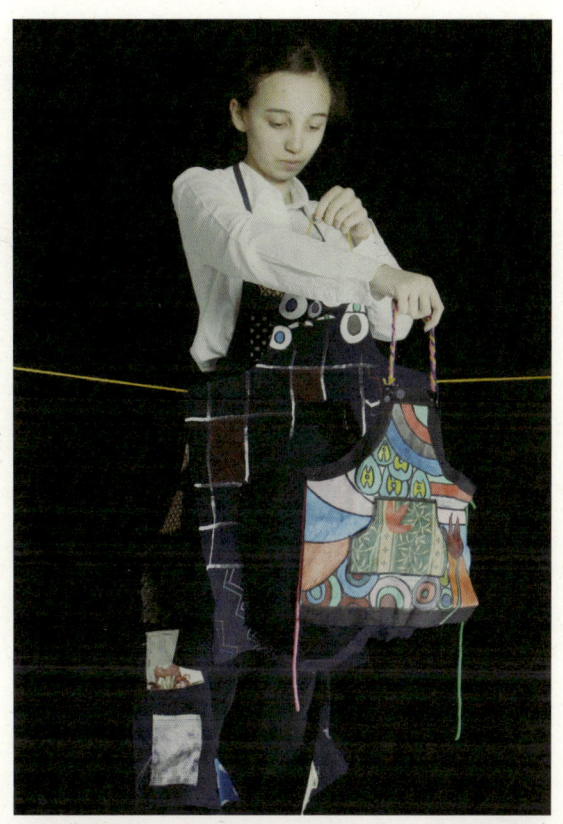
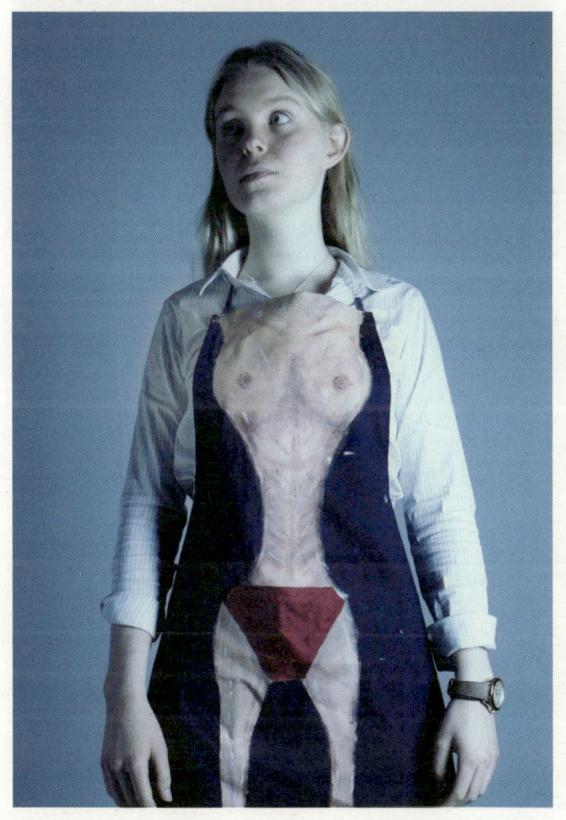
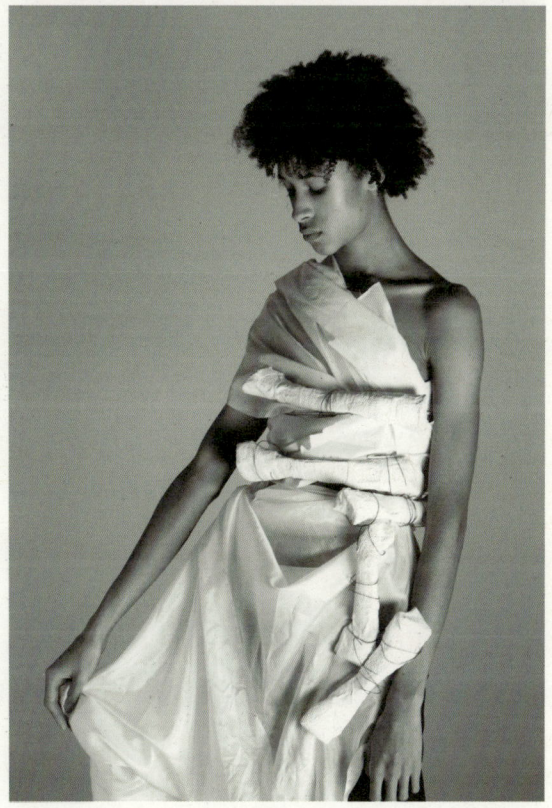

49

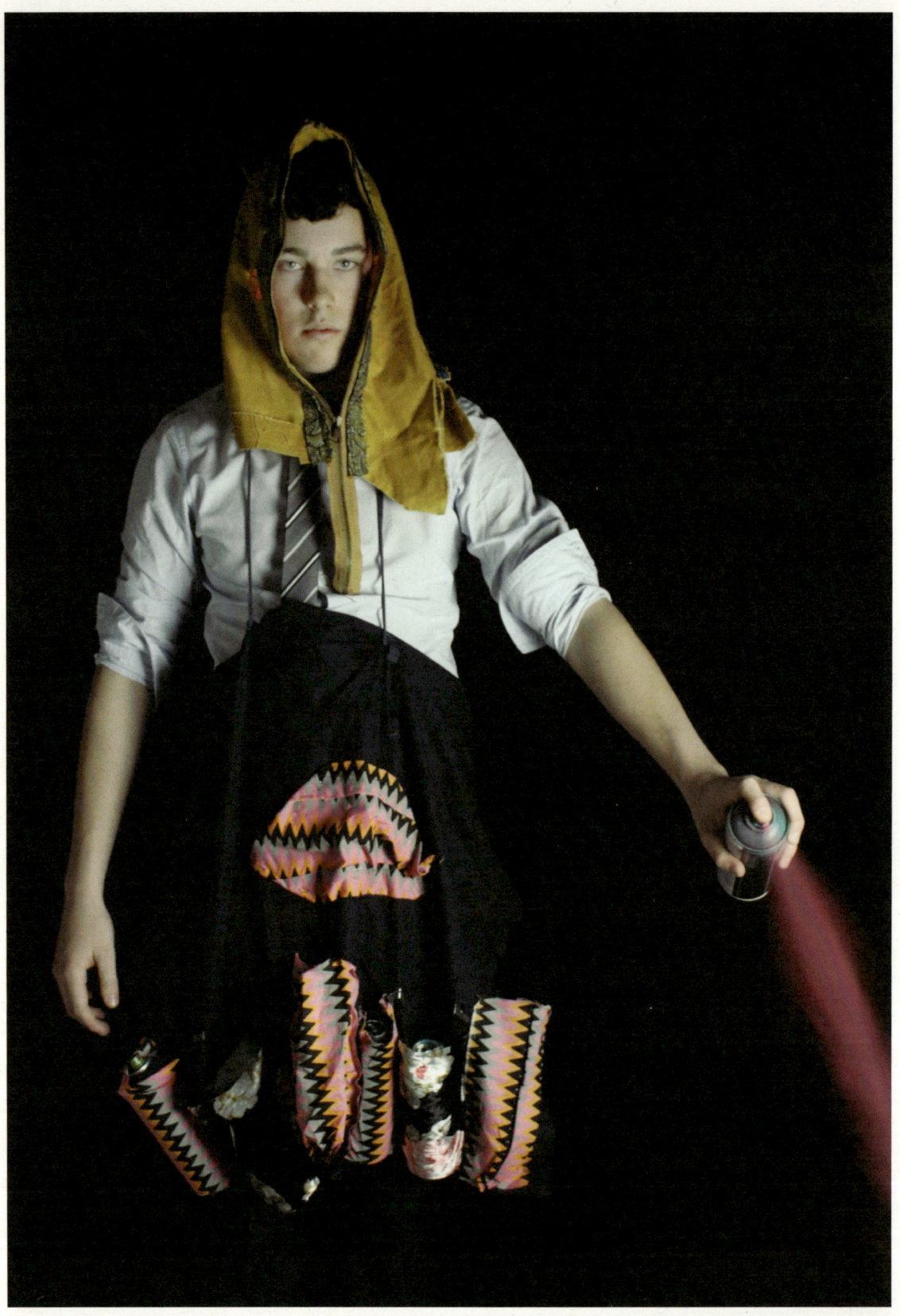

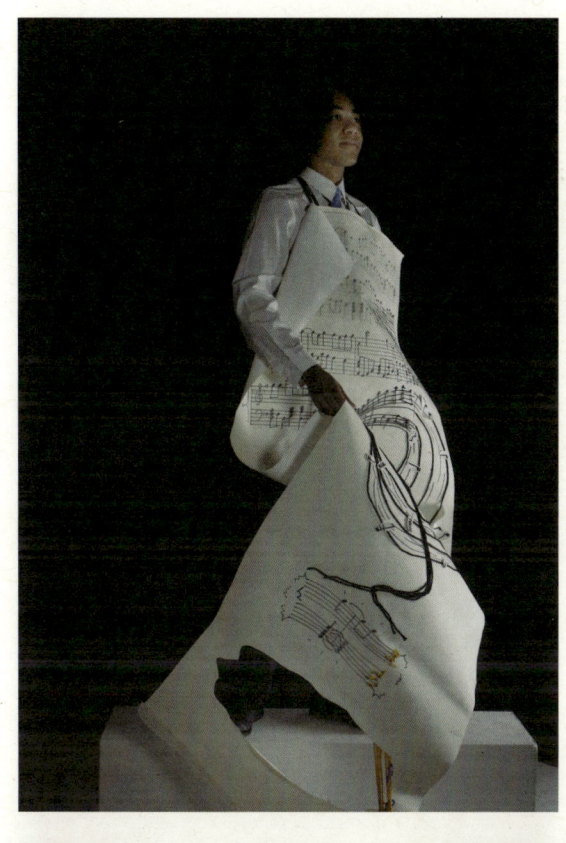

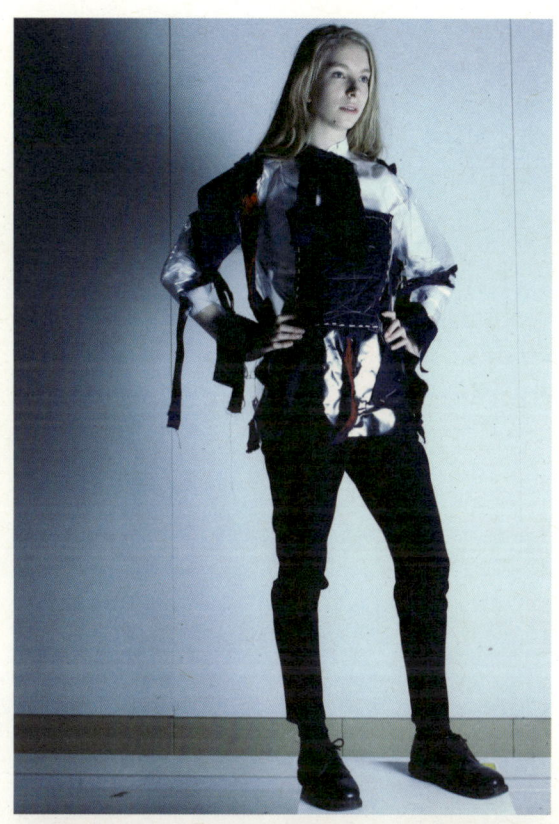

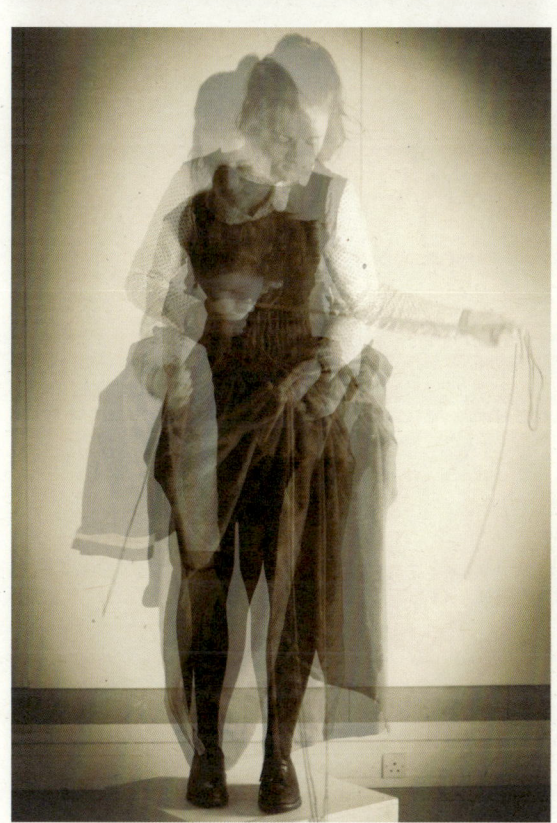

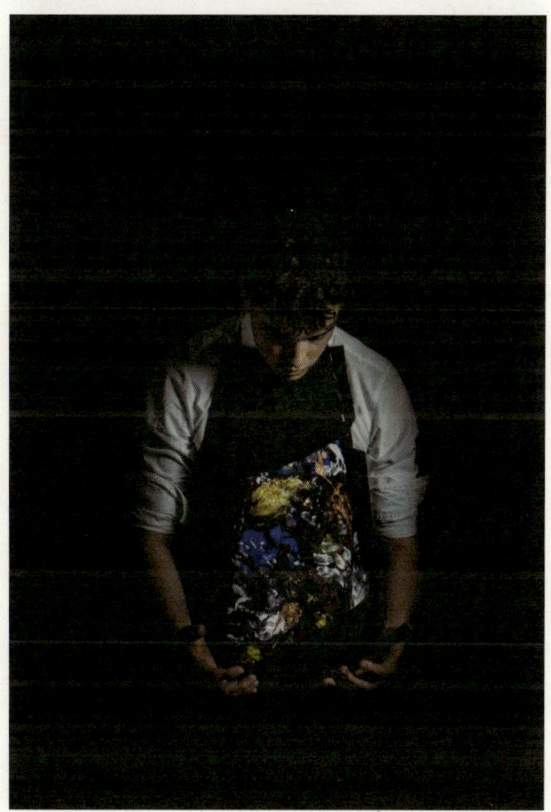

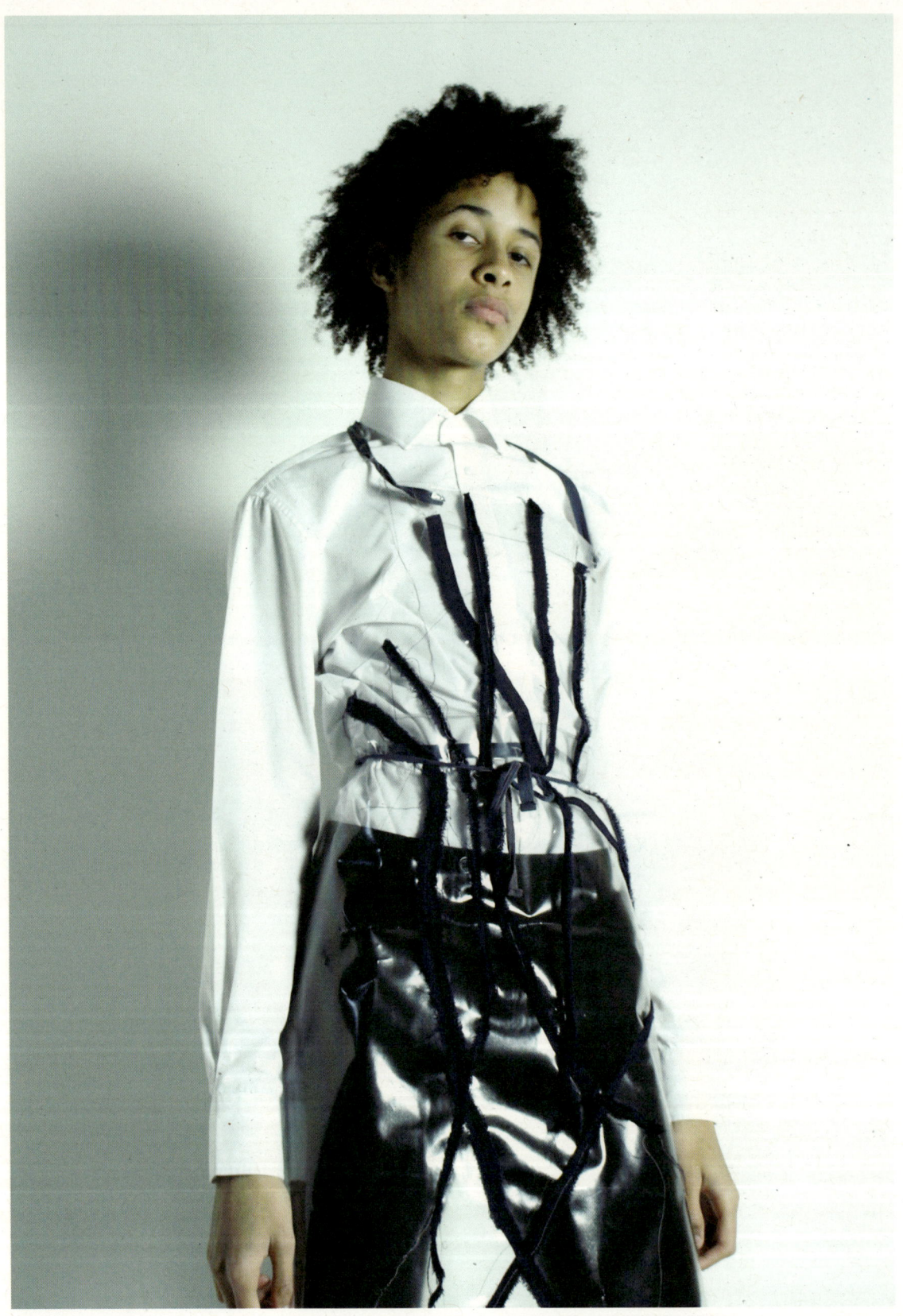

According to Bob and Roberta Smith (2018), there are two main pre-requisites for making art.

> 1 *Peace…*
> *You can't make art if people are*
> *dropping bombs on you*
>   *and*
> 2 *Freedom…*

In the wake of funding cuts and tyrannical performance measures like Ebacc and Progress 8, 'freedom' and 'peace' for secondary school students to make and experience art is wandering further and further out of reach. The stills you see here are taken from a short video shot by a GCSE student at the back of school. It was the first response to a task I had set, to take a print piece made in class, reinvent it somehow, and document the results. The more I watched the video, the more strongly it began to resonate with the position of arts education in our current climate, felt most acutely of course, in the context of school.

The student stands at the back of the institutional building (itself a symbol of arts diminishing status) like a political leader on a protest, back lit and silhouetted, he waves the flag for the 'freedom' and 'peace' to make art. A few moments later the phone was confiscated by a senior teacher, despite the student's attempt to explain what he was doing. However uncertain the future of art education may be, perhaps one thing is clear, make videos at the back of school which look like a protest is starting, and you will be sent back to the confines of the classroom, where 'real learning' is taking place.

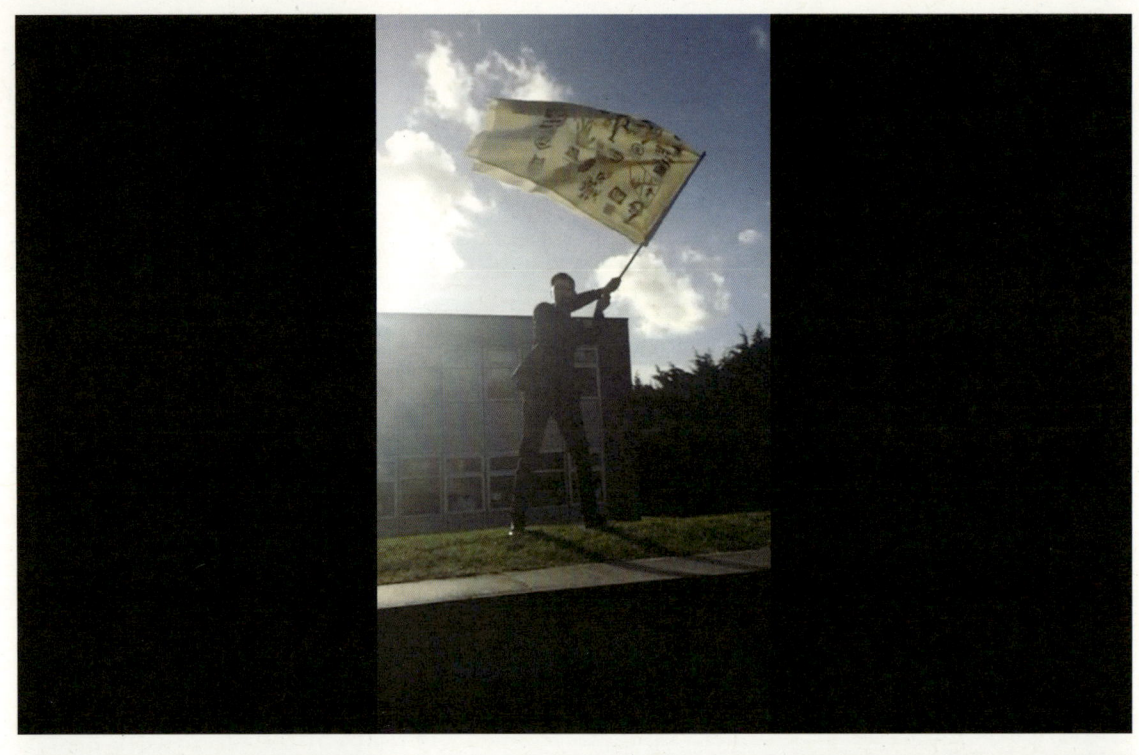

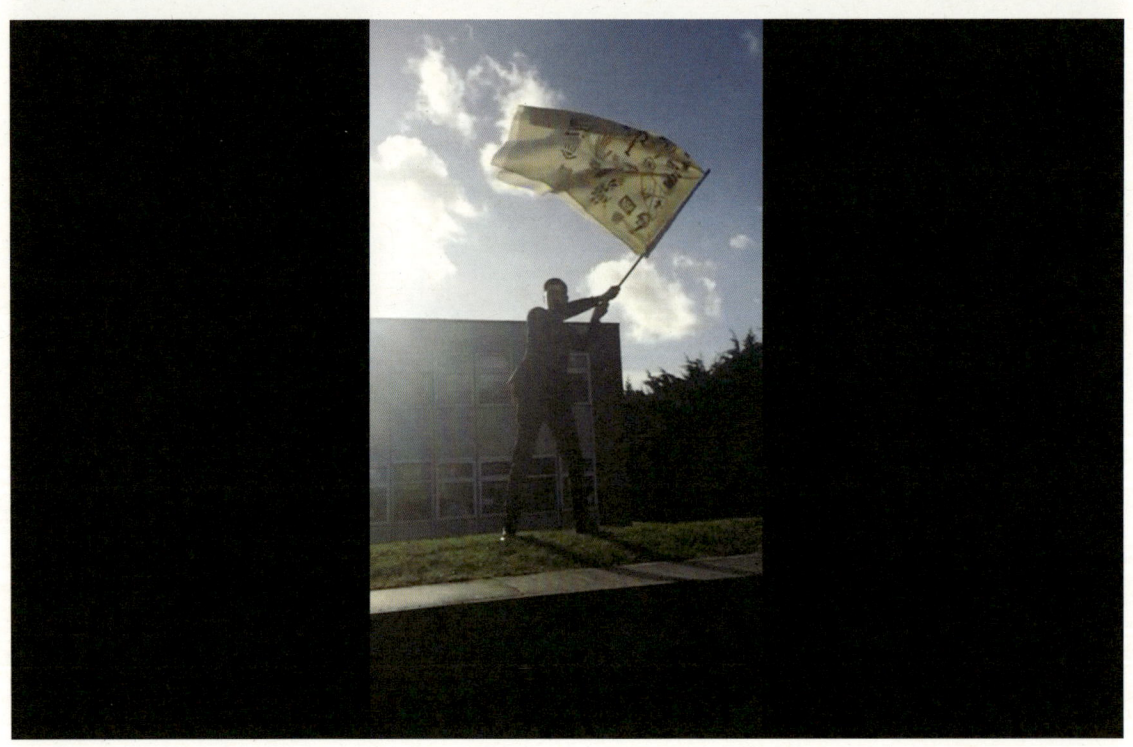

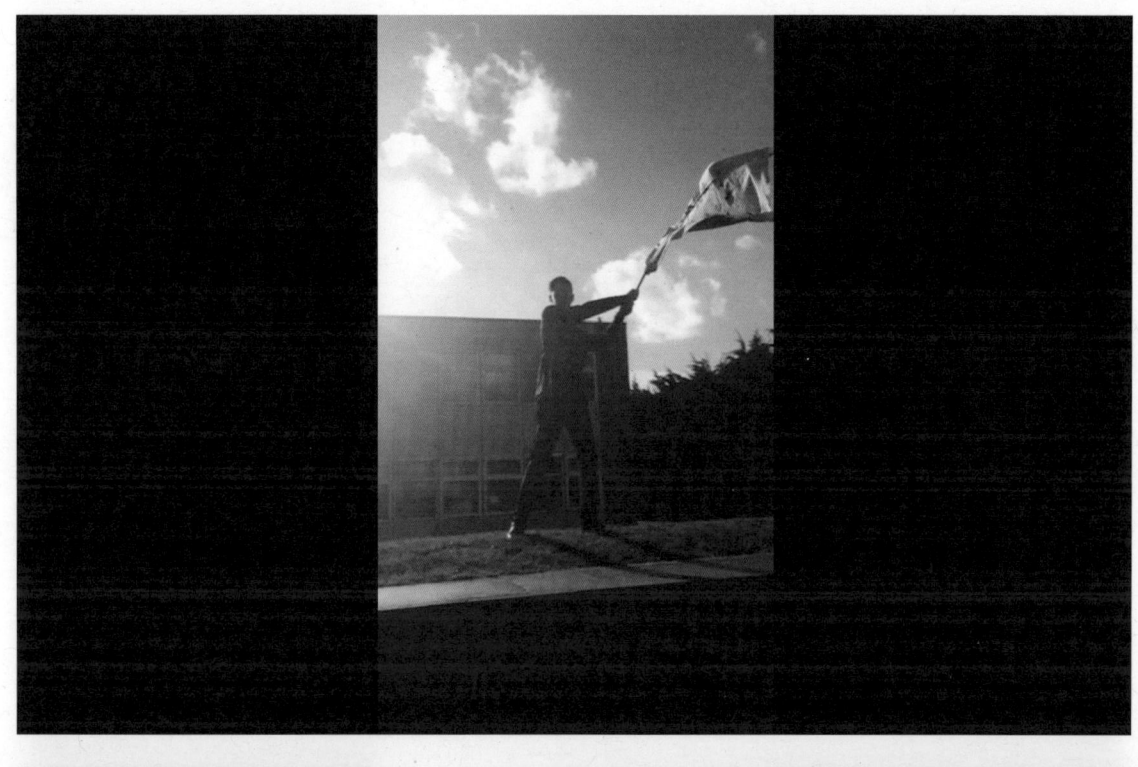

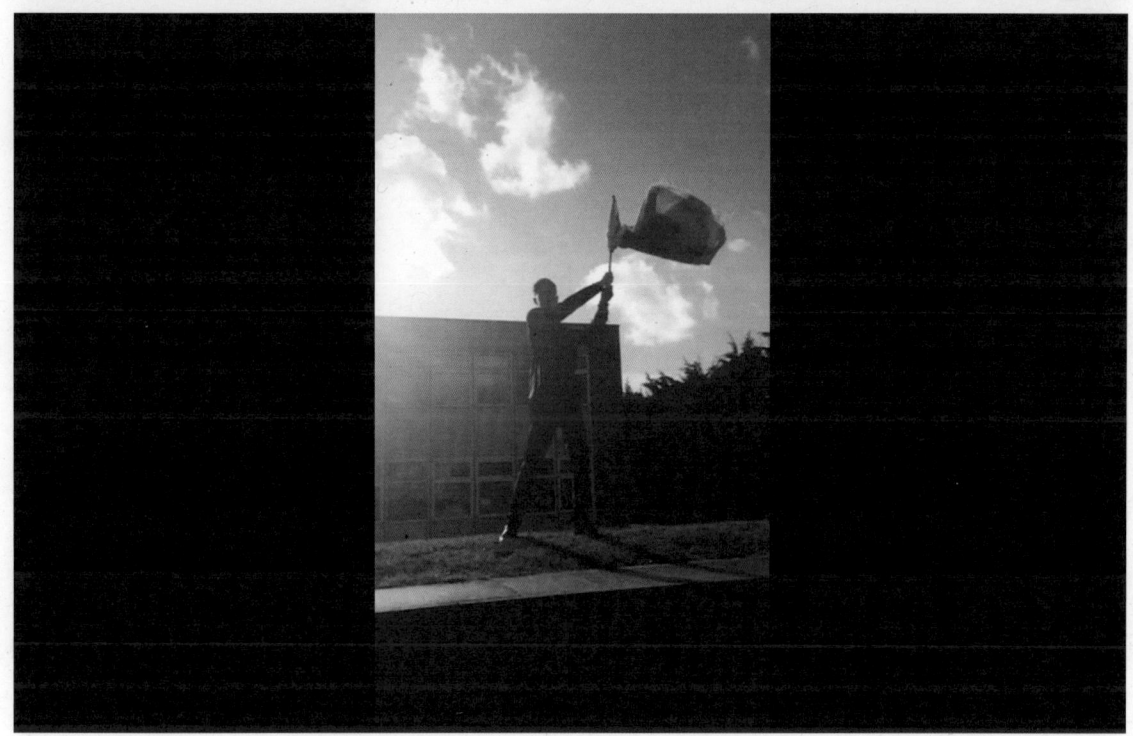

55

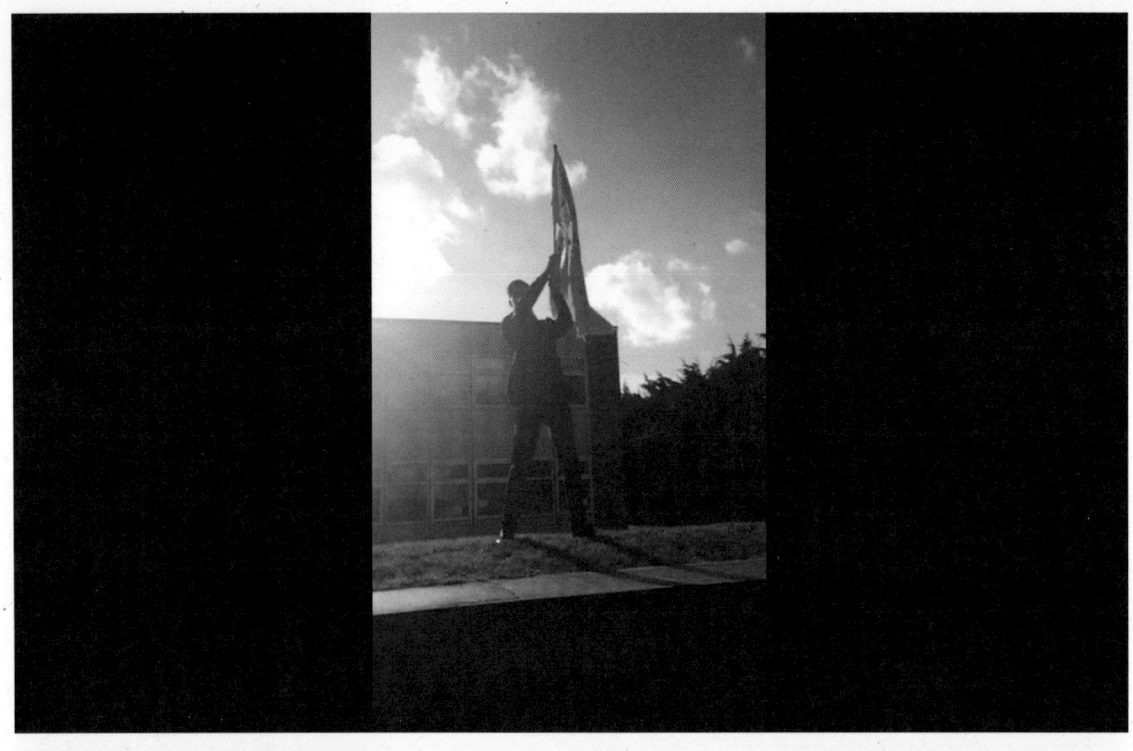

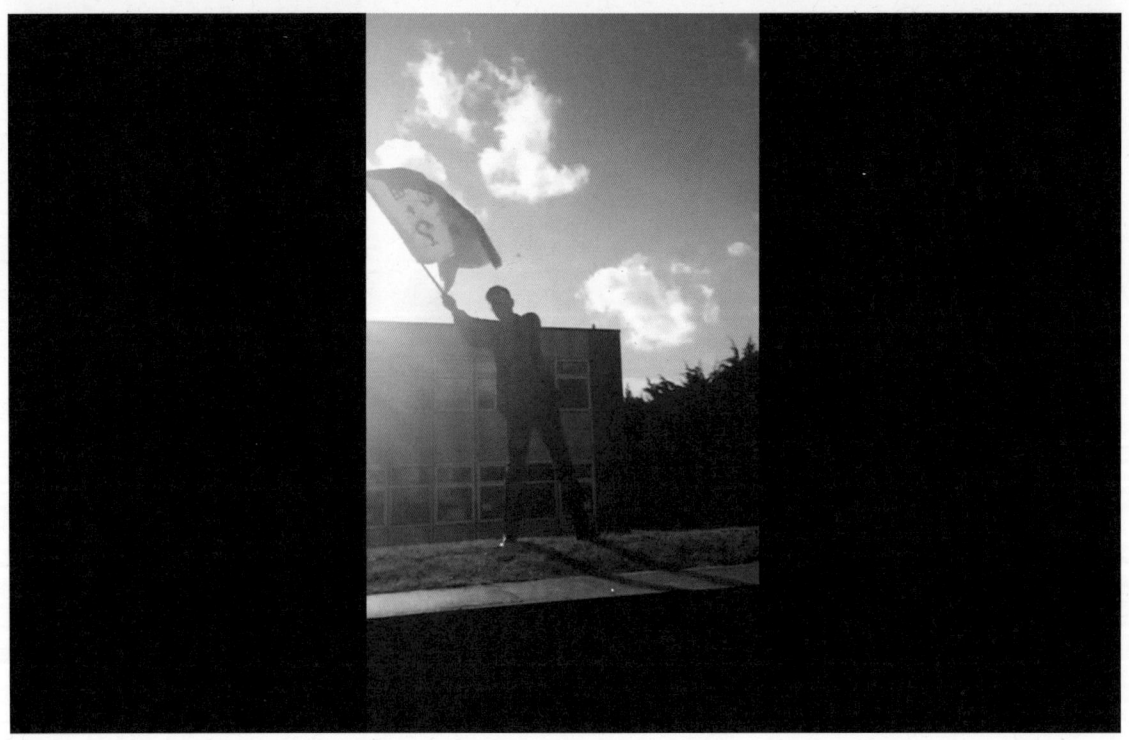

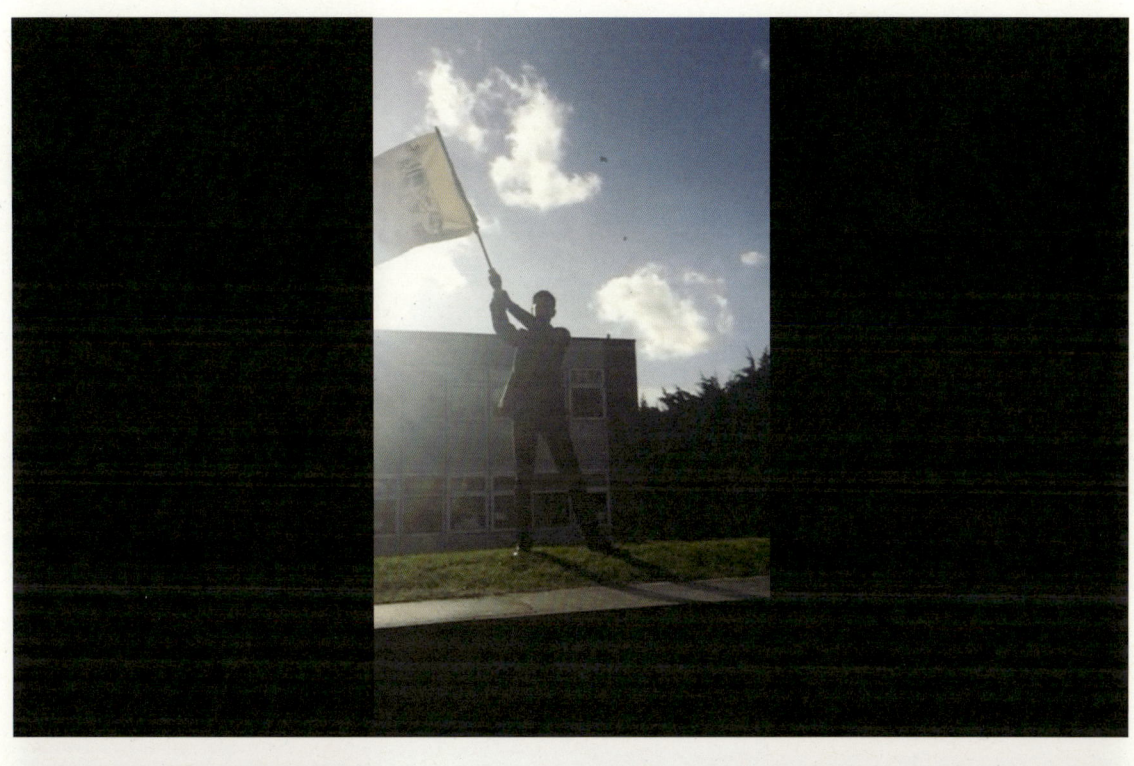

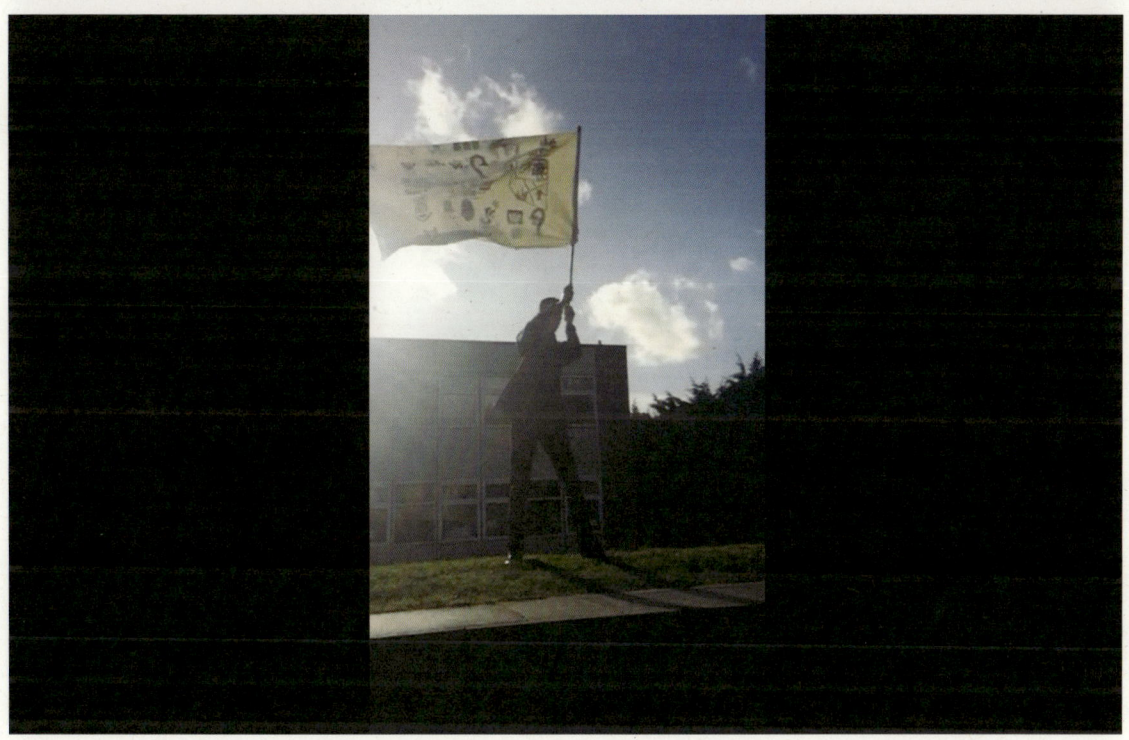

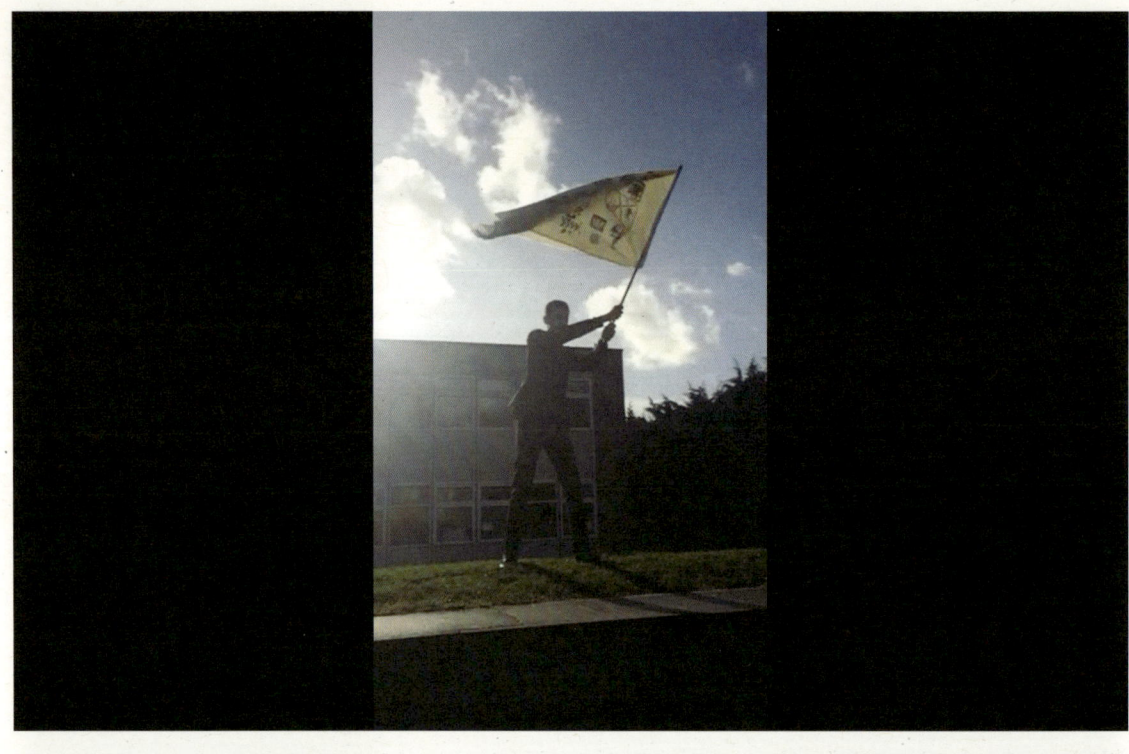

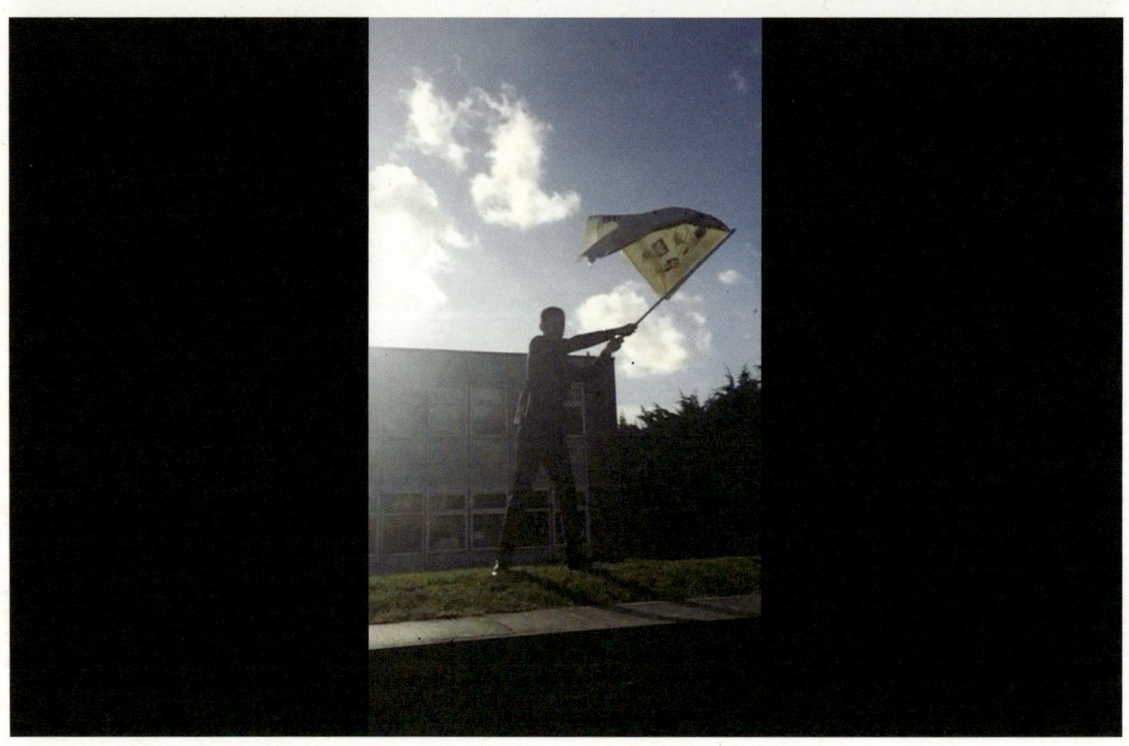

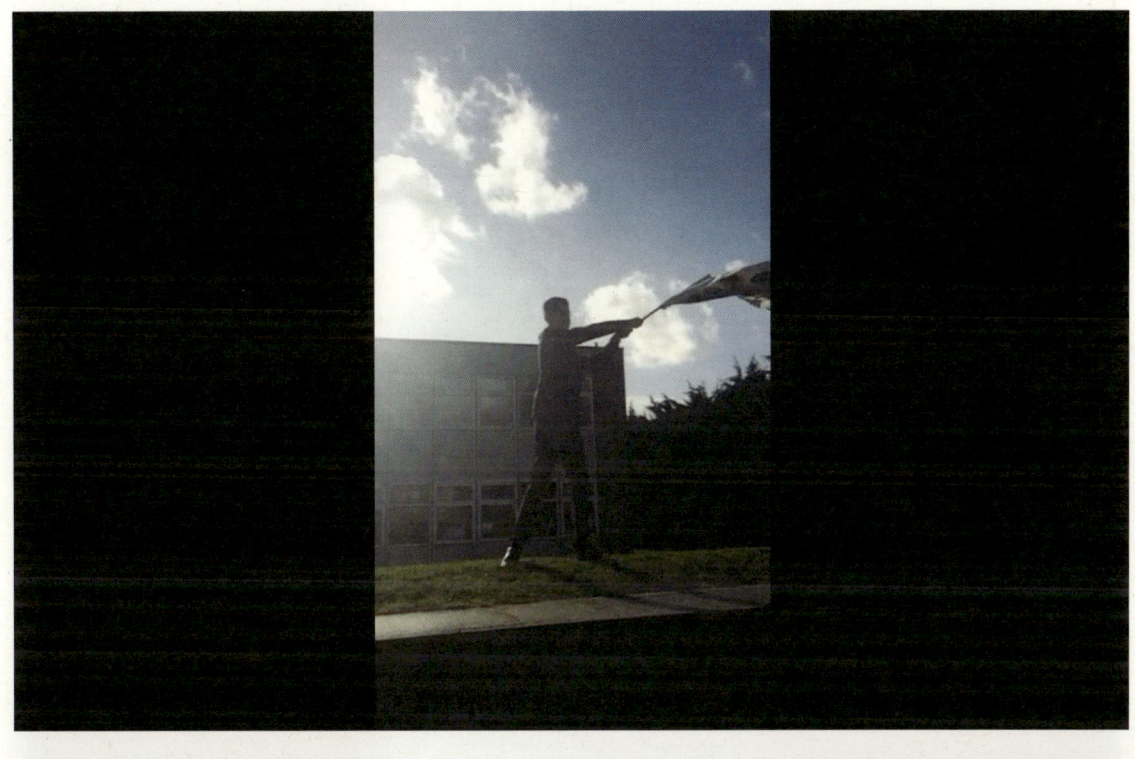

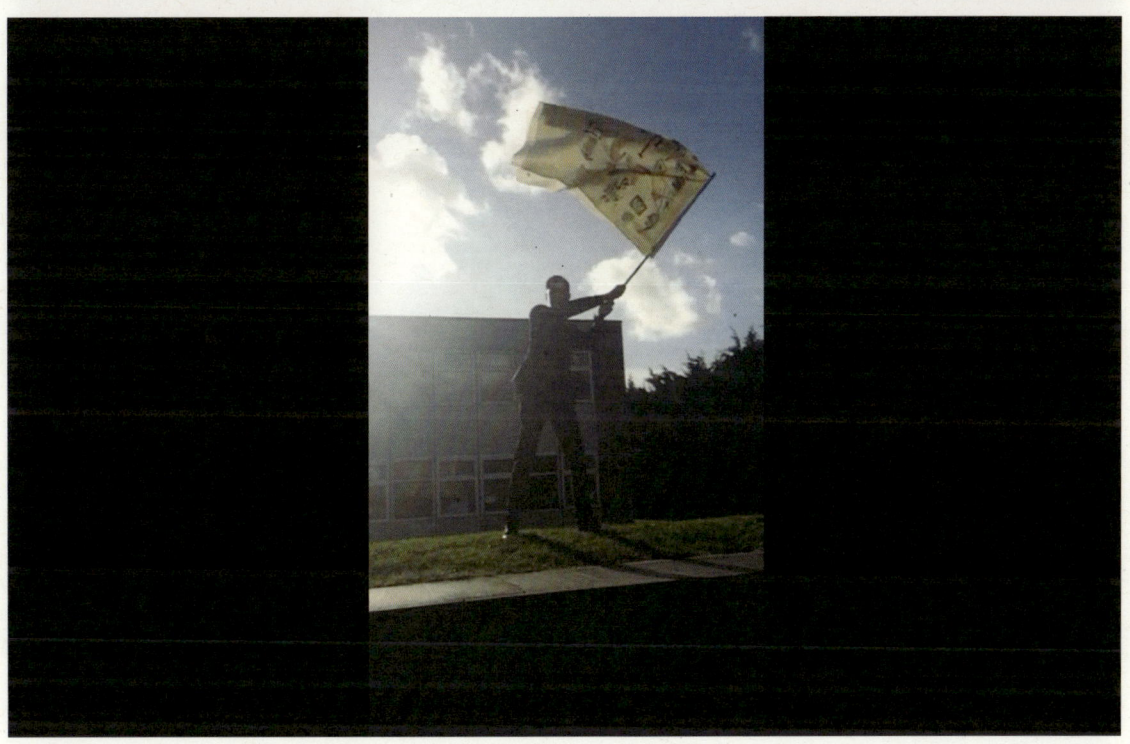

JENNI SNOWDEN

I feel so superior walking round holding a cup cake

you're old still

Miss, did you know ...ner miss was ...g down ...ning you said ...sson?

girls get more points because ...e teachers are ...h and oney only ...iris.

...nany ...had...

Are teachers allowed to faint?

Mis... dyed ...air? ...onde! With bleach? Is this your natural hair colour?

Miss, every time I come into the art office you always have ...ner a biscu... ...ndu...

...have ...ff

miss?

...u put a fish ...ld it

I can't find miss anywhere. She's like a ghost, especially because she's old and has grey hair.

...u're a ...!

c... ca... we ... agai...

I need art ther... after that art lesson

Teacher... Wh... were...

If Adam and Eve were the first people to be made and had their children, how were the other people from the bible made?

My resolution? To be me

What was the time when the first clock was made?

Sensible is my middle name... I lied

Teacher: Wh... the middle? Student: The equator...

Surrealism lets me get to the imaginative side of my mind

In 2018 i'm going to be independent

So, I wanted to use the idea of the strangeness of school as a way for the students to re-evaluate their own experience. Whilst picking up on the strange things I'd noticed about the school myself. The horrid digital BLEEPS, full of black and grey uniforms and a lack of boys weren't things I was accustomed to. Pips, campus buildings, uniforms, music on Fridays chosen by students played throughout the school (blaring electro alluring voices; odd in the hospital corridors), teacher's swift 'traffic warden' gesturing. It was all rather stifling and kinda odd. Routines and order and sameness, leading to unusual manifestations of uniqueness and character. All smooshed together. Symbols of my transition into enforcer and authoritarian, rather than watcher. My clothes were businessy, but my movements weren't quite swift or smooth enough and sometimes I'd jig down the school's

walkways envisioning myself as the toddler intruding on her father's BBC news broadcast. Naïve or nay, I wanted to lead my students on a reimagining of the school. Something akin to the terror tunnel of the Wonka Chocolate Factory. I imagined the school pips reverberating in our ears as we trekked the school's winding tracks, rainbow through our homemade physical filters (cellophane pipe cleaner glasses). Our 'looking tools' would help us navigate our way through the location. These tools becoming increasing useful. Magic sunglasses for a wider view, utility belts and mini transforming pianos (boredom reliever). These defenders of the self in this scenario, these 'looking tools' a strange support or a way of allowing others in on your filtered vision. I wanted to cover myself in colour. Crafting my own tool/ suit from felt squares, cellophane, newsprint and art storeroom scraps. My costume in my momentary role as Willy Wonka / Joseph Beuys. Beuy's own felt suit a gesture of unattainable comfort, warmth and itchy, decaying, moth eaten formality. I'd always wanted to wrap myself up in one of those suffocating looking blankets.

But here the comparison sat almost too comfortably in my new teacher brain. Willy Wonka and Joseph Beuys. Inventors, tool users, teachers, thinkers, gesturers, holders of eye glimmers, wearers of 'ensembles' and a keen sense of hat. Perfect.

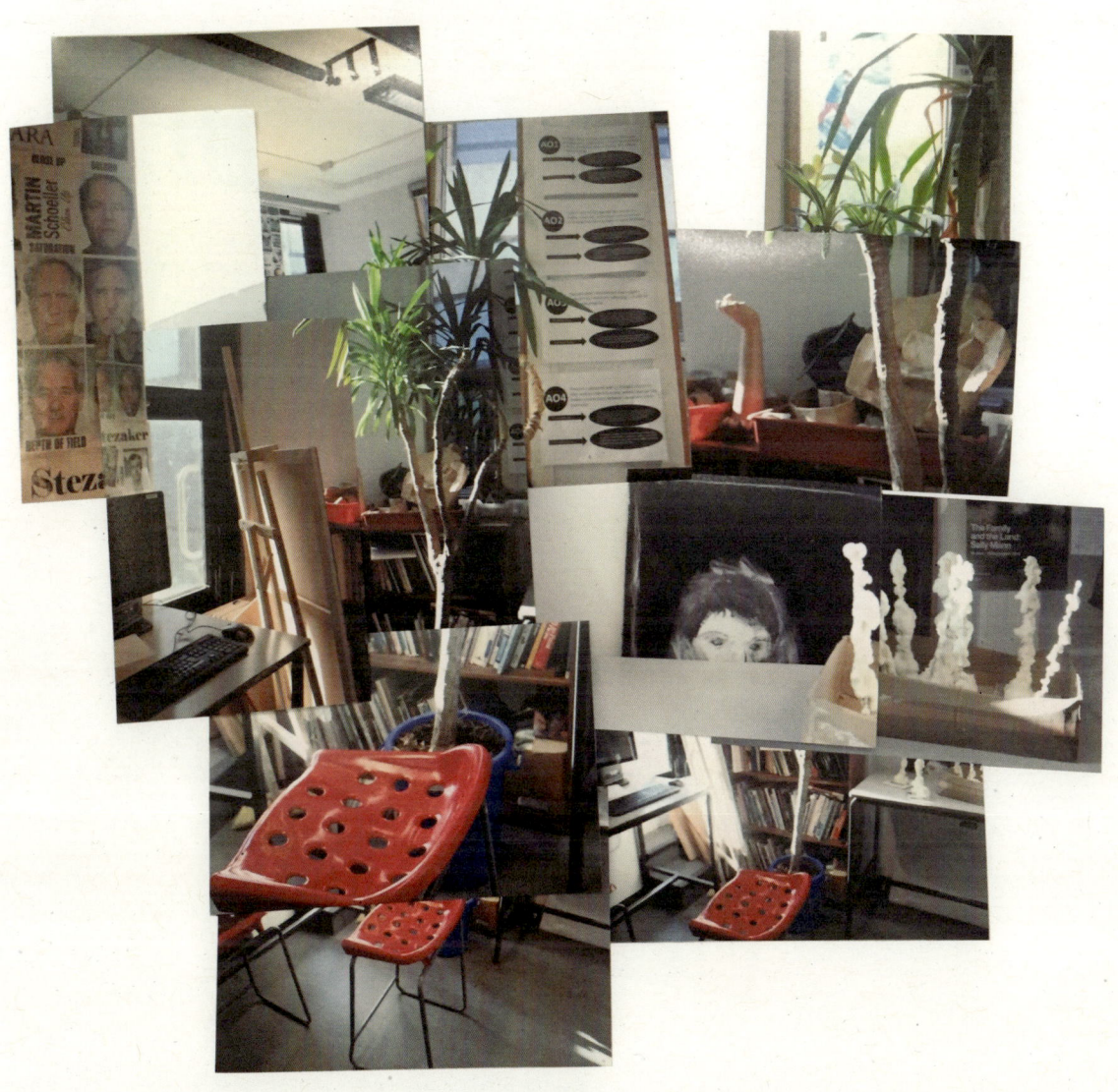

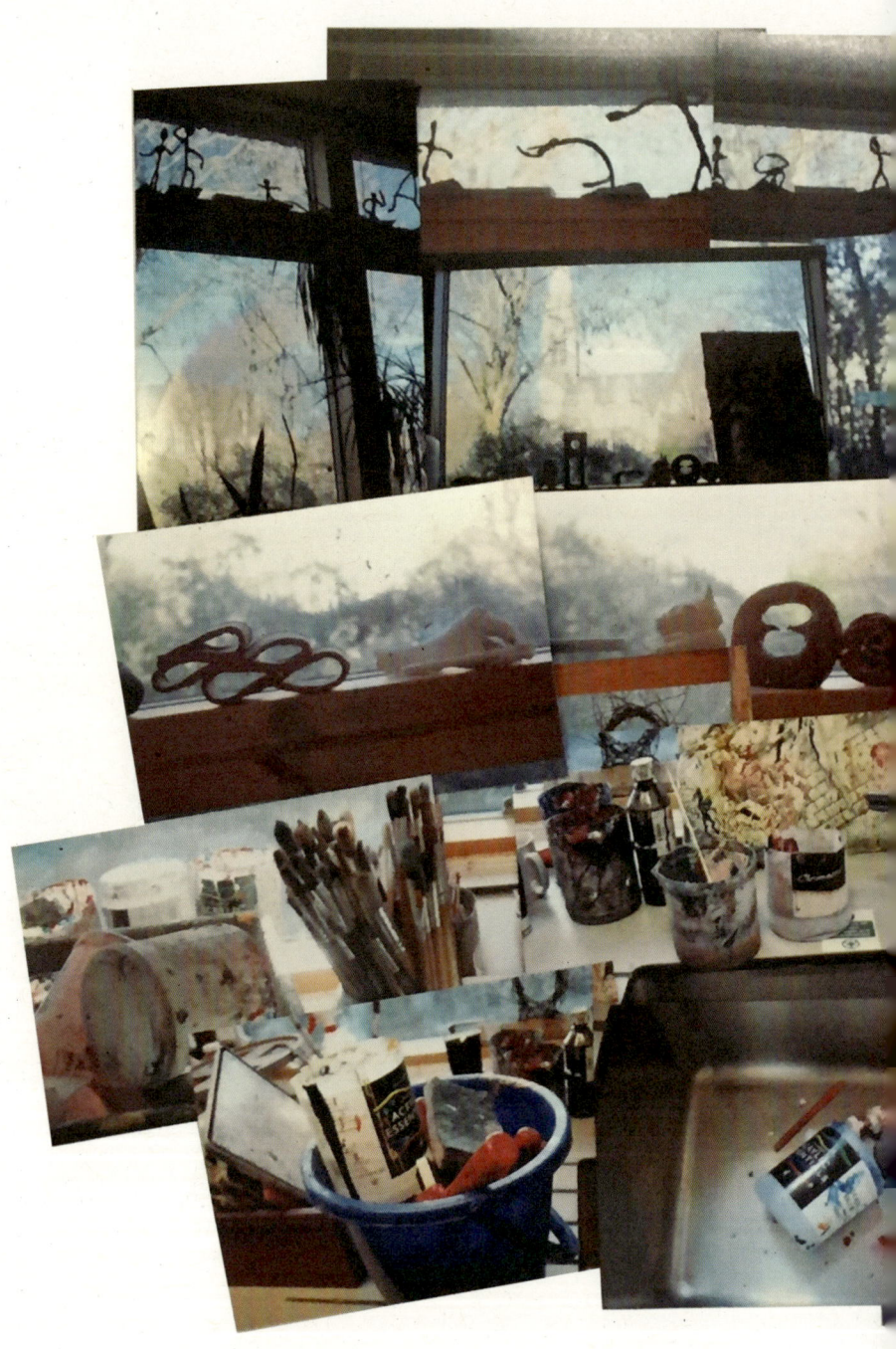

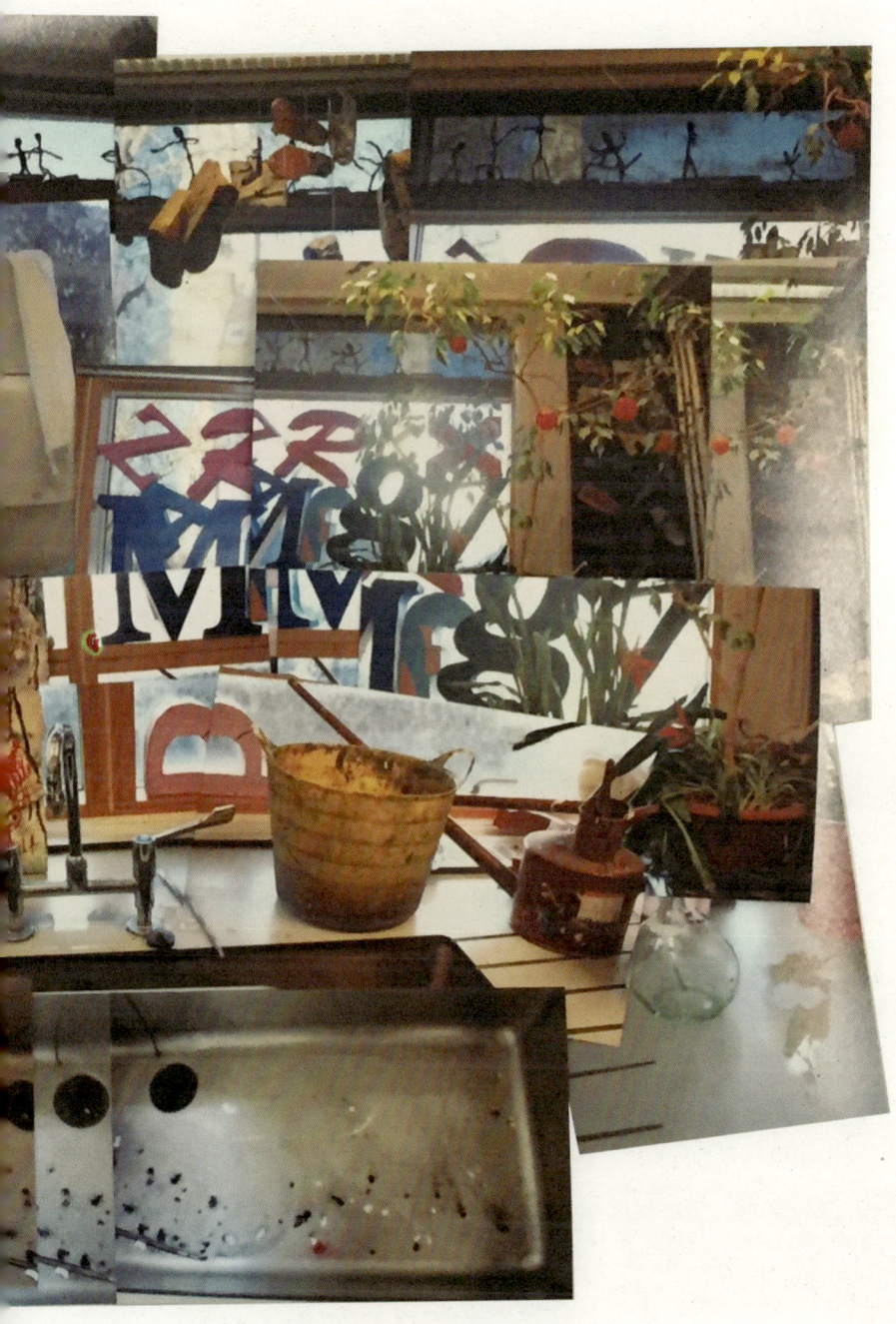

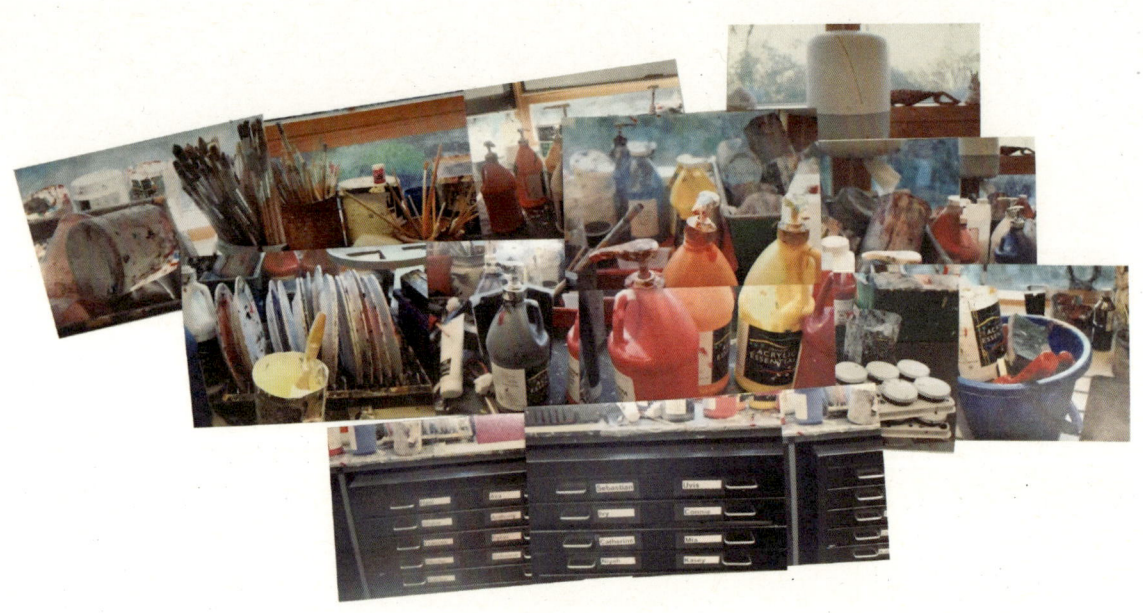

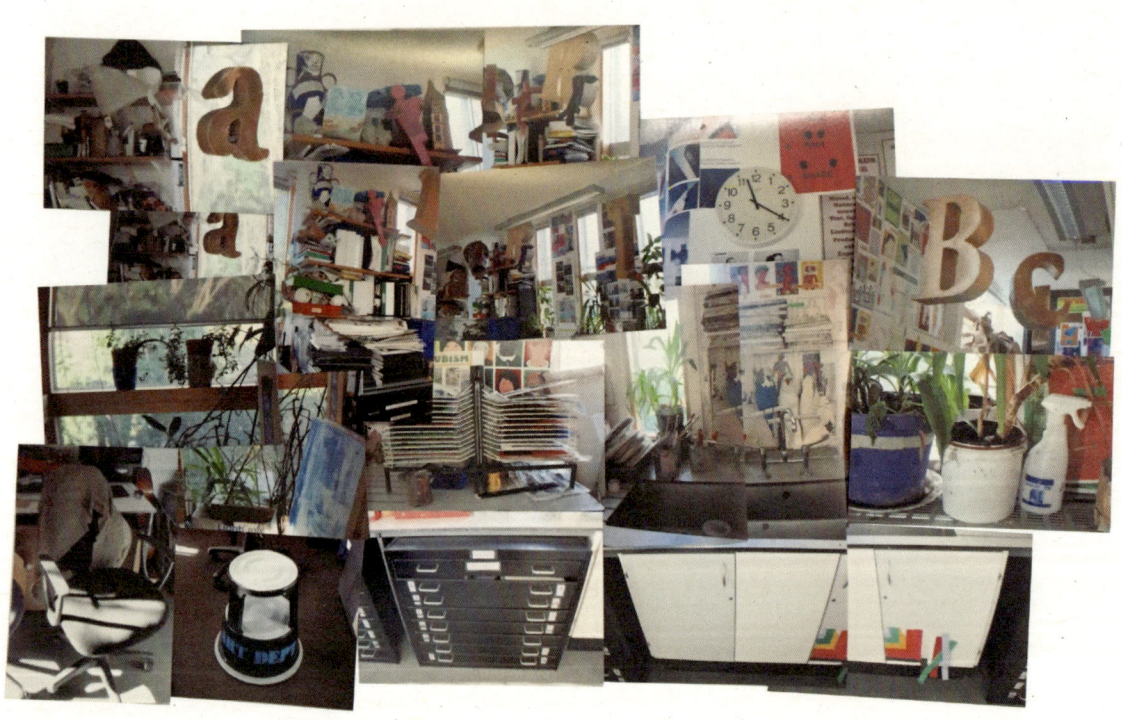

One of my responsibilities during my first school placement as an art student teacher, was to take an 'Art Enrichment' class once a week for a Year 7 group. The students had opted to take 'Art Enrichment' over other subjects. This was allocated time for them to enjoy the subject within a workshop-based capacity. I observed my mentor take this session for a few weeks before I began running it. In all the sessions I observed, the students were told to paint numerous roses for the set of the upcoming school production 'Beauty and the Beast'. They sat in silence, week upon week, as they painted identical roses. Once the roses were finished, they were allowed to draw shoes.

There was an interesting air of contradiction surrounding this session and the position of the teacher within this context. After all, this was not a lesson. This was an opportunity for the teacher and students to play and explore the subject. Consequently, I decided to ask the students what they thought 'Art' taught them:

'new skills',

'learning to do things better, like drawing',

'creativity'

With this, I decided I was going to explore the role of the art teacher, ownership of work, and the consequent responses from students. First, I adopted a similarly directive role as the teacher I had observed. It transpired that none of the students knew how to sew. As the 'teacher,' I would teach them how to sew. Initially, they enjoyed it.

They showed enthusiasm for working with a new material and the challenge that it entailed. They battled patiently and quietly for the hour-long session, threading the needle, making repeated knots and getting tangled.

Gradually, they all demonstrated good progression. Box-ticked. By the third session of sewing they were definitely 'doing things better'. However, it was clear when talking to them, through this basic repetition of 'honing their skills' they were no longer stimulated. When asked what they thought about this process of learning, they answered robotically with words that would fit well in an assessment capacity. They were bored. For me, this pulls into question the notions of learning and teaching. They were learning a new skill, they were demonstrating progress, but there was a distinct lack of creativity and ownership over their work. I asked them, again, to consider what art teaches them and this time, to sew their answers into a piece of paper.

Second, I became the facilitator. This was in the fourth session I had with the group. The only instructions I gave the students was that they were to work in groups of six, to pick a word that had been sewn the previous week to work from, and to only use the materials supplied. They had an hour to create a response to their groups chosen word.

The materials I supplied for them were non-school materials, such as latex gloves, glow sticks, bin bags, tin foil, rubber bands and balloons. The words that they had laboriously sewn during the previous session were now a stimulus for making. A mad dash to grab materials ensued and debates erupted between the groups. A fever of creativity was clear. When talking to students about what they were making there was no stumbling over what they thought I wanted to hear, they had ownership over their work and new what they wanted to say. Some students started dancing when they realised they could blow up the latex gloves like a balloon. The teacher told them to 'stop it, or they would have to sit out'.

At the end of the session they curated their pieces on black card, placed on the floor in the middle of the room. Their exhibition complete, each group took turns to present their work to the rest of the group. An exciting discourse began, surrounding intention and interpretation. I asked them which word they would use to sum up this creative process: 'Fun.'

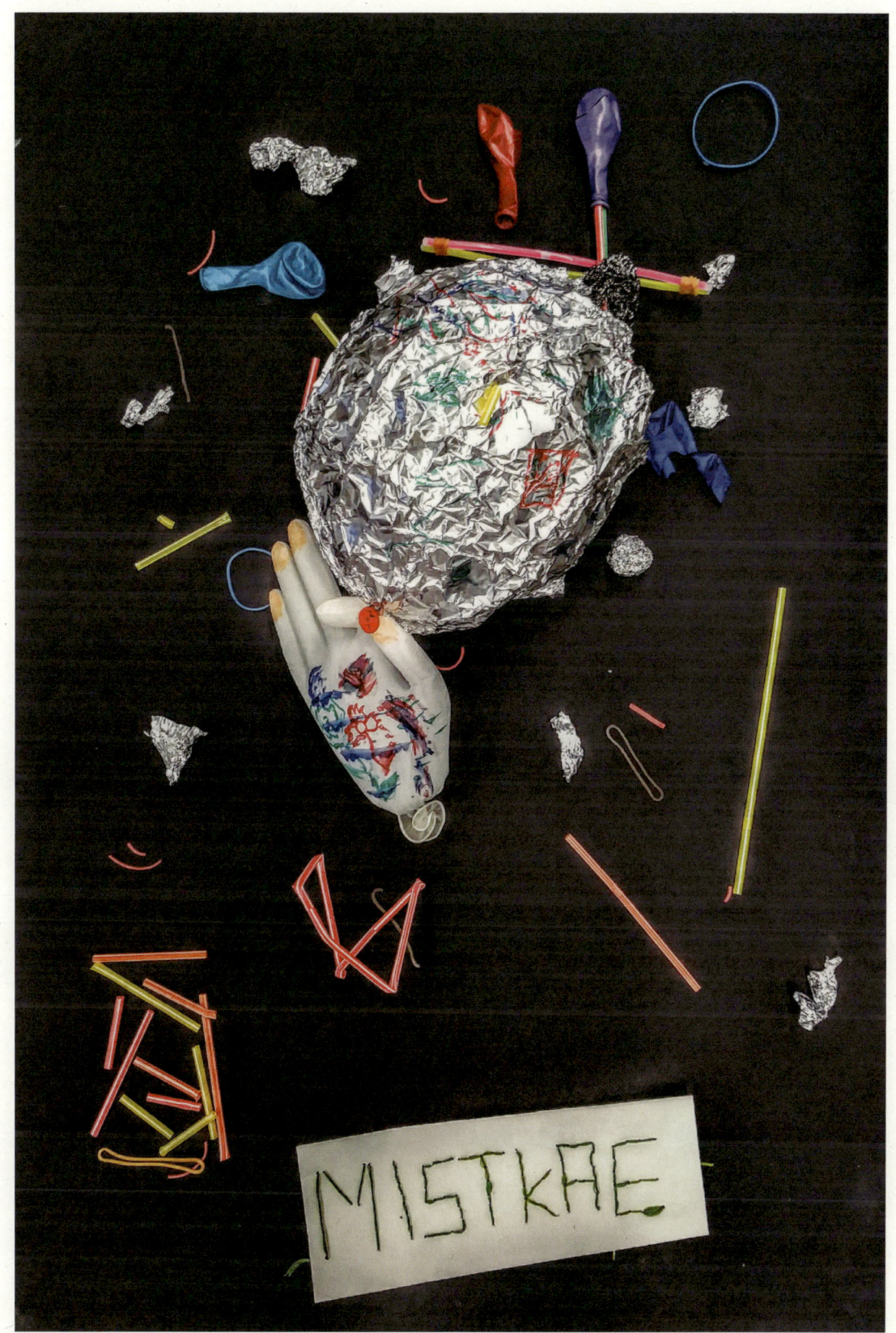

In 1993 the United Nations Educational, Scientific and Cultural Organisation (UNESCO) set up the 'International Commission on Education for the Twenty-First Century' as a way of addressing globalisation and rapid techno-logical change. Three years later, the commission published a report outlining 'four pillars of knowledge', around which education should be re-framed in order for it to respond to the new millennium.

These four areas were: learning to know; learning to do; learning to live together; and learning to be. Since publication, these pillars have been hugely influential in how national governments formulate their curricula. They are considered indivisible and co-dependent from one another and, in essence, viewed as symbolic of a need for a new global, experience, both for the individual and communities at large. It is now common for cultural platforms, governments and organi-sations see learning as a life-long endeavour. Quality education, and good schools, are seen as a first port-of-call for acquiring skills in being creative, cooperative and resourceful, beyond the classroom.

Since the UNESCO report, there has been much discussion about the need for students to obtain core skills, specifically in terms of developing digital literacy and creativity. Critical thinking and citizenship have also been on many educational agendas, as emerging social and economic trends overturn traditional frameworks for employment. Programmes such as Connecting Classrooms, from the British Council and the Department for International Development, believe that through sharing experiences of other cultures and building international networks of learners and teachers, these opportunities will not only broaden horizons but also tackle issues around employability and inequality.

The National Curriculum in England mirrors the sentiments put forward by both UNESCO and the British Council insofar as it requires for schools to promote spiritual, moral, cultural, mental and physical development, preparing pupils for life outside of compulsory education. Expressed within the 'Purpose of Study' for Art and Design is a requirement that 'as pupils progress they should… know how art and design both reflect and shape our history, and contribute to the culture, creativity and wealth of our nation.' In these times, it's easy to see this statement as a double-edged sword – it seems to reflect not just the plurality of British culture, but also a growing nationalism that wants to embed our notions of nationhood and ergo of education through the prism of the past.

Nicholas Addison, from the University of the Arts, writes that history has been about exchange and diversity rooted in Europe; and included within this rhetoric are issues around colonialism, diaspora, post-colonialism and transatlantic dialogues. This makes it imperative that we as teachers understand how important it is to treat and teach works of art produced in, or by artists, who reside outside Western European frameworks. As both a student and trainee teacher, I've seen schemes of learning entitled 'African Art', or 'Aboriginal Art'. From one point of view this is laudable, it helps learners make sense of the world and understand the multitude of lived experiences within different communities of people. However, these titles seem to repress complex societal structures into a narrative of Otherness that re-asserts Western dominance in the field of art and design.

It's important to recognise that fundamental words used in art education, such as 'depth', 'form', and 'tone' – words that are supplied to pupils to critically analyse their own work and that of others – can impede their understanding of how others view themselves and their environment. I have seen works by Australian artists like Amanda Nakamarra Curtis, be dismissed as good examples of landscape painting because her work isn't recognised as having the qualities of perspective; and yet, hers, like many others of a similar background, would not only value these images as indicative of their landscape, but consider them also as cartographical resources. Whilst Nakamarra's work may not imitate a three-dimensionality we see in European traditions of landscape, it's important to realise that the use of key words can often delimit explorations of practitioners who reside outside these Western art traditions, reinforcing a cultural hegemony. As Addison writes: 'Apply aesthetic criteria to art objects that hold no direct relationship to those criteria and you have a recipe for reinforcing difference and inferiority'.

The same goes for the inconsistency to which art and design teachers frame Western art into movements and periods of history, and yet, those works made outside Europe or North America, are categorised by region or continent. Distinguishing maker and work in such a way diminishes a deeper understanding of cultural and social histories; it places art and design production within an a-temporal framework that is often biased and outdated.

It's also important to remember that most classrooms house within them pupils who have connections to these parts of the world as well. Notions of cultural identity are an opportunity to expand points of view. By comparing art ethnographically, there is a tendency to generalise aesthetic values, belief systems and collective histories that not only do a disservice to makers and their work, but also to the students in the class. Art and Design teachers need to think carefully about how they select their makers and the most effective way of framing their work within lessons. Teaching to a diverse classroom is an opportunity to give voice to the numerous cultural identities and lived experiences of its pupils, and teaching art and design is an opportunity to address the diversity and similarities of human creativity.

Art and design has become the right
of a privileged few, who often don't recognise
or care about their advantage.

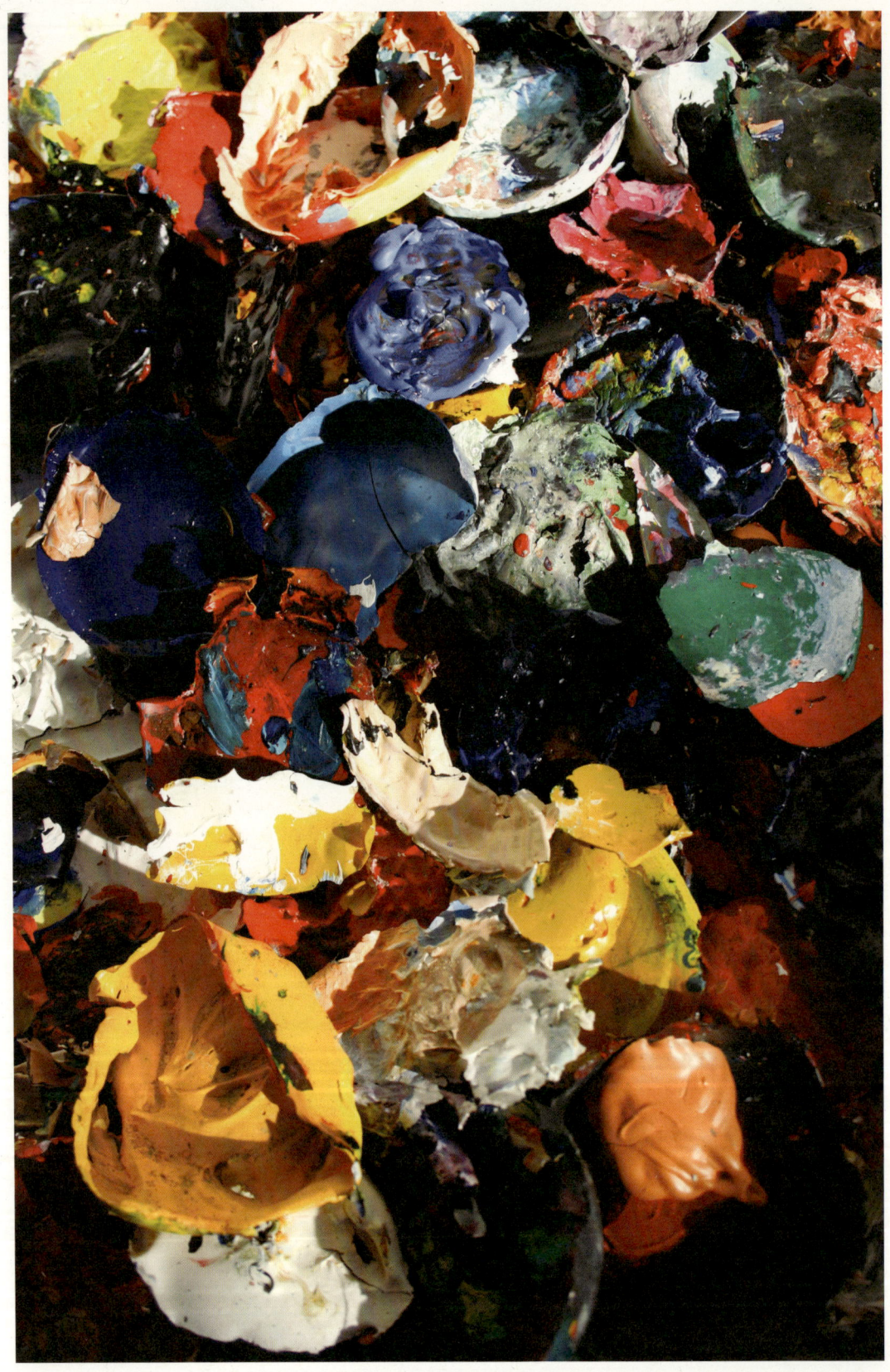

ALICE HAVERS

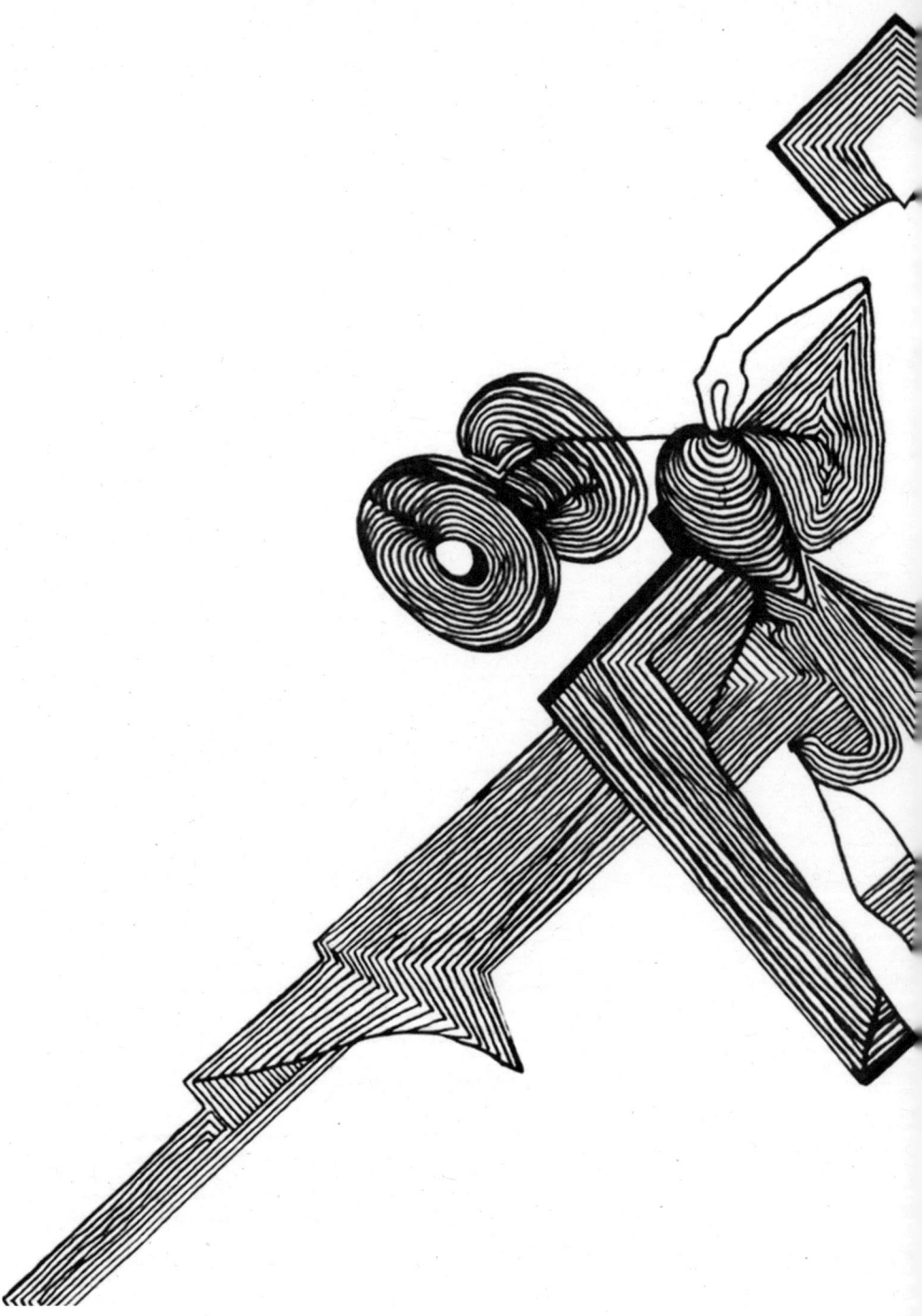

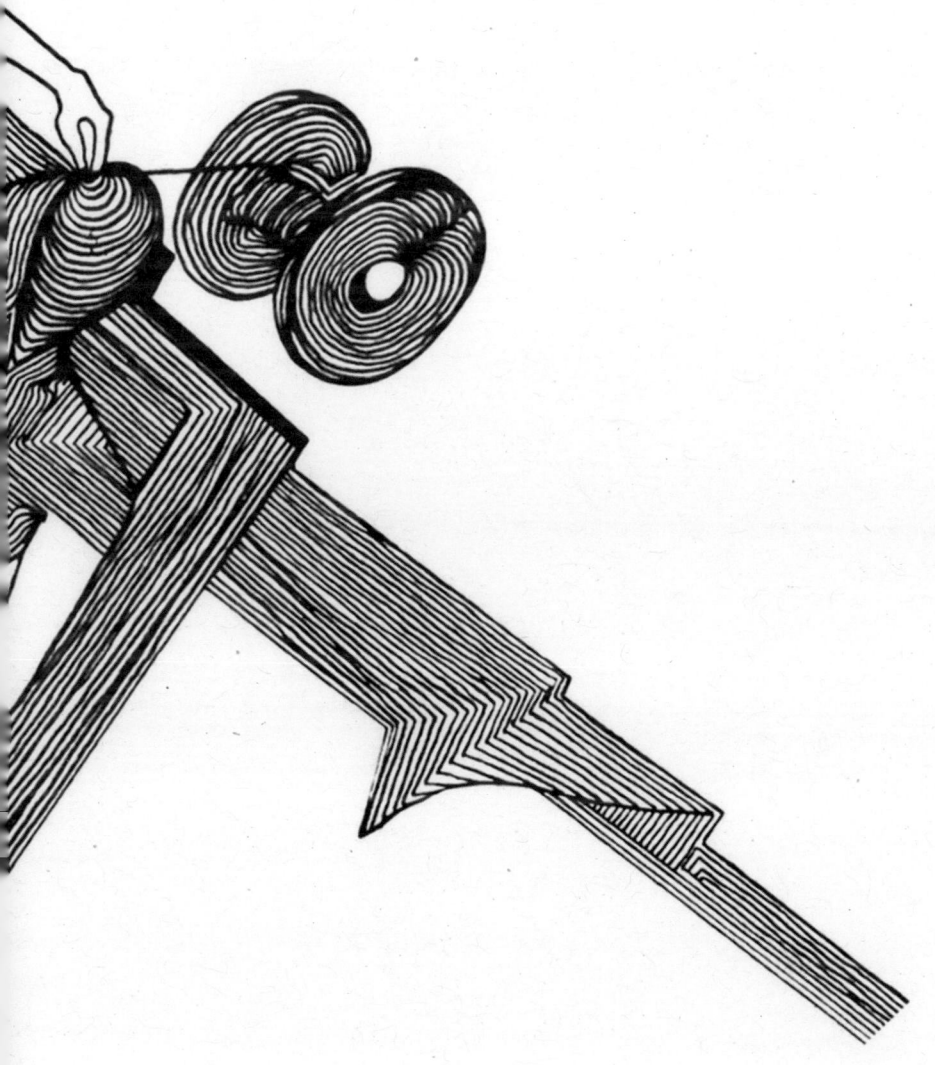

Professor Macintosh commanding
the functionality of all students

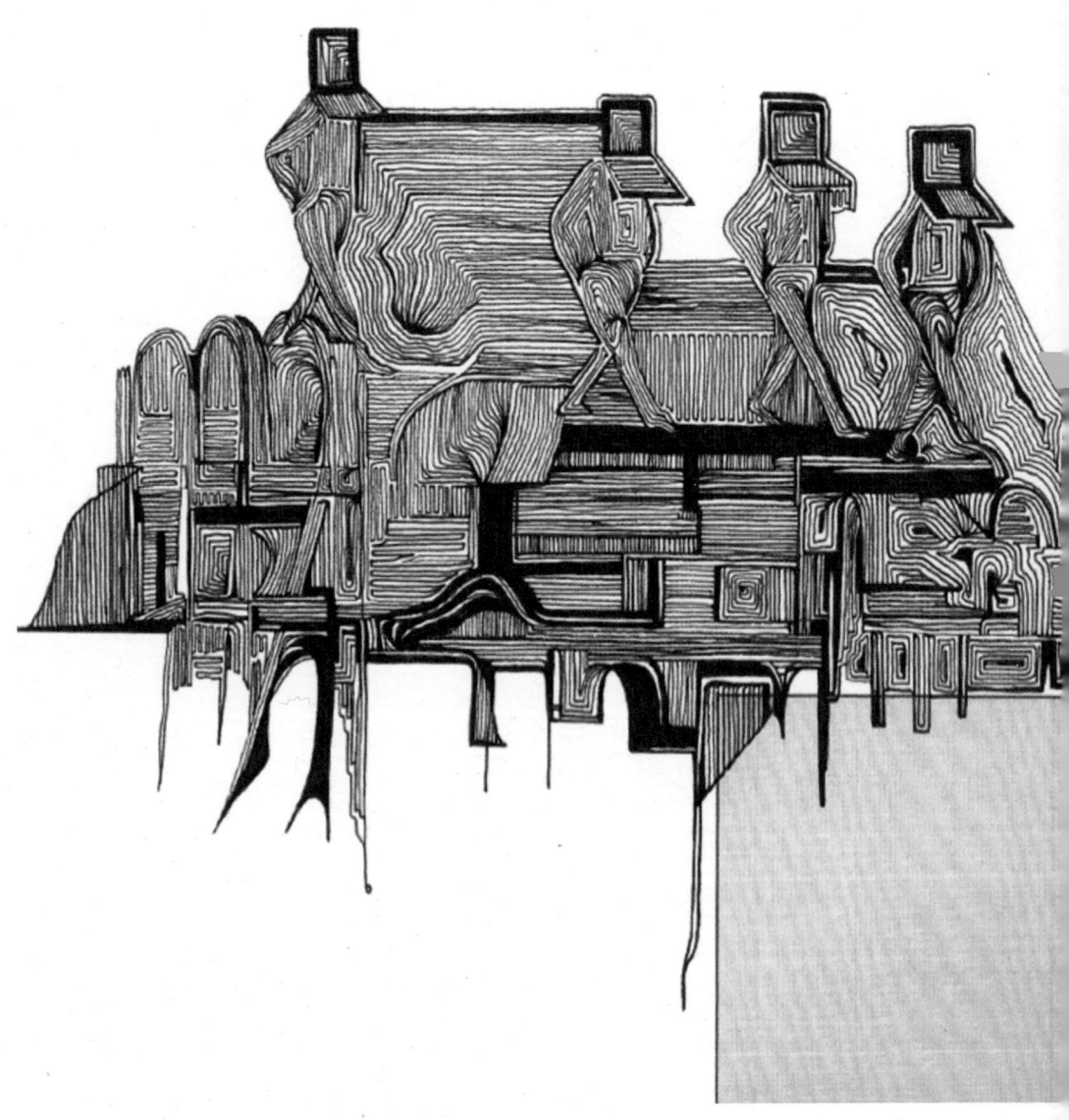

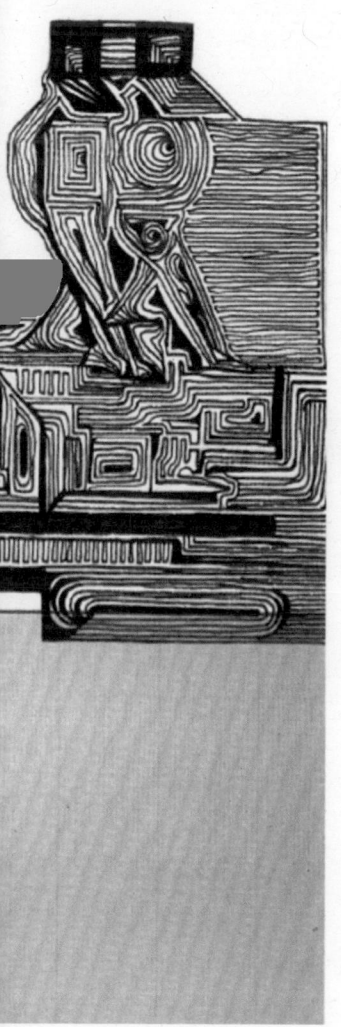

Students in a technological haze
promenading the corridors from
pod to pod

85

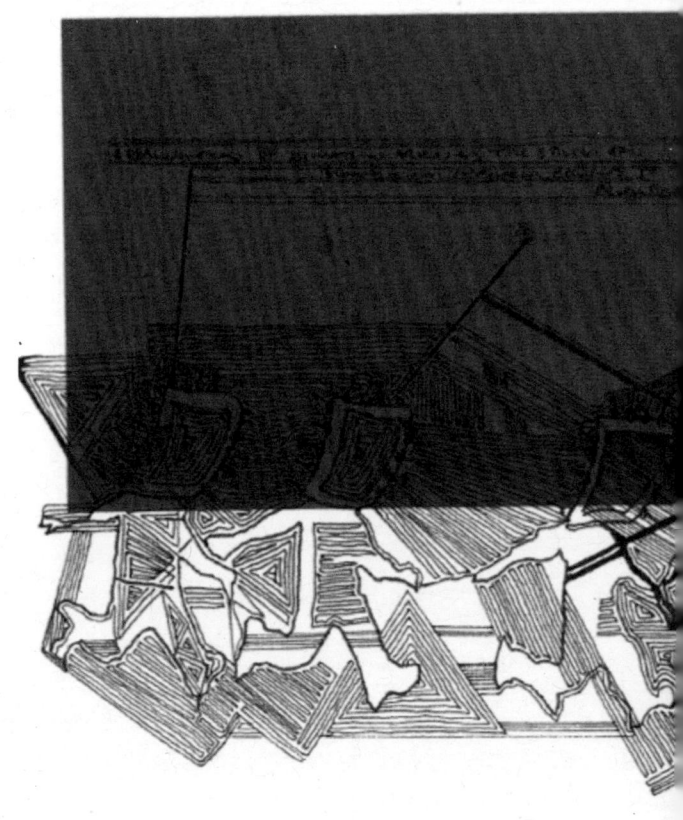

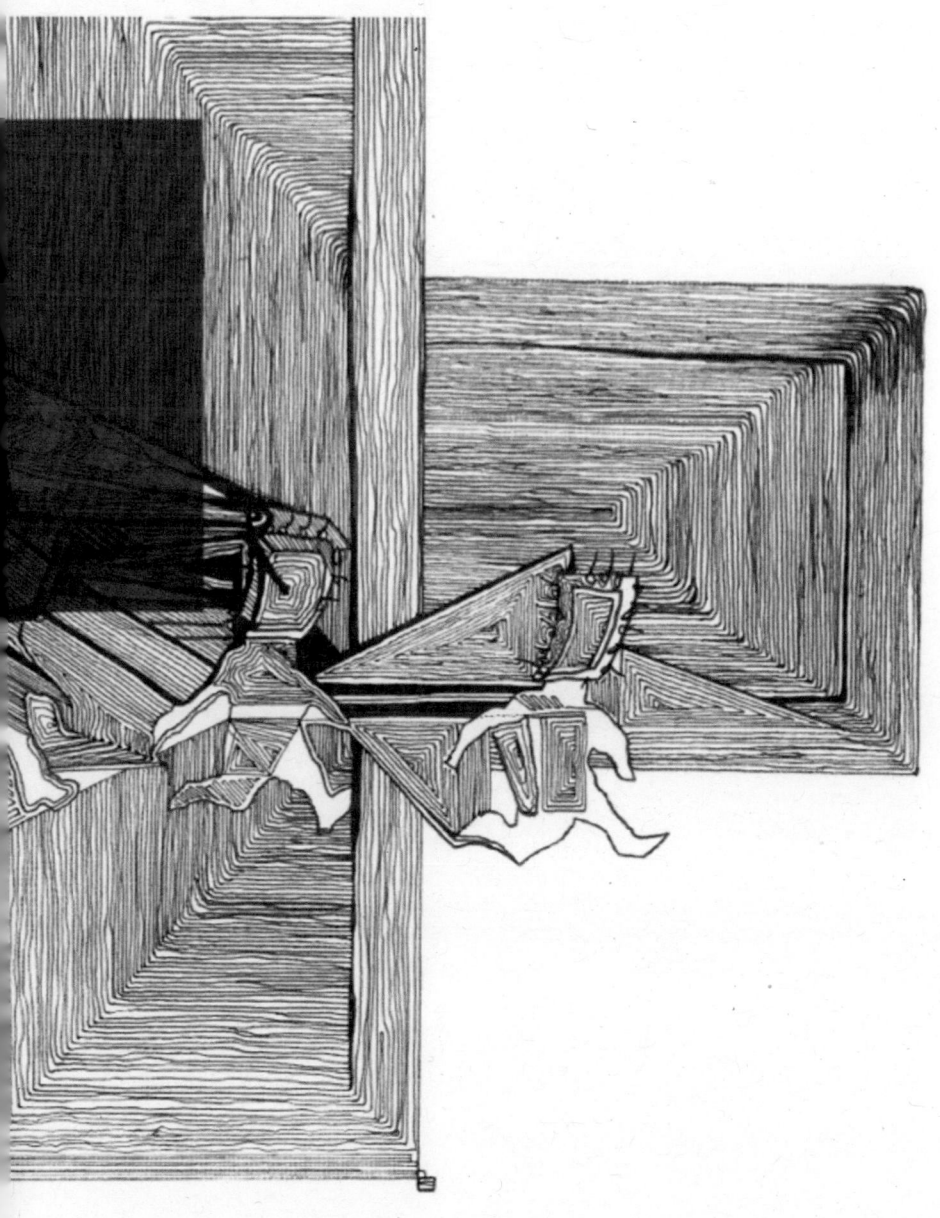

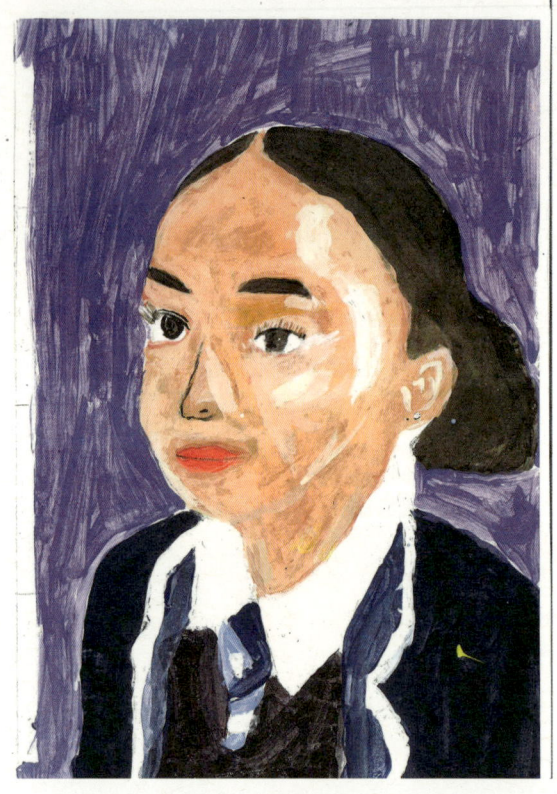
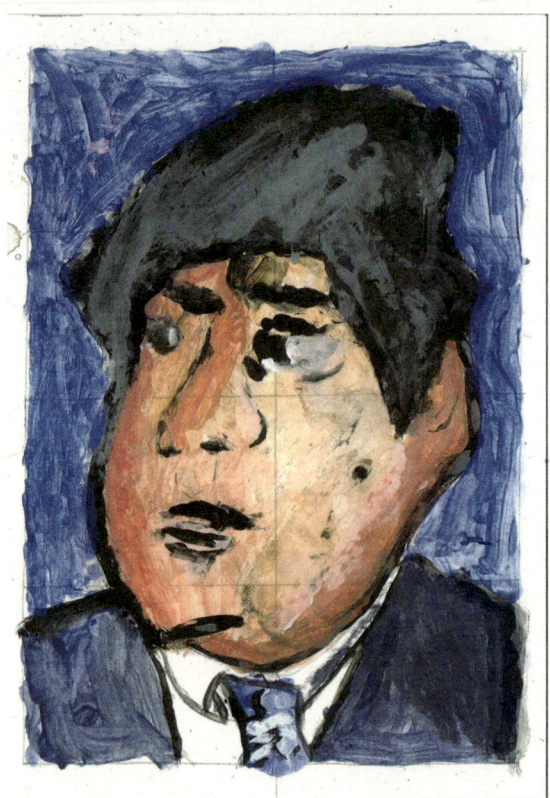
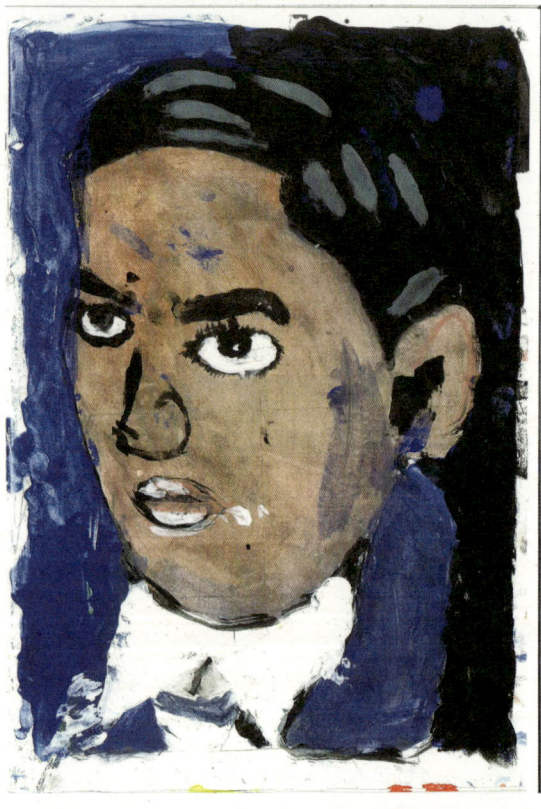
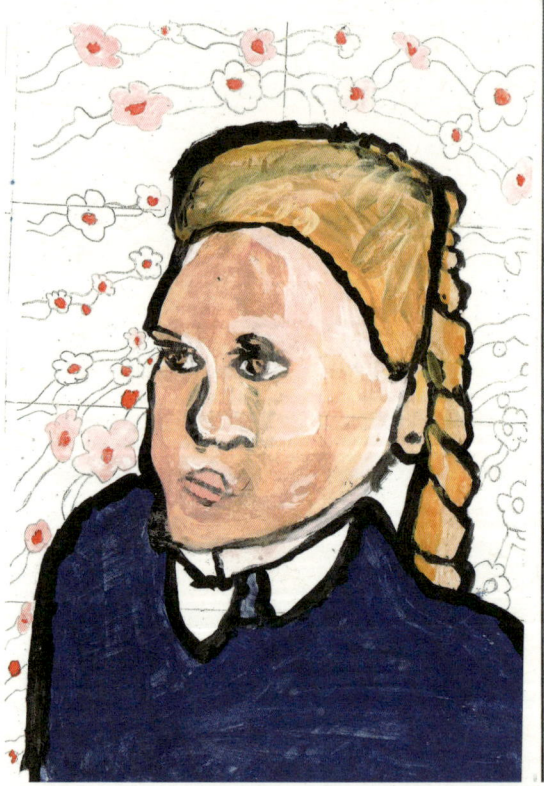

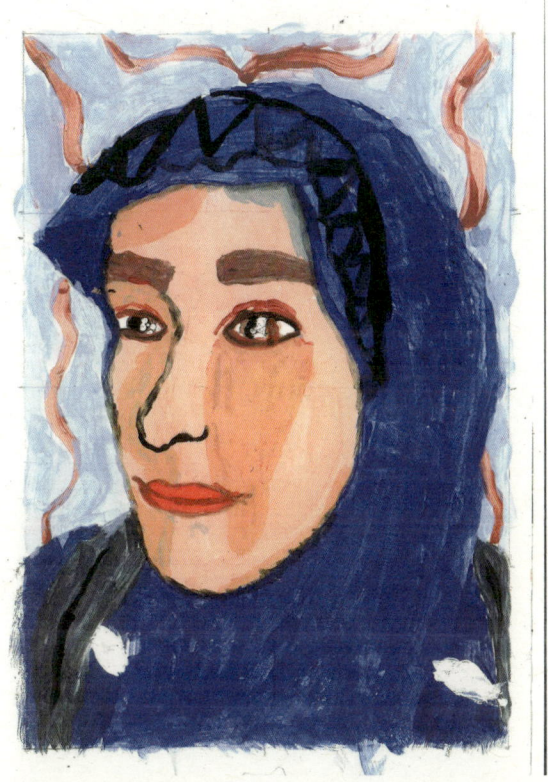

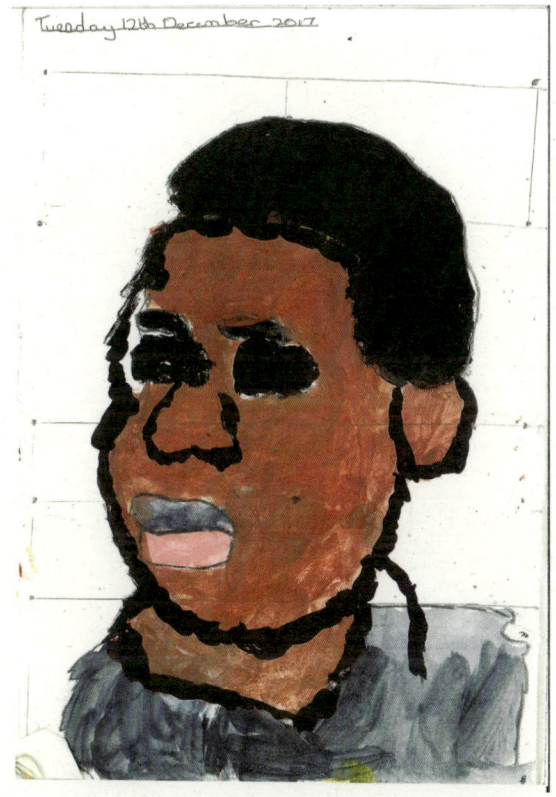

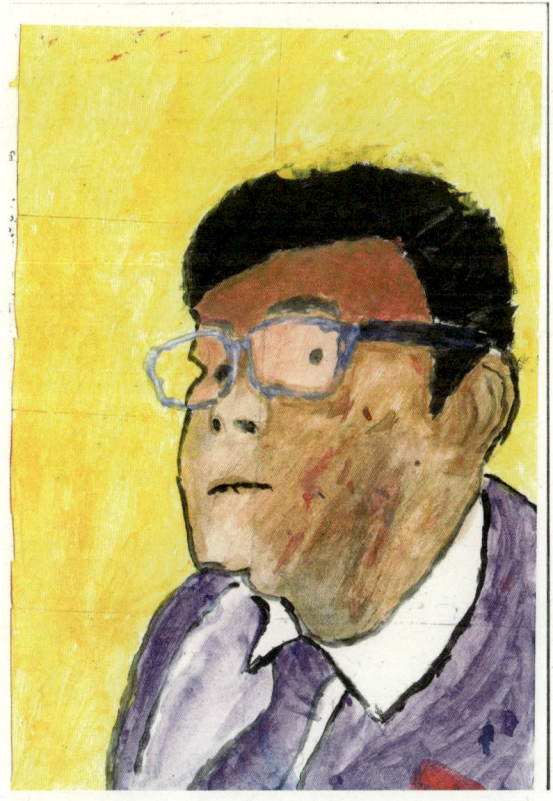

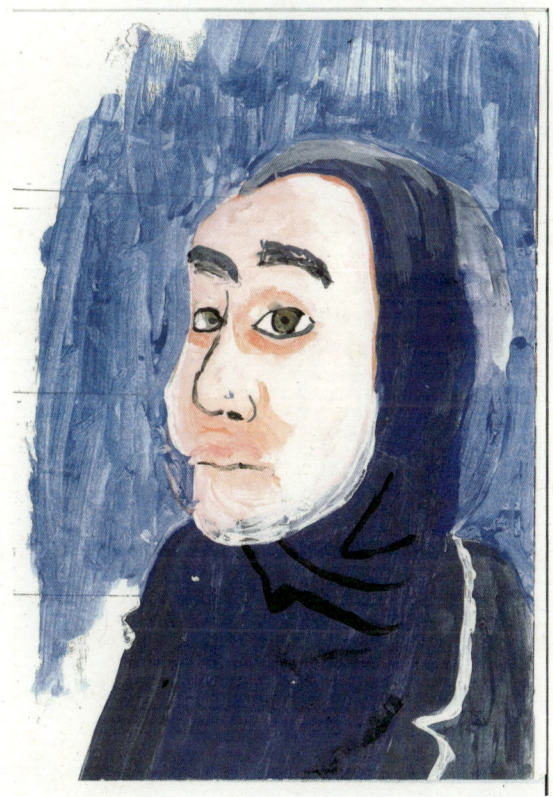

91

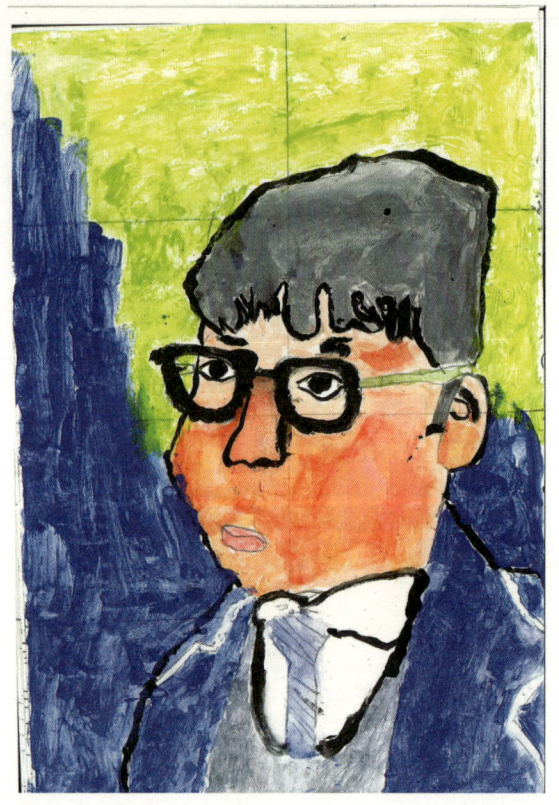
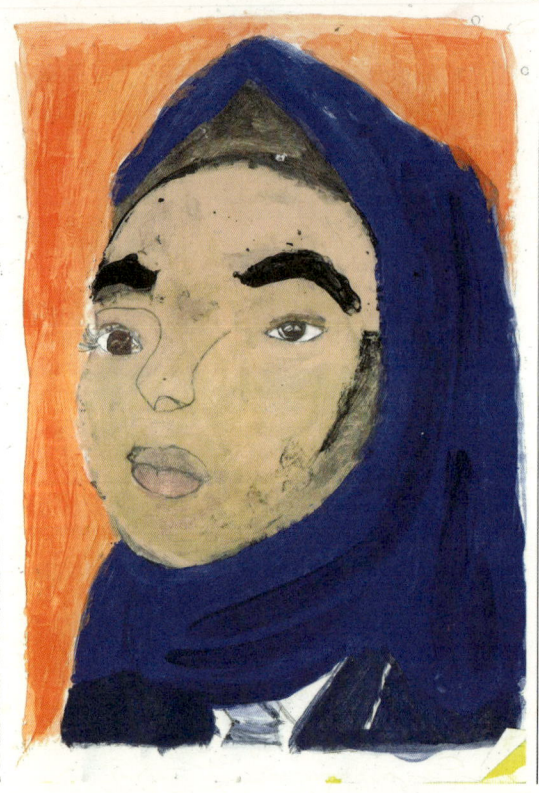
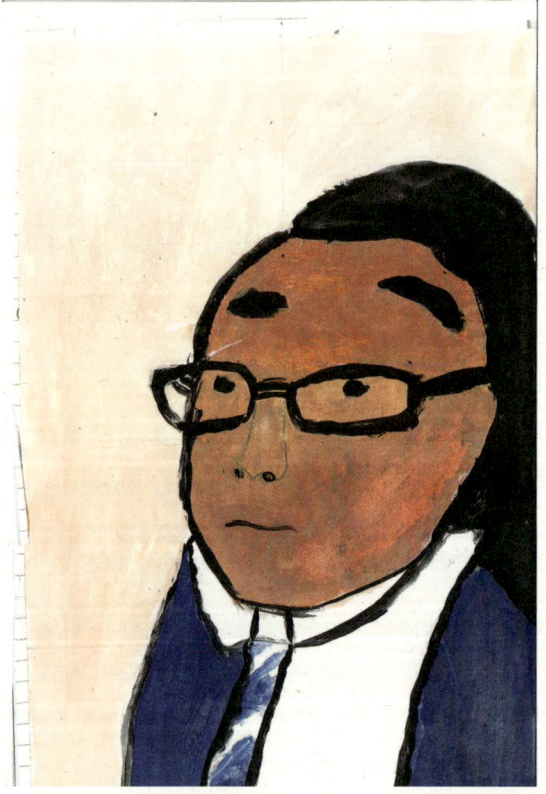
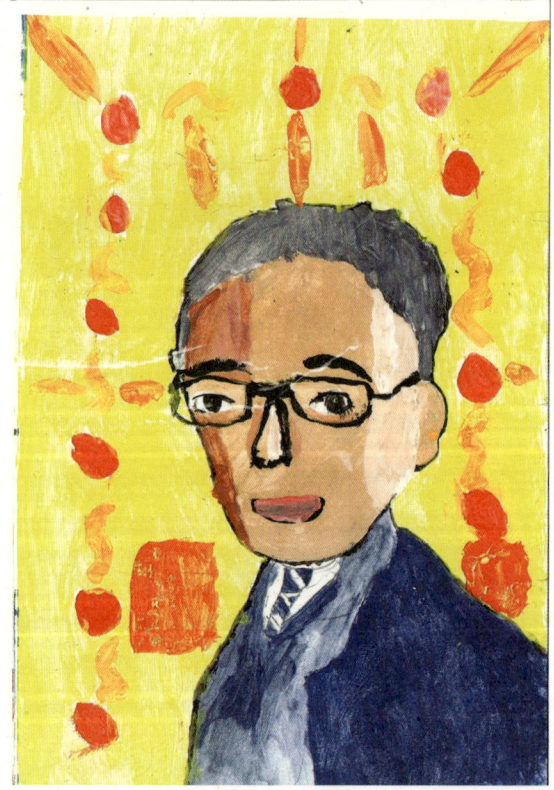

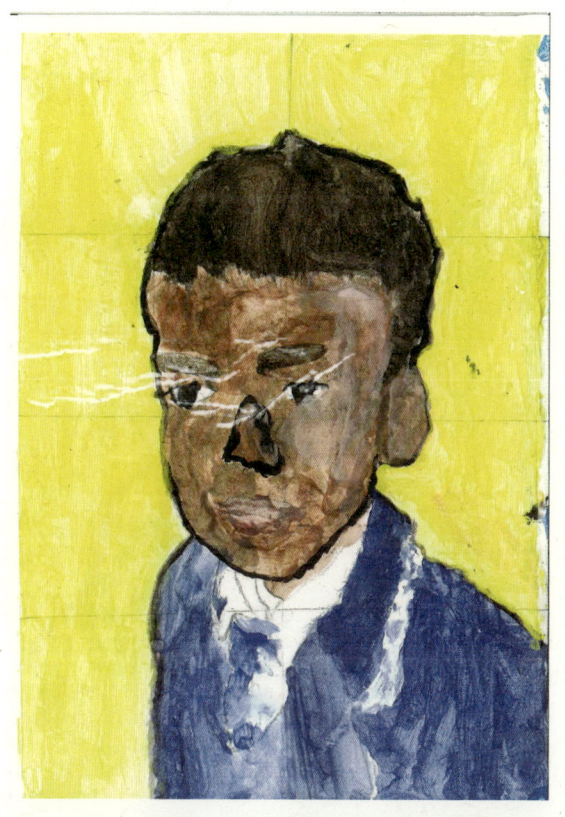
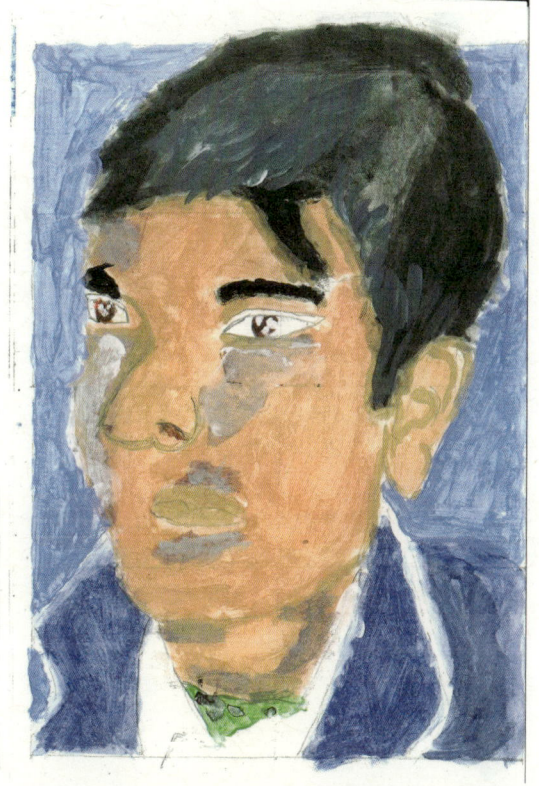
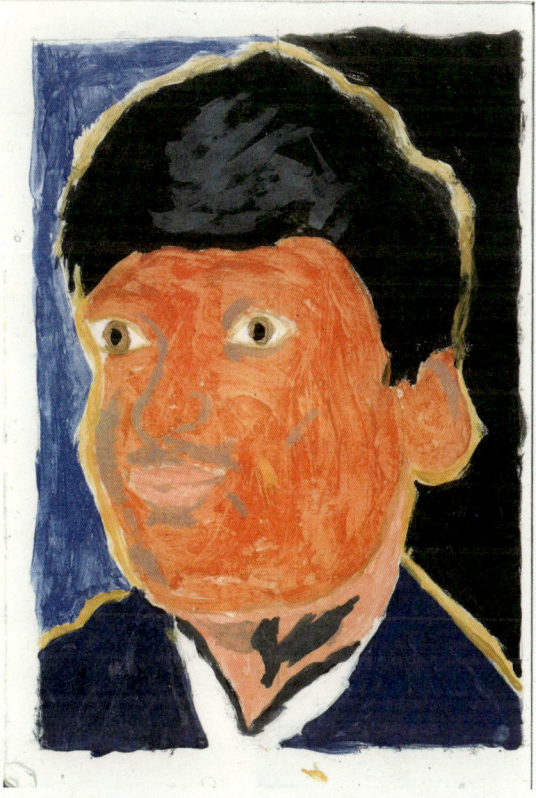
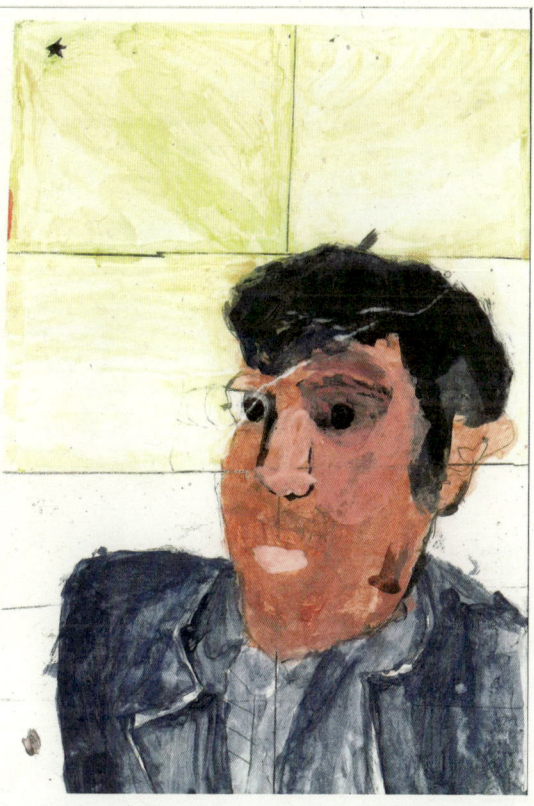

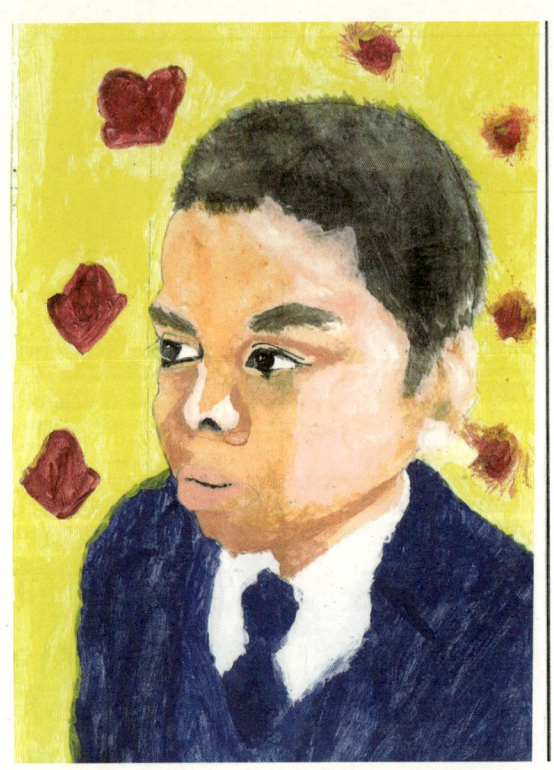

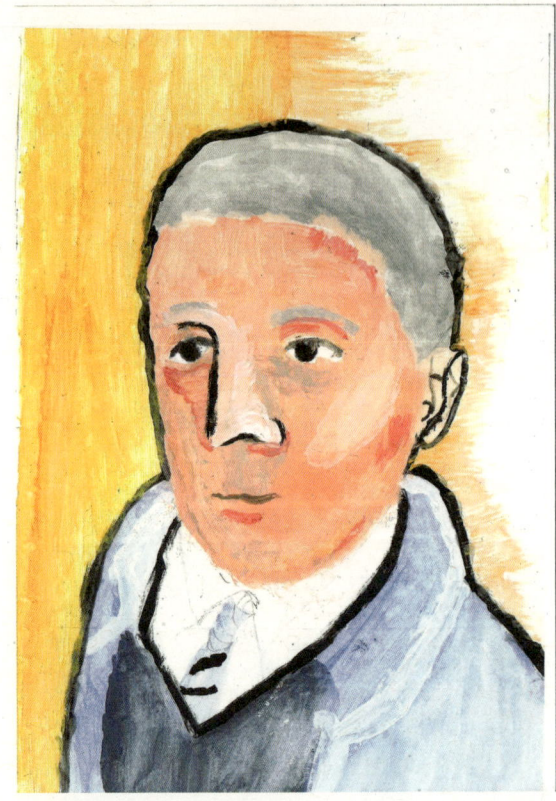

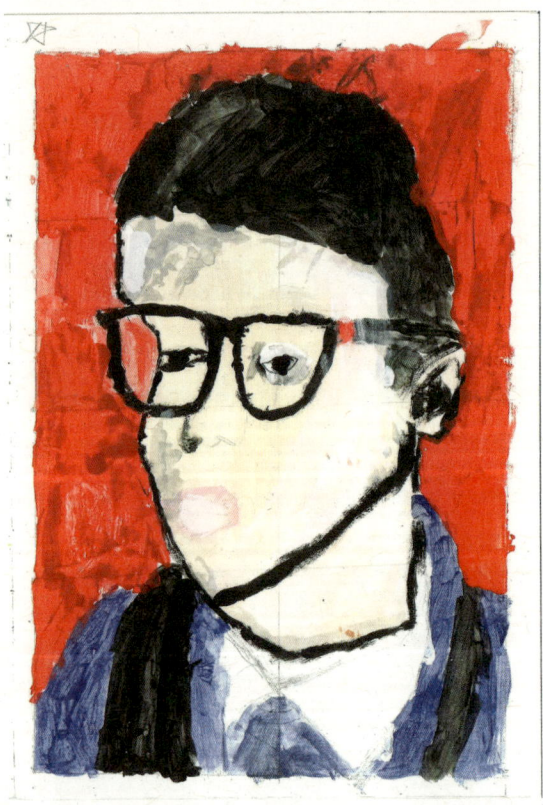

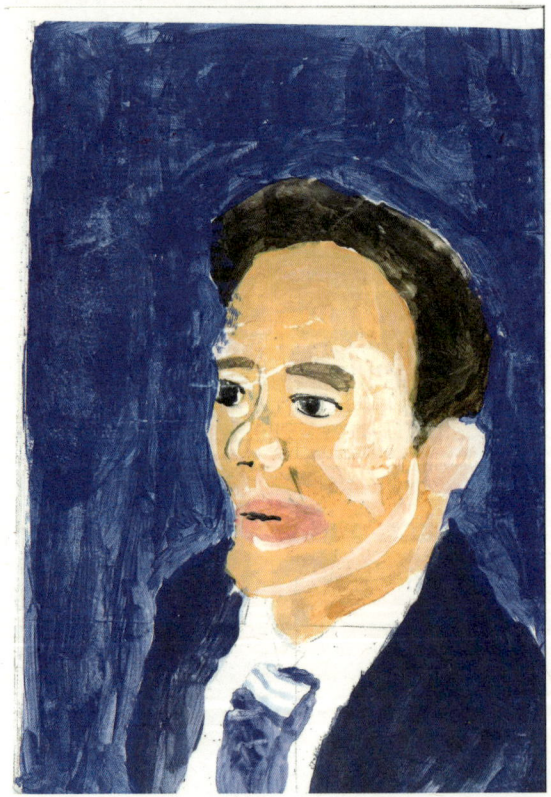

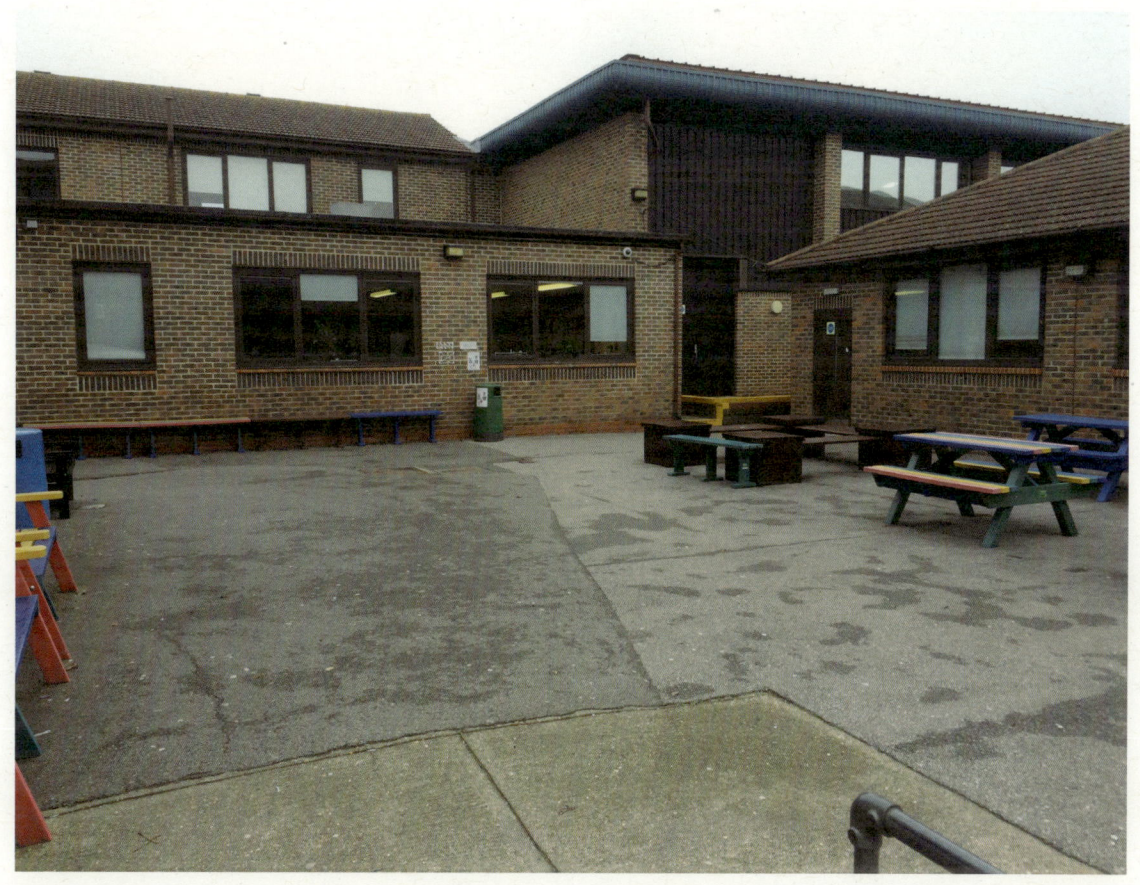

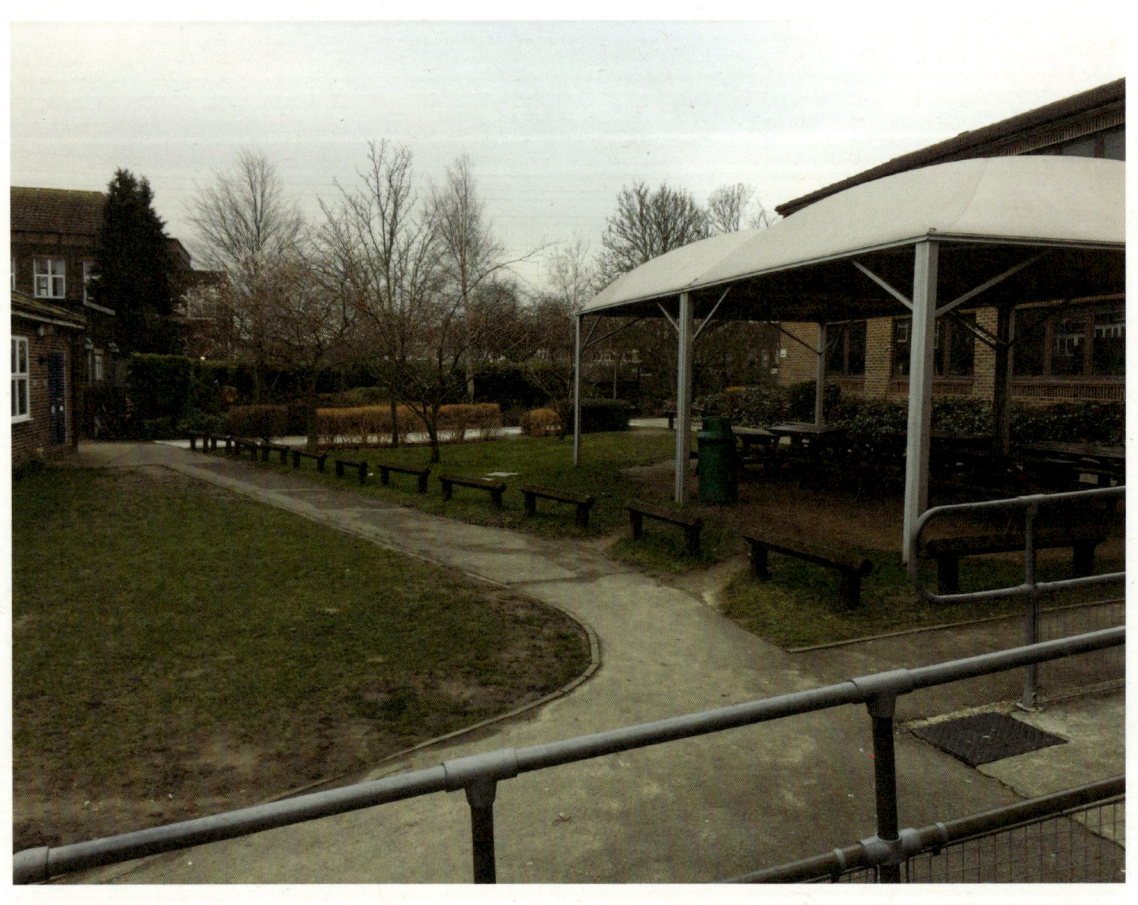

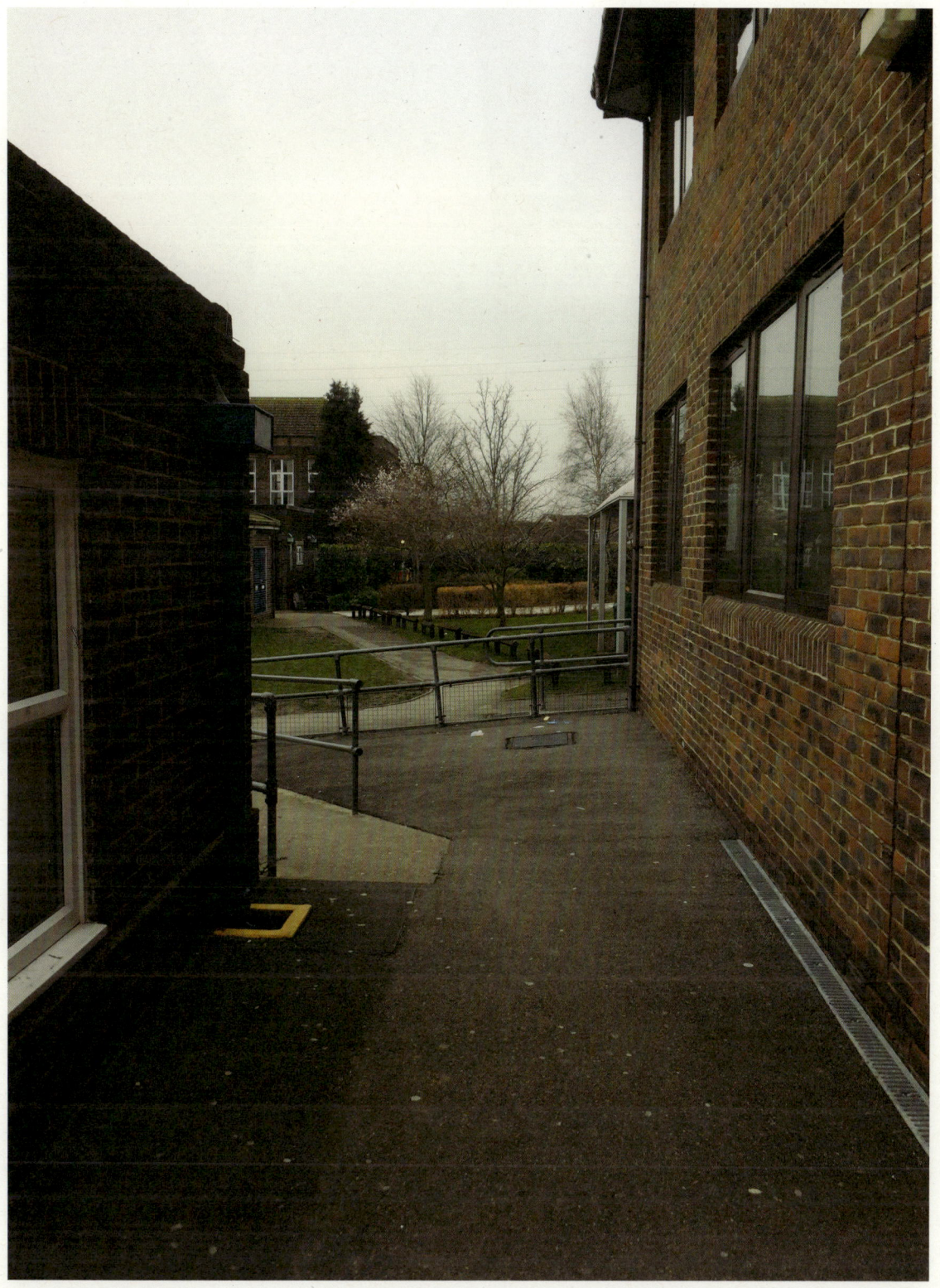

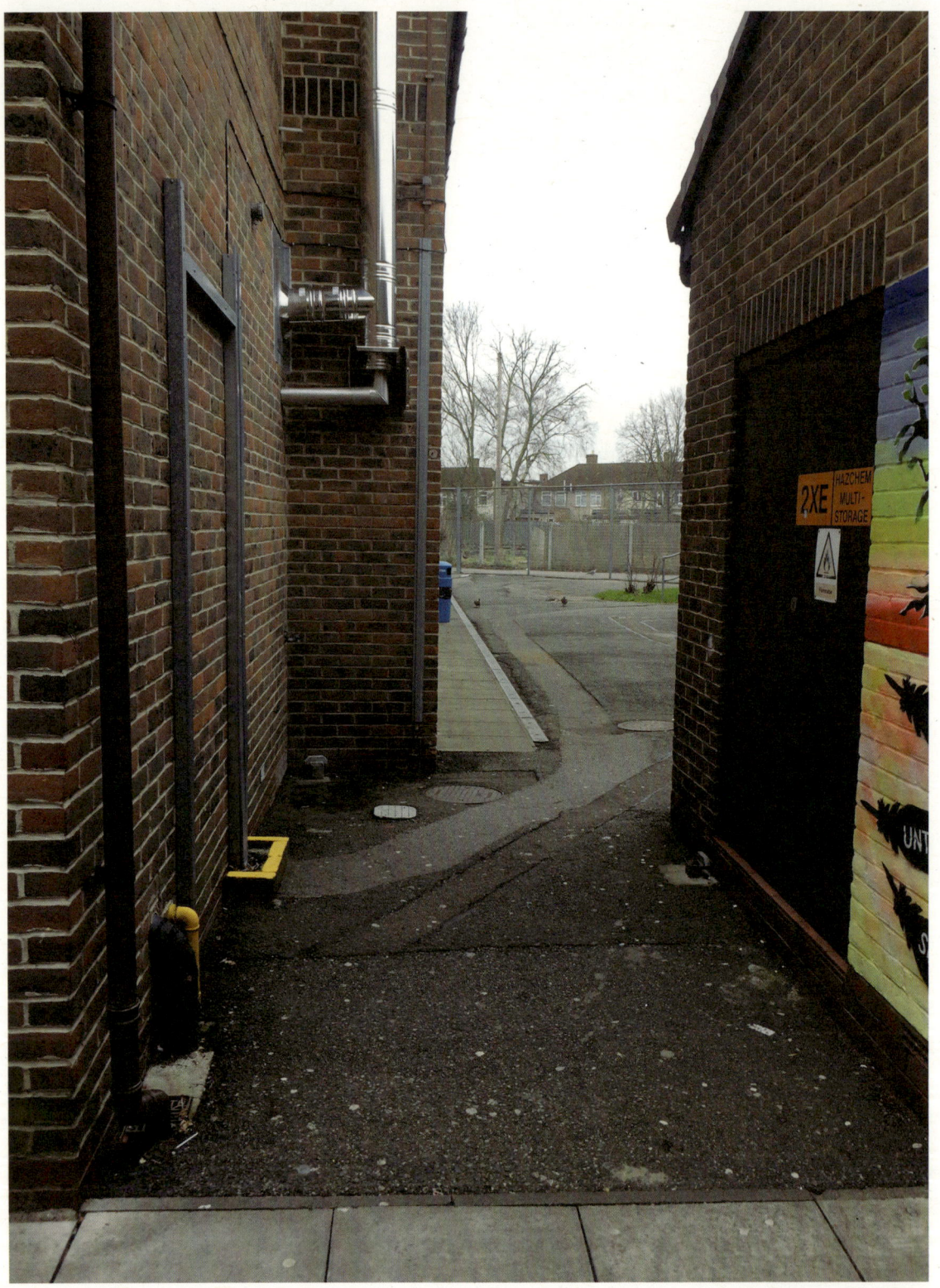

As a result of the layout of a cluster of buildings and huts, this school's 'play area' was a sequence of small passageways with breaks of small squares with tables. Walking around these spaces at break and lunchtime I would never see anyone playing games or running. I remember my school breaks were filled with sprinting after my friends, playing basketball or generally being quite active. I asked a pupil why no-one was playing any games, and she replied 'we aren't allowed to run'. This inspired a sequence of small workshops working with the girls to develop a booklet of rules to games which they invented with their friends at primary school, trying to re-inject that love of playing.

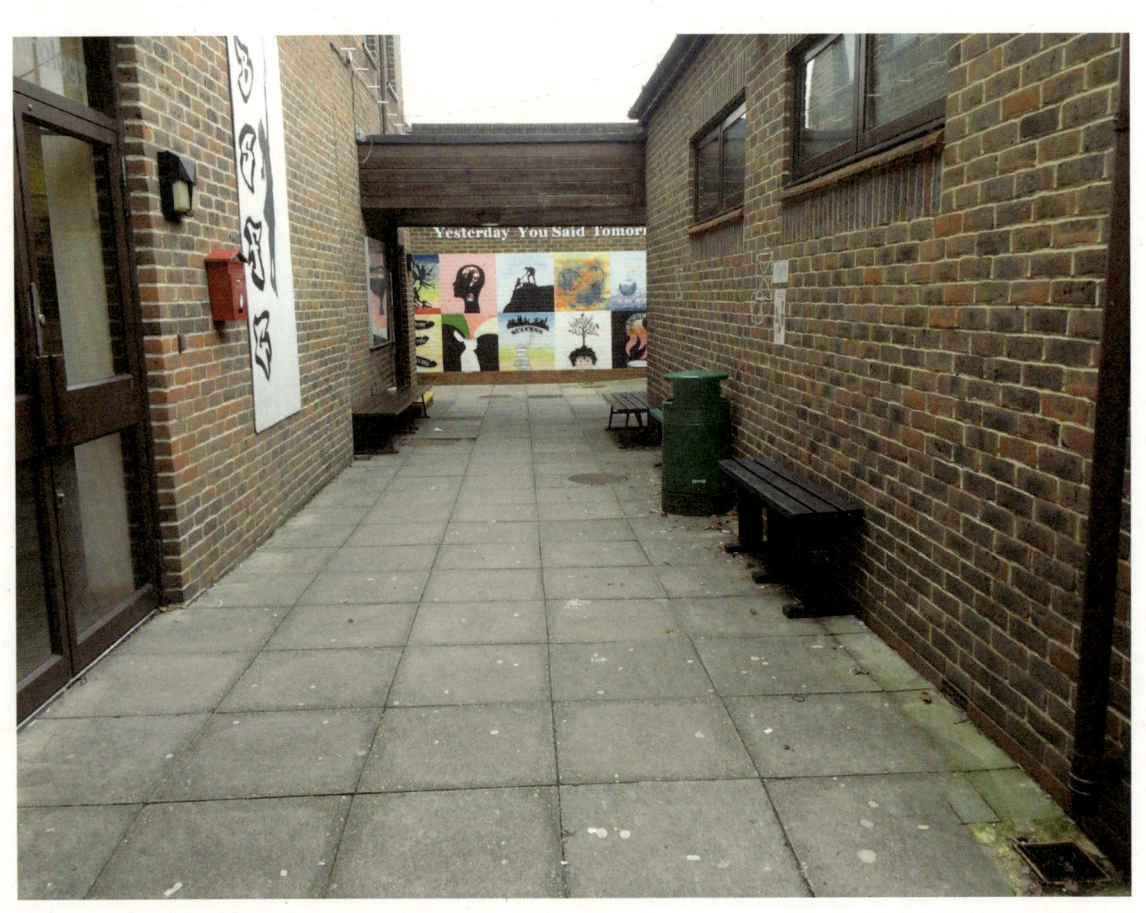

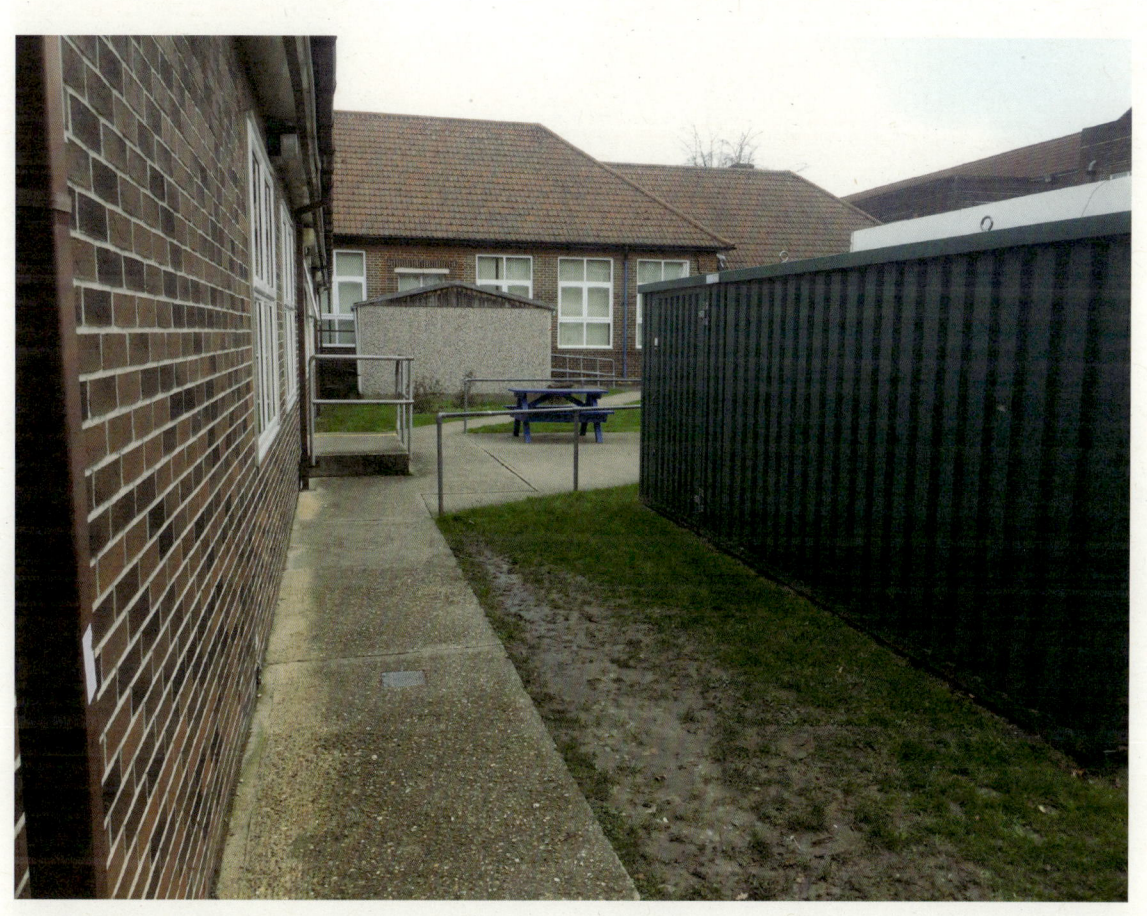

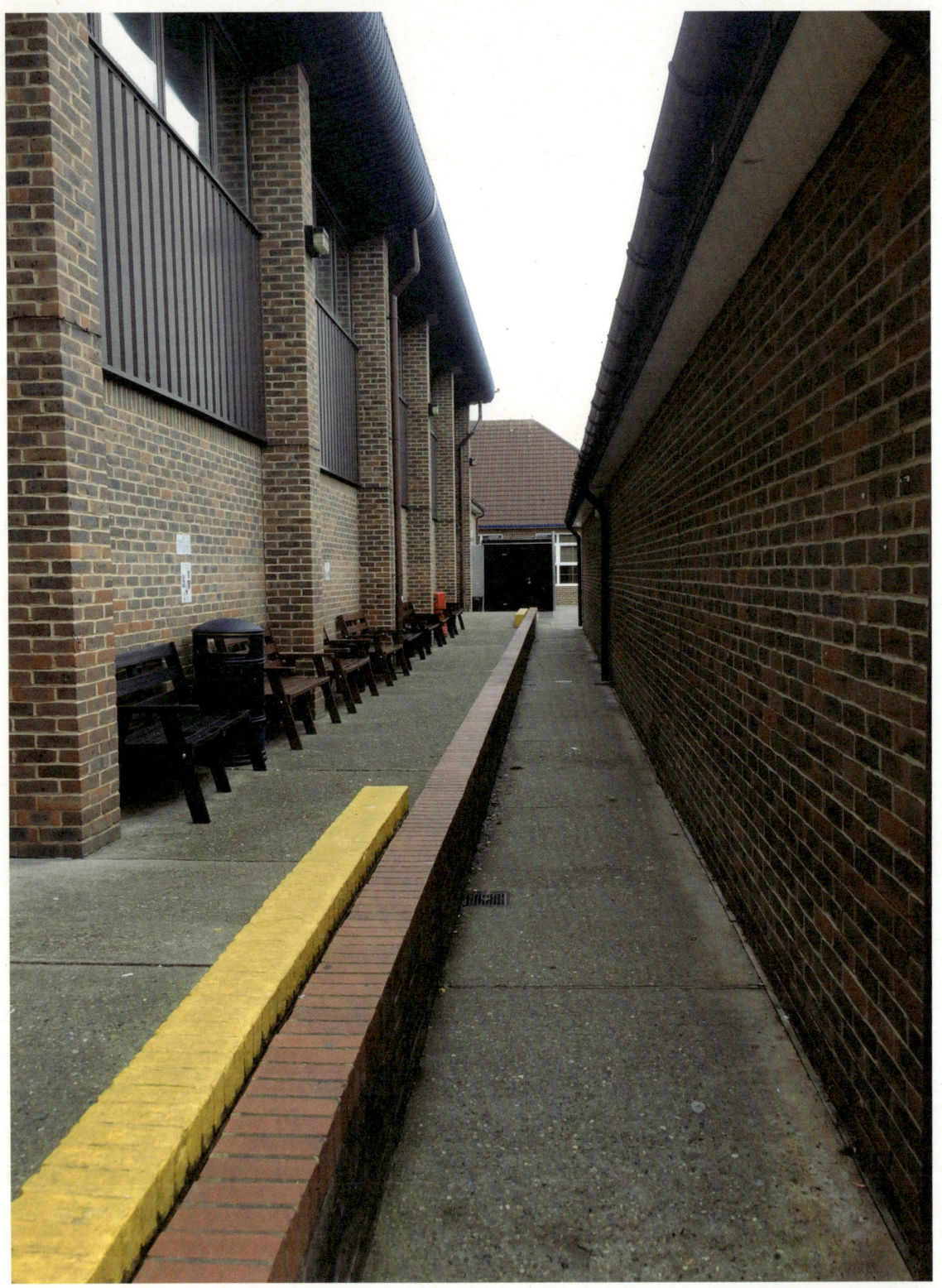

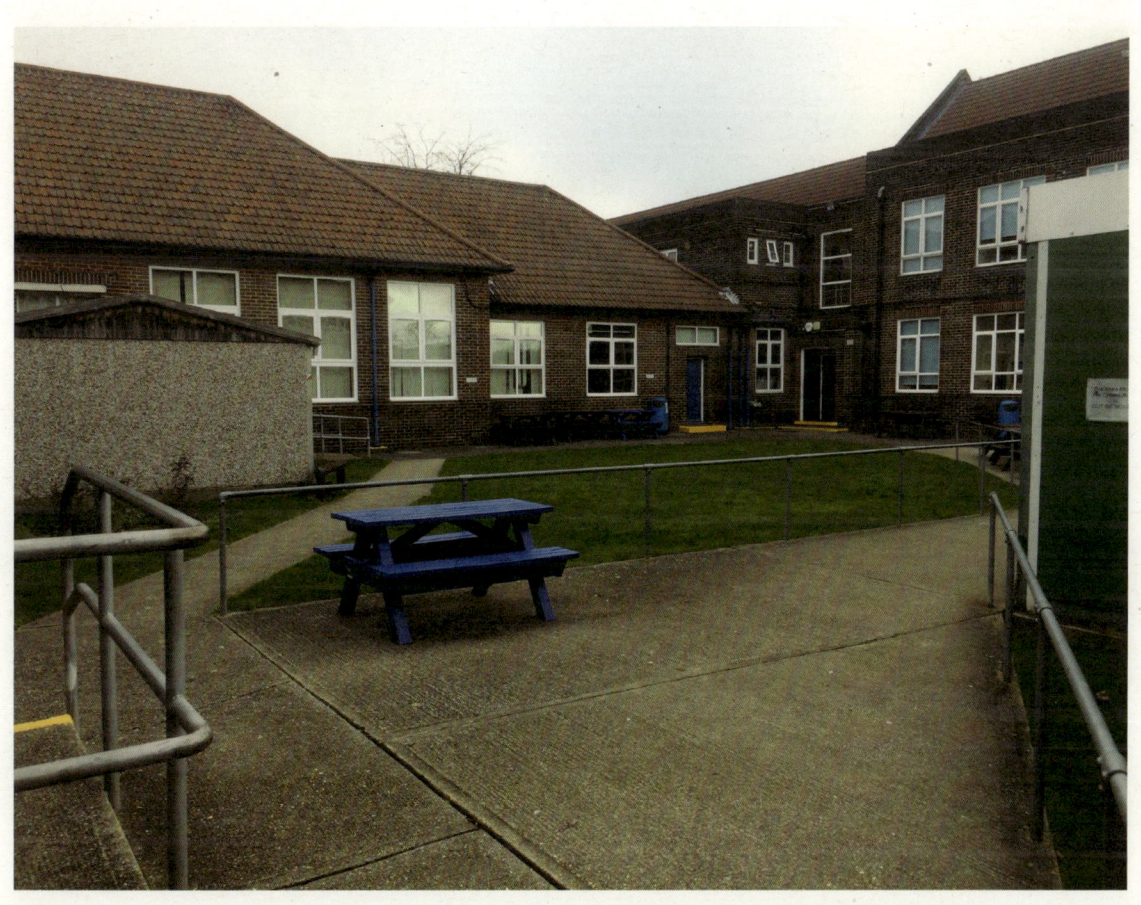

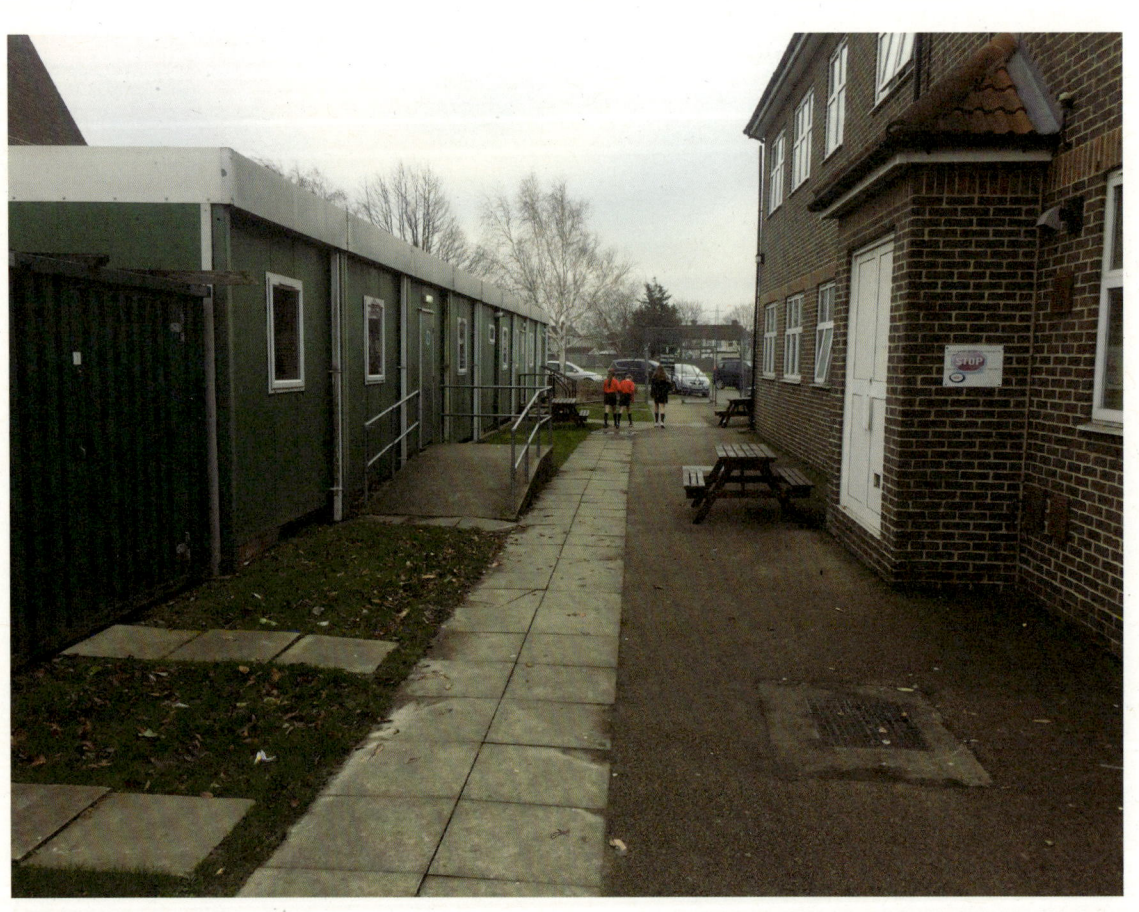

SUSANNA McALPINE

FACT
Face
fate
fame
farm
~~fart~~ fart
FAST
tart
test
test
Best ???
Beat
bear
BOAR
boat
float
flute
flume
FLUKE
flake
~~flake~~ FAKE
MAKE
take
TAME

Fame
FATE
Face
FACT

FACT.
ACT
ace
RACE
Rice
rice
NINE
fine
FIRE
WIRE
HIRE
HIDE
HID
LID
lip
slip
SLUT
SLIT
slice
nice

My project intended to facilitate students to engage with artwork as an experience instead of strictly an 'image', to challenge perceptions of what art is, and increase accessibility and interactions with contemporary art. I wanted students to perceive art beyond the classroom and outside the confines of printed images or projections, often of varying quality and sizes which portray inferior copies of the original. At my first school placement, it was evident that most students' interactions with art was confined to the Art and Design department, and a majority had never visited an art space or exhibition, despite frequent referencing to artists' work through printed images and development of personal responses. It occurred to me that this limited their understanding of the dimensions, materials, context and techniques attributed to artwork as well as their own interactions, emotions and

criticisms. In response, I decided to compare the 'image' seen in the classroom with the experience of visiting a local community gallery, where an artist in residence was exhibiting work, and investigated their reactions to the visit.

Before visiting the gallery, students were introduced to a single painting by the exhibiting artist and worked collaboratively to answer questions about the work. This activity applied prior knowledge of painting, and stimulated new thoughts whilst considering assumptions of the exhibition and equipping them with some critical questions. They were then set the task of photographically recording the journey to gallery, and they further collaborated by deciding upon a concept they would capture through the photographs, for example capturing movement of the sky as they are walking there, or recording the context of the journey through

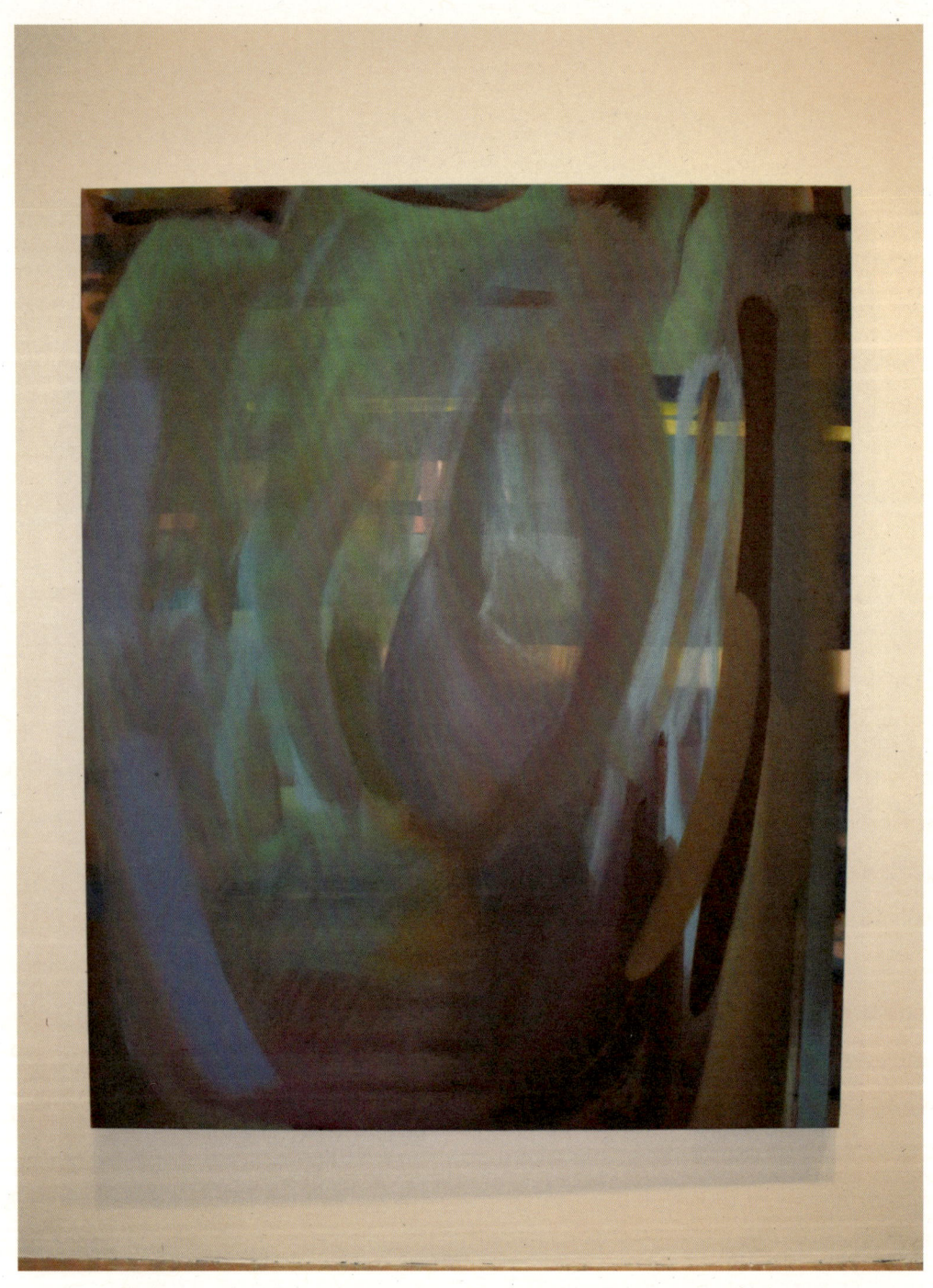

architecture. The task aimed to emphasise the journey as an experience and explore the possibilities of a concept through photography, and to develop an awareness that artwork outside of the classroom could be the journey to the gallery, as much as the exhibition itself.

At the gallery, students initially viewed the space freely, before being met by the curators, who were eager to talk to students about the exhibition, and explain the dynamics of being an artist in residence. This generated curiosity from students, who were intrigued to know how artists live, work and earn a living, and consequently built a context for the role of artists in the real world. Students were then set the second task to record the artwork individually, they were given A3 pieces of paper, folded into six, and a view finder, which they used to isolate a small part of a painting/s and drew on one section of their paper using pens, pencils and crayons. They moved around the gallery, working on the floor and standing, mingling with one another and exploring the exhibition space as they worked. The objective of the task was for students to concentrate on small areas in order to examine elements of the artists' paintings, in relation to style, colour, layers and techniques. At the same time, observe the abstract paintings as complete compositions and consider the narratives inspired by their ethereal titles.

Students responded to the trip with enthusiasm and interest, and our discussions showed they had realised new perspectives of looking and seeing art as they expressed the value of being exposed to art in a local gallery. Many students commented on their enjoyment of recording the journey through photographs and recognised this as art they had produced on the day. Additionally, I encouraged expression of both positive and negative opinions towards the paintings in the exhibition to develop a critical dialogue that acknowledged all preferences, reinforcing the validity of their thoughts and fostering a relationship with contemporary art. For the students, interactions with the wider community are invaluable, and any experience that promotes accessibility and a feeling of ownership of culture around them is extremely meaningful.

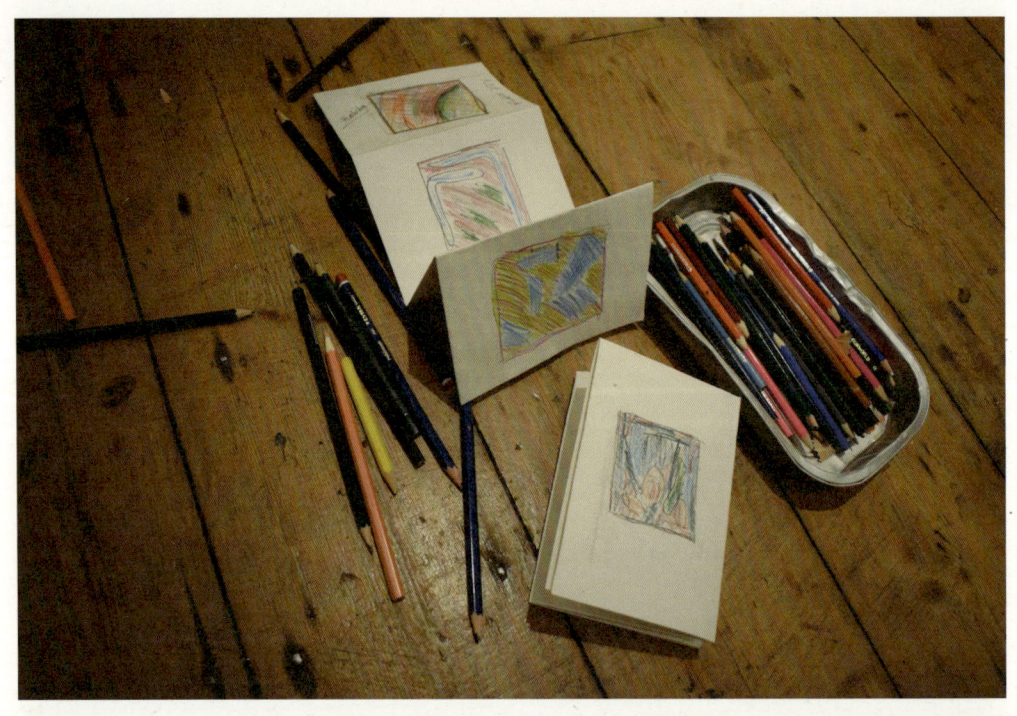

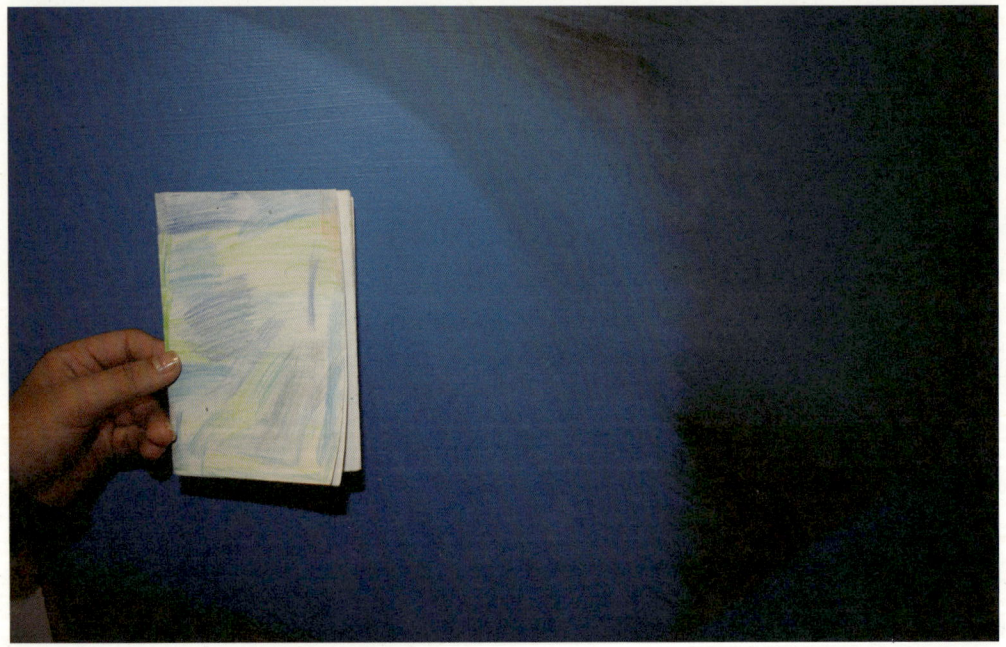

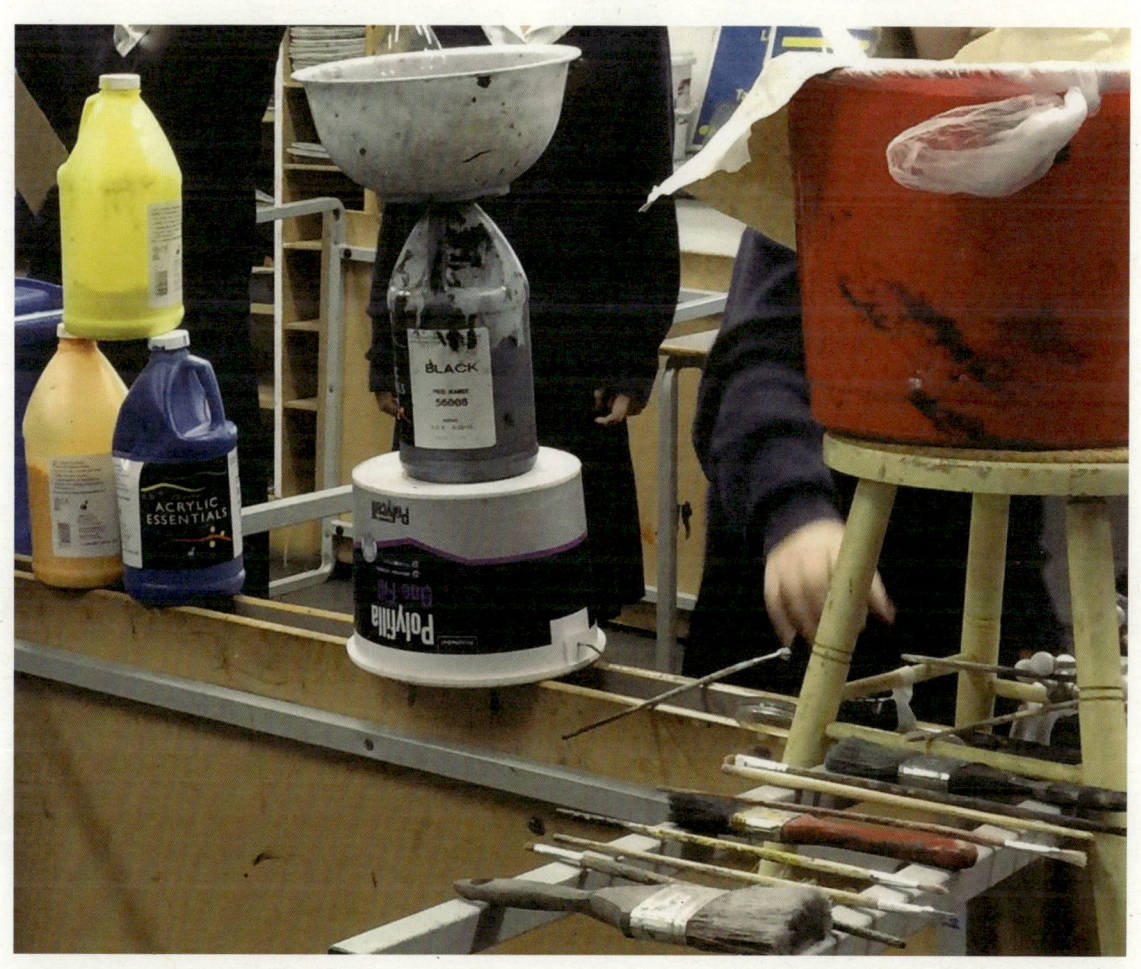

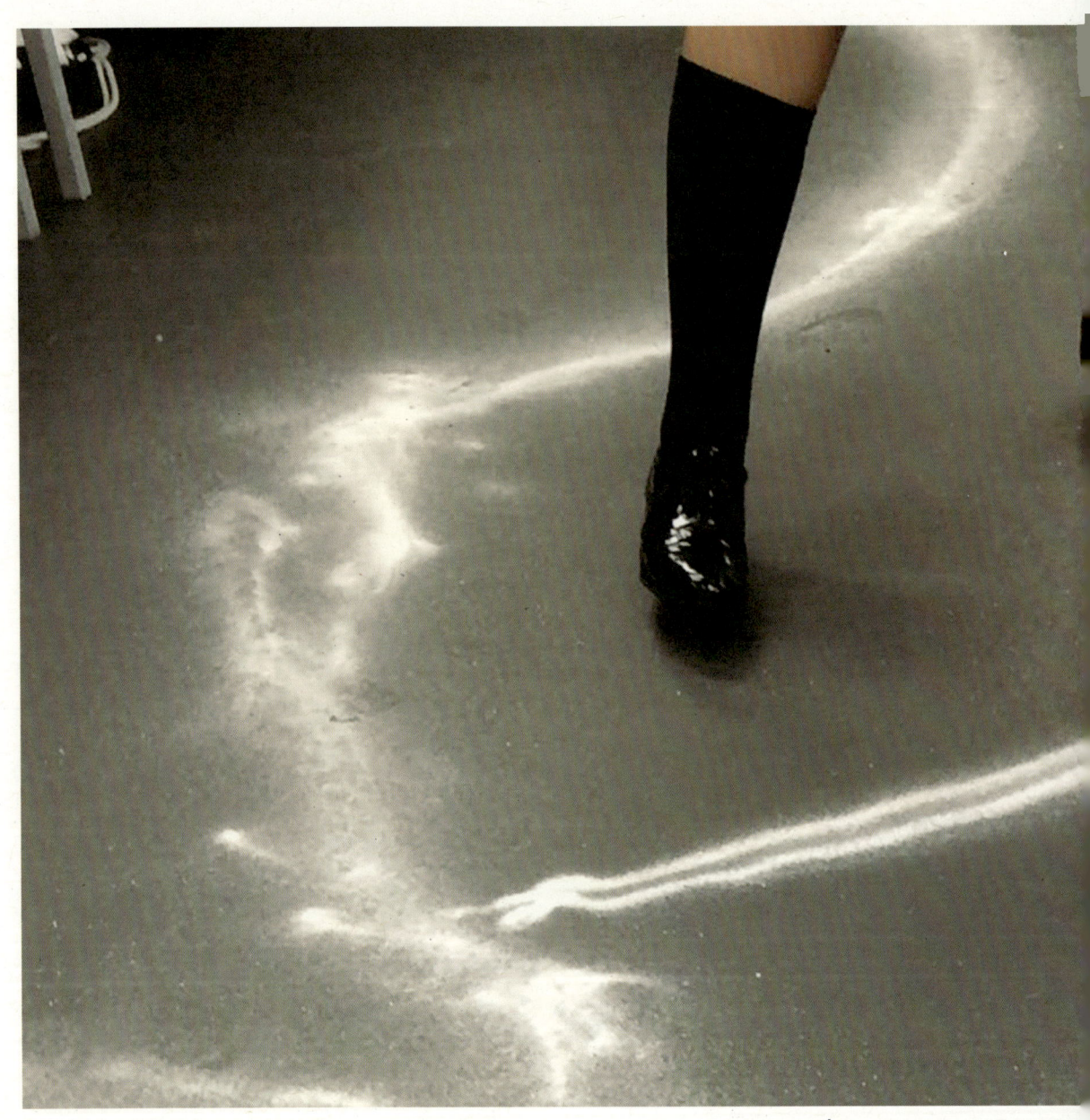

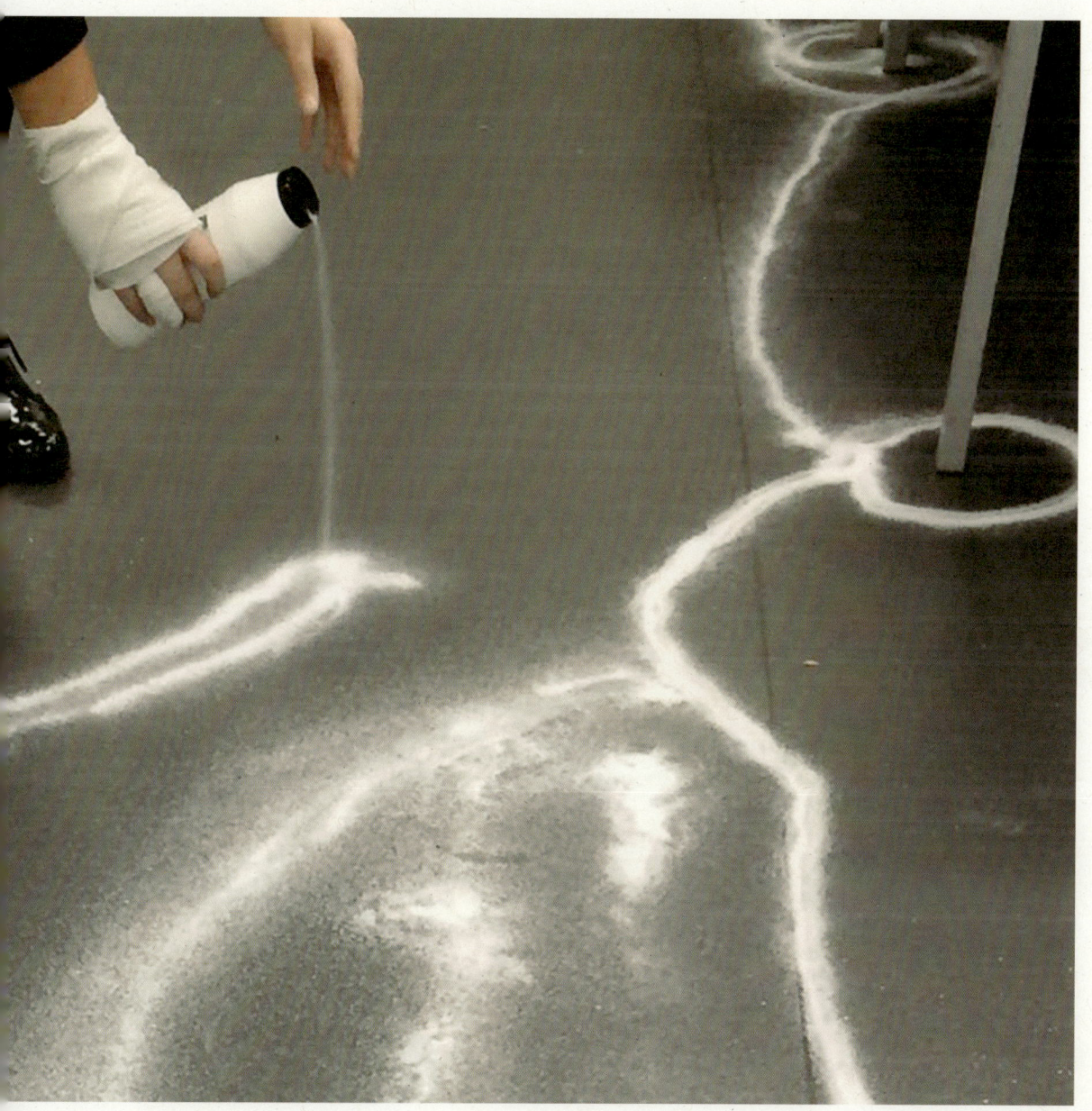

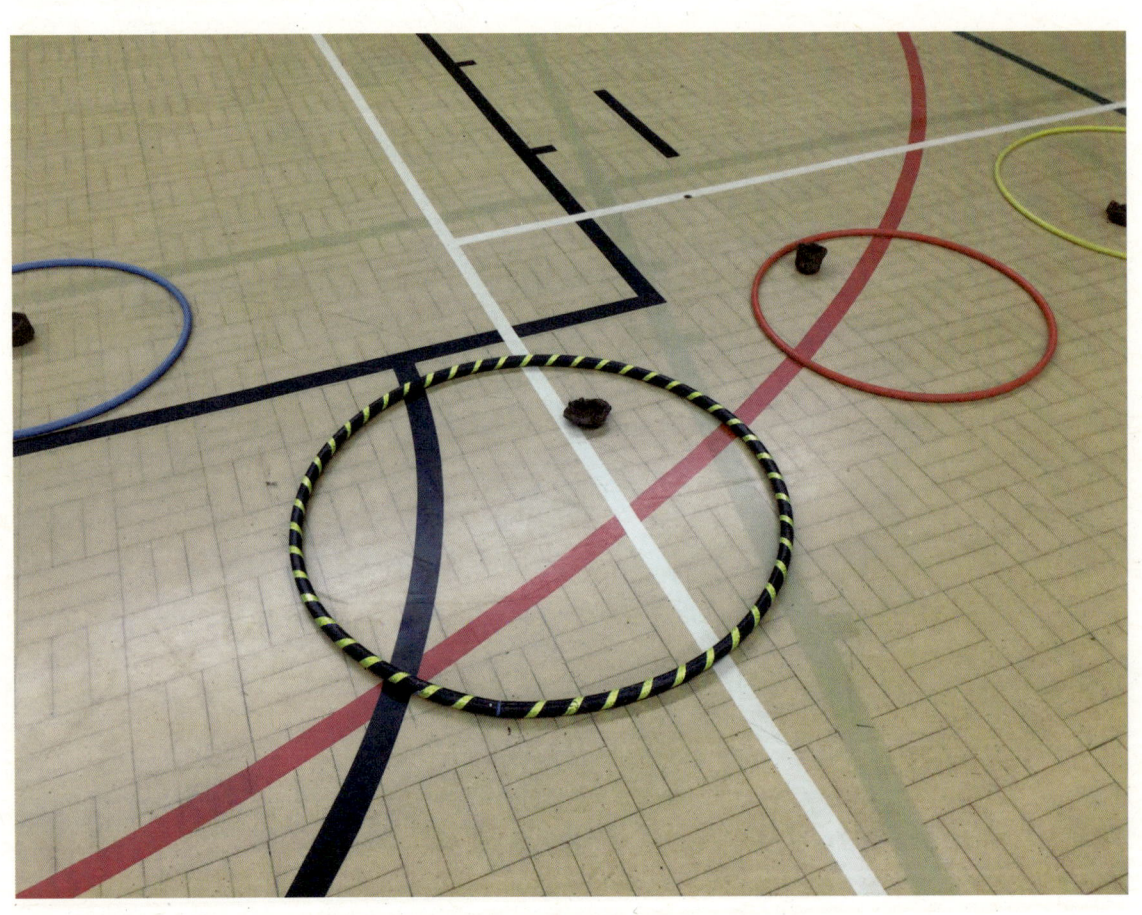

VICTORIA McGILLICUDDY

Oh I killed the moon it's bleeding.
The red moon. The balloon
and you've gone for red. Yes cos
I'm special.

Do you reckon it's sticking.
If it's sticking. That's what you call
a print. No that's what you call when
someone dies. No. Right I'm gonna
leave in a bit. Cos I want to. Yeah
in about 2 mins. Yes cos I help the
librarian and she wanted me to
come to meet the author but you
have to book it in stuff beforehand.
Just for a few minutes. But I'm gonna
come back.

I'm gonna miss you when I'm gone
doo dooo dooo doo

You d do do the whole of the back.

Okay can you just stop now.
Oh from the too

Miss do you like this art? No you
can't use this. Cos it's full stem init.
Put paint on the thing. Put paint
on here. Oh yeah. Get some more
yellow yah!

It's art look. Oh no! Wait why didn't
you put red man. Because were all
doing different colours. Exactly *red
is like the best pepper colour*. Are you
using that? Hahah are you using this?
This guys slicked. Budge up, budge up.

Let's mix it in with a bit of yellow
cos its too bright. Not too much
though. Use this for the bottom.
Do you want to do the anus? After
this I'm gonna have to do a bit of...
stop man I'm doing it.

You're painting the paint man move
the red paint.

No no no no look you painted the paint. Thank you.

If I said that to Jibble he would just punch me in the face. Jibble is this guy. And I'm Brendan!

My painting is sick init

Don't paint their faces this time. Except for this one. Keep on hold of it. Ahhh … nooo!! Look it's green. Not here though. Get it for me.

Oh yeah

Miss did you know I had white blood today? He had puss… he thinks it's cos I pushed him and I had to explain that I didn't.

I had puss white real ones – because I got earrings. I got them pierced in Sri Lanka. Sri Lankan earrings?? You went to Sri Lanka? Yeah I'm mixed raced. You're half Sri Lankan? Wow I didn't know that. I didn't mean to do that man I swear.

What is this? Look look this is the reason for it. It's because of the lanyard…

What time does English finish?

I love yellow. Yeah but we want it to be lighter. Yeah but is there. Just use the deodorant colour? You should've added a bit of white.

That way it will go lighter.

I don't paint like that I don't paint like stupid retarded. Do you know how Brendan mix? And this is how I mix?

If you feel like you're a badman then it kind of makes you a neek? A neek yeah init.

You know Hamza? He calls himself hard. Hamza chicken. I'm the boss I am.

No no he blame me it's cos I'm like yeah I got this car. It's not like its bad blood. It's like it's my blood. Get up get up get up get up.

I made a really good painting back in India.

You get gassed cos that teacher in French he goes is It meheheemhehhh. You know who miss Lanky is?

Wait what what what's the name?
You know who ms Lancaster is? I
know everyone calls her miss lanky
haha it's funny.

This is your favourite song haha
yeah but it's not my favourite song.
What's your favourite song, swalla?
Yeah swalla – swalalala

Aren't you gonna wash it if you put
red? *Aren't you gonna put red?*

Do you like this song? Yeah. Let's
make chocolate. Chocolate! Yay

Ah you're

Why you singing? Stop singing.
Stop singing it! Nah seriously. Why
you singing it for? Stop singing it
seriously.

I thought it was water I'm sorry mate.

Will it be alright now?

I want one more. Can I have that
plaster? Everyone has the plaster?
Ask miss if she has one because I
don't have one.

Did you actually know if this is mine?
This is mine.

He has the puss yeah he has the puss.
And he picked it too hard.

How did blood come so quick?
Because yeah you were picking. Kind
of gross looking. Mouldy pepper.

Do you like my nokia brick?

There's this guy in

Give me your finger then. You don't
even help. Ah man help me.
How is that disgusting it's a plaster.
Good boy.

Can you help me paper mache my
box? Im paper macheing one. He
made it bend man. I didn't do that!
Do you know how I feel? I've had
it for 2 weeks now. You had it like a
week ago. Exactly we always go to
form init. I like this song. Oh yeah I
took it. I didn't listen to it I'm sorry.

It's not even your favourite team.
You know in the news about.
They were talking about man u. is it.
I swear im gonna punch you in

the face. I sjdhkas. that's how you talk. No no don't glue it no. move this way and then you die. Can we get the paint. He wants to paint it basically. And I just do everything. You're not even taking it home though. It's going library.

Beatboxing

Do you think you'll do this before the lesson? Before it dries?

We need to make a whole book. Nothing about you. Whispering I promise it's nothing about you. Josh be helpful. Come and help me. If you get star on paint.

If we don't if we don't. okay fine. Exactly what's the point. Actually yeah. Well we both get homework. Before 6 minutes we have to do it yeah. The body, the body. The folley. Okay let's put the time for 6 minutes. I am man, we have 4 minutes. Starting wait stop stop stop. Wait lemme stop.

I don't play that game yeah. Hi saggy.

Or punch me

Okay fine fine the bet is sports hall or nah nah I'm not coming all the way to ur house. Or that 20p thing. Okay I'm challenging you. Okay 10 minutes yeah, 10 minutes and 8 seconds, no seconds yeah no seconds, just 5 seconds. What? Ah. It's gonna be here just watching.

Green lets go. What shall I paint on the pepper?

The highest I've ever done is 20. This game is on 30 blocks. I would not be safe in this. Cos the stairs will just be like that. This game was made before though. Nah fortnight copied it. Well actually all these games… ahhhhh! Why you shouting like a chicken? You can do it you can do it.

Mate I am class at this. On my phone. What radio station is this? My town is now a small city. What was it before, a mall? It was just a city? Wait noooo??

Wait okay I've almost got 8000.

This is the best. I'm out already! Can I try? There's a new version of this. A rare vehicle.

Can you stop playing with the phone and start painting that. You need to wait for about 2.5 seconds and then you can paint it. You're like my brother you're just like. You're not very good at this. You keep pressuring it. You're gonna die on this.

Yeah with some people annoying me and taking the glue.

I wanna draw the adidas sign. Then it went to puma and then to nike. Next week – ralph lauren. Going higher up in the ranks. *I need to I need to finish off my pepper.*

Massie where are you going? I'm going. Oh yes. It's right there. You're not very aware. Wait where should I put it? Here.

I am not going football training tonight. I had the best day on Sunday. You know it was raining? You know it was snowing? I played in that. My whole face was in the snow. I went for a slide tackle. Ooh

No because you tied me up to the table. And then Massi started doing

it again. It's all Massis fault miss. Oh Glen!

I did not do that. Its glens fault.

Miss they were washing their hands with washing up liquid.
Miss is this done? Guys have we done the bottom?

I'm leaving a finger print all over the place.

What are you doing?

We need to cover it. This is all your fault. You destroyed our pepper. Destroyed it? I made it look architectural.

Can I have the green paintbrush please? Or just a small one? Will you need a small one just in case?

Will you turn into the hulk because West Ham aren't doing well in the Premier League? Oh. There ya go. Why you hiding your face?

Can you tell me the meaning of that? Okay? Okay. You don't have to.

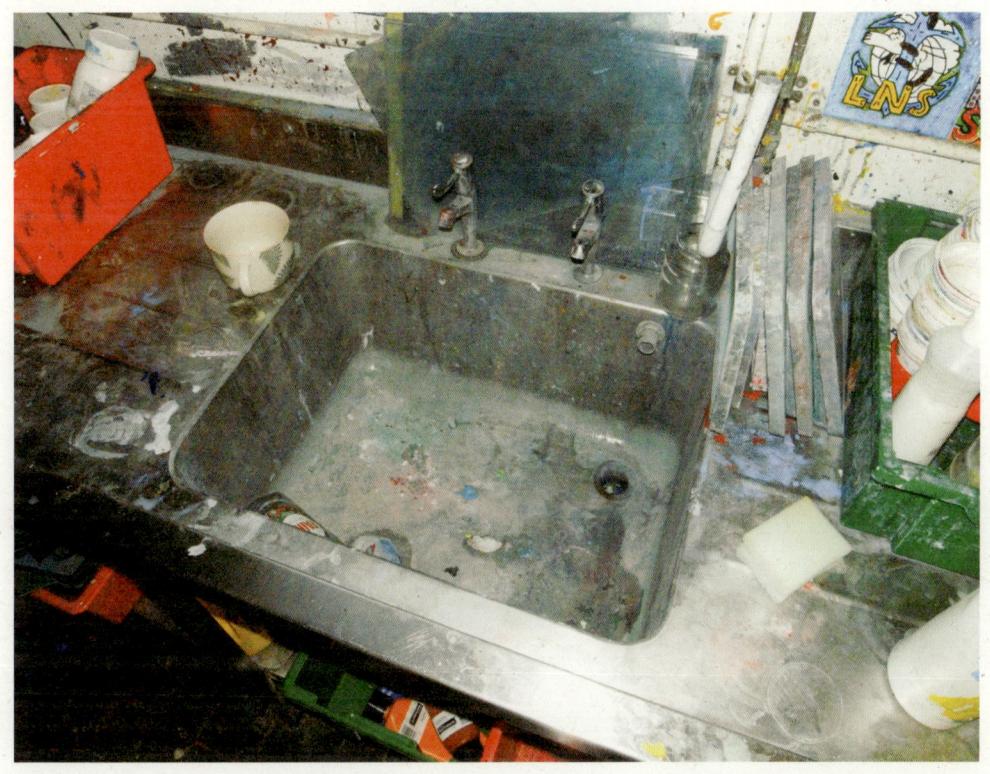

The sink was blocked for a week.

'Sometimes, I purposefully walk into
cigarette smoke. It's a gross habit but
I secretly love the smell'

Year 8 girls like the smell of…

Bleach

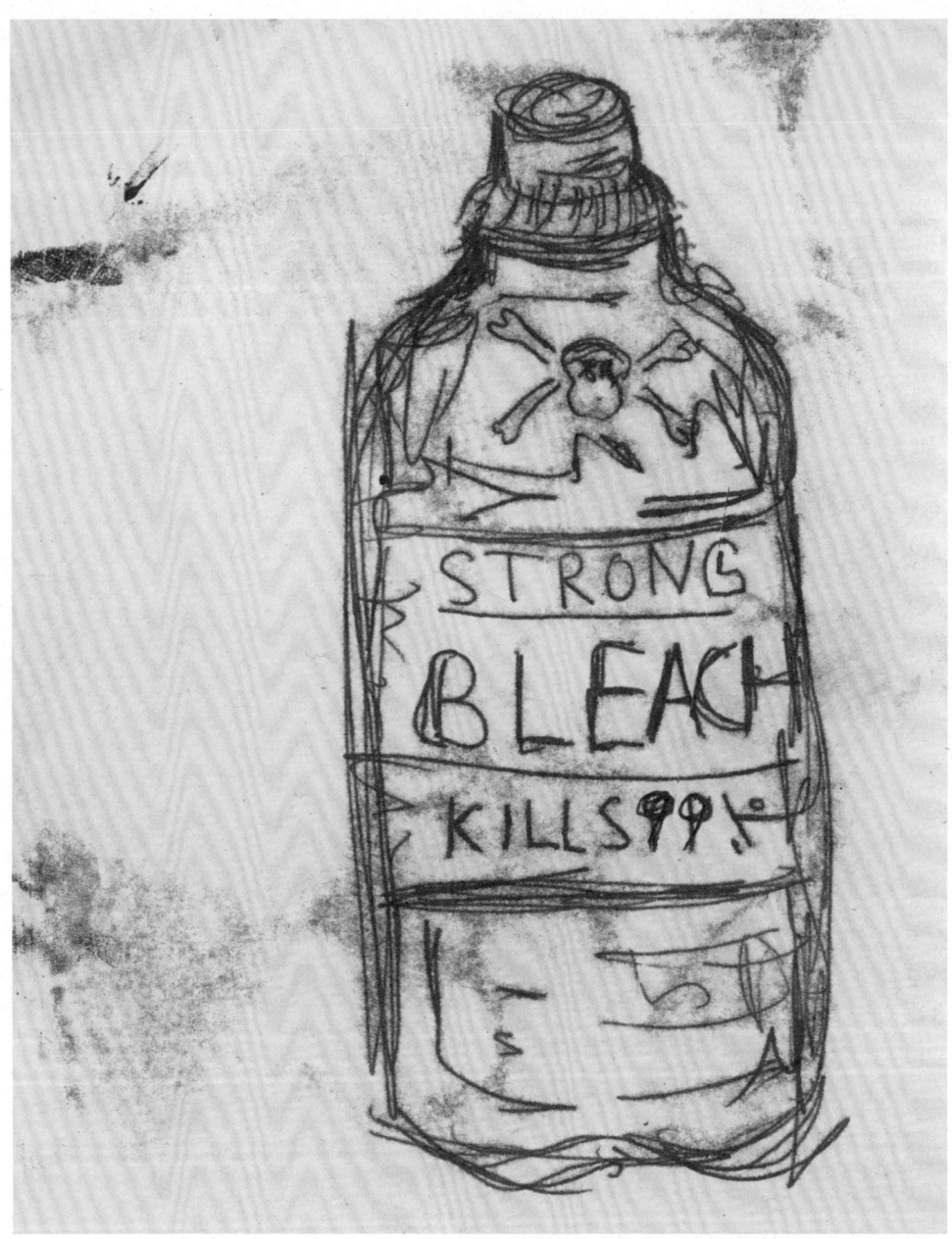

Burning
Cigarettes

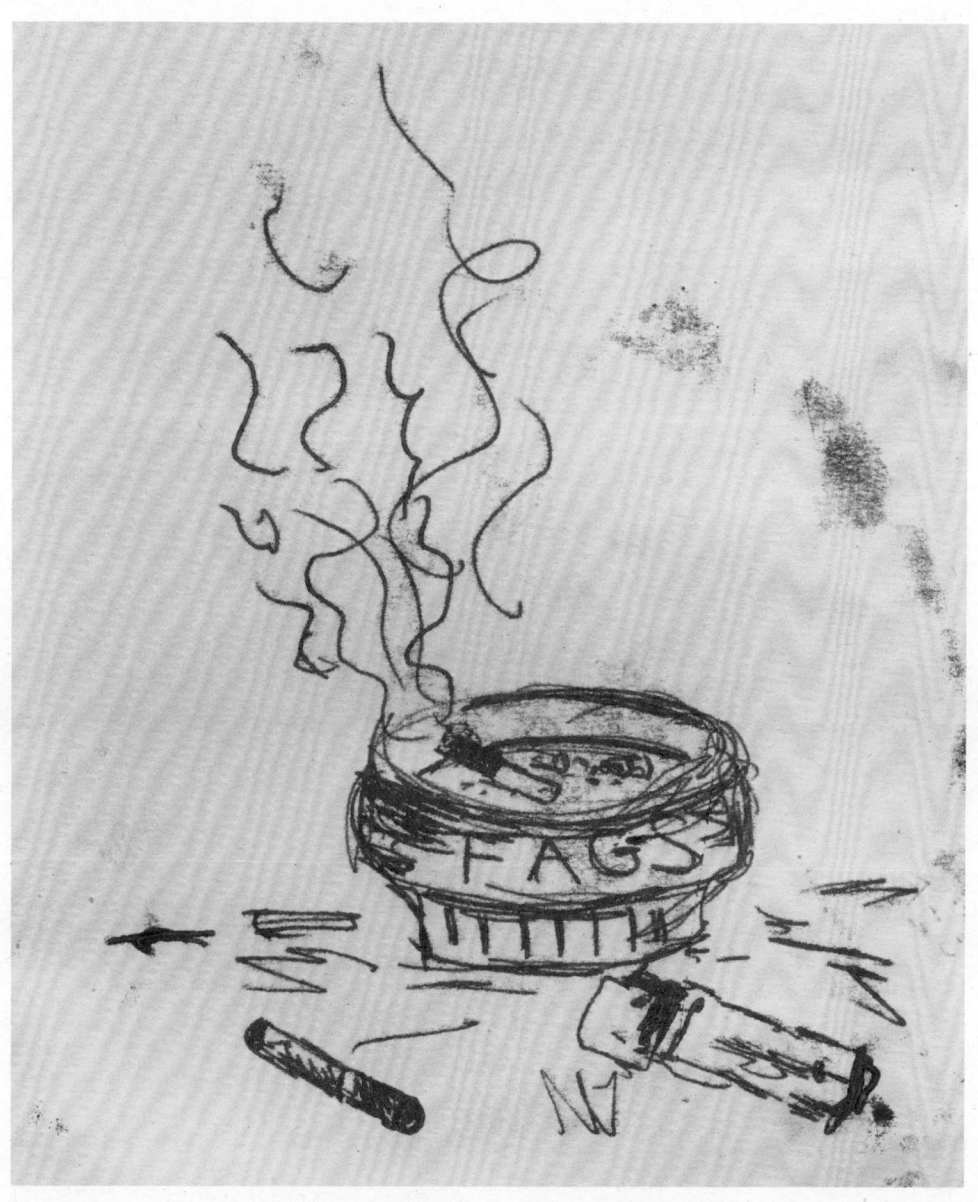

Cleaning Products

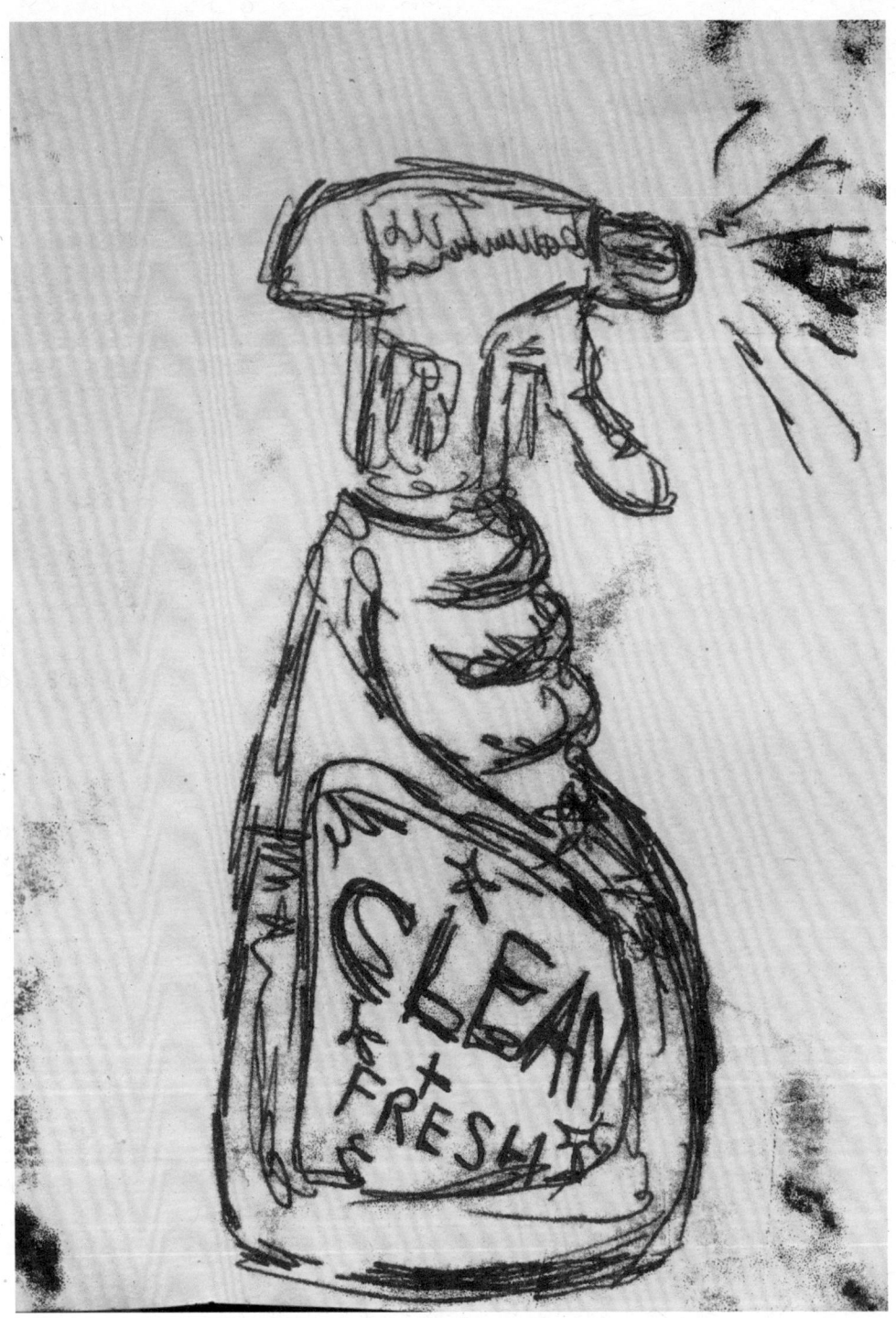

'I don't think art can be taught but I
think a situation can be created where
art might happen'

John Baldessari

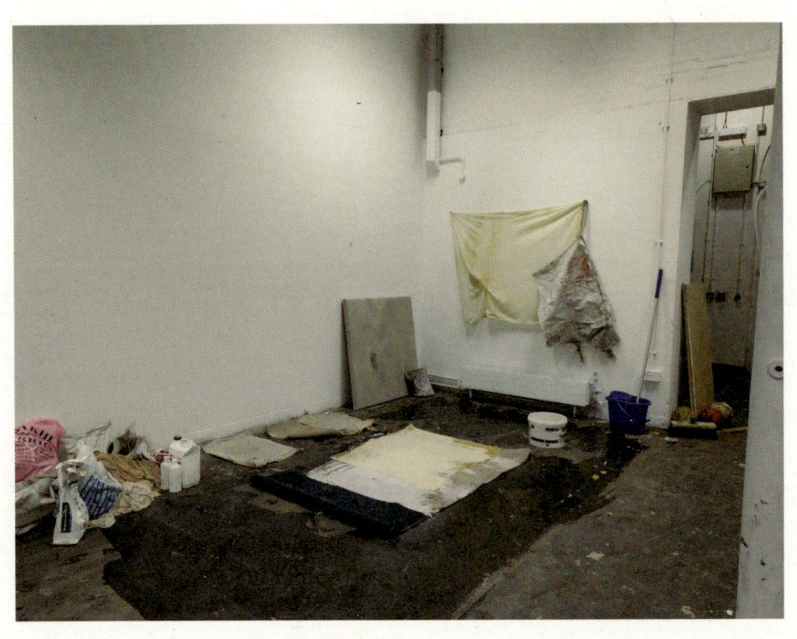

Define conventional

What is the conventional use of a material?

What should we learn about a material?

What do we need to teach about a material?

What are we teaching?

What are the limitations of a material?

Are they really limitations?

Is there time in education to discover limitations of a material?
Do we need instructions or can we explore?

Is there time to explore?

Is there time to play?

Can things go wrong?

Define wrong

Define right

Do assessment objectives limit us?

Do we really have time to experiment?

Should experiments be under timed constraints?

WWH: I liked the way you taught us and I learnt alot from you!

WWW: I really like how you always demonstrate what we are doing.

Miss Hasnat: what went well
You were a nice teacher and you explained things clearly. You praised everyone's work and ~~were~~ was very positive. I will miss you. Plus you gave me a Christmas card and that was very nice of you. :)

WWW:

Miss Hasnat really helped me improve my work. When I didn't understand something She always made it clear. She was a great teacher and She was always prepared for every lesson. She was a great, inspirational teacher!

WWW: You have explained and showed us how to try new styles well.

WHAT WENT WELL... ♡ ♡ ♡

I think Miss Hasnat was a really good teacher, She explained everything really well and made the lessons really fun as well. WE WILL MISS YOU!

WWW:

Miss Hasnat always helped us when we needed it!

WWW: Miss Hasnat is very enthusiastic and makes us interest by being interested and happy.

What Went Well:

You always knew the best tips to give us, and explained how to do things really clearly. I loved all the tutorials which helped explain alot clearer than just words.

WWW: Altogether I thought that Miss Hasnat, was a great teacher, her lessons were planned out very well and they were also quite successful. ☺

134

EBI: Try to let us help you a bit more.

EBI:

Miss Hasnat is a very good teacher. However sometimes she sets us a little bit to much homework. She could sometimes give us ittle time to finish a task. If she gave us a bit more time and a bit less homework she would be a perfect teacher.

EBI: To Show more Videos.

EBI: Miss Hasnat Could be a little more strict but still made the lesson fun.

EBI: Not to make us work in Silence, It helps us wind down! WR Will miss You!!.

EBI: Miss Hasnak could maybe explaine things more clearly.

♥

EBI: I think you could have tried to start us off sooner so we had more time

EBI: It would be nicer is you gave us more time to finish our work.

EBI: If your sytems of tyding up was better. e.g Ionitors.

EBI: In your next school you should show them more videos and when they are done a task you should get them to do creative drawings.

KIRSTEN ADAMS

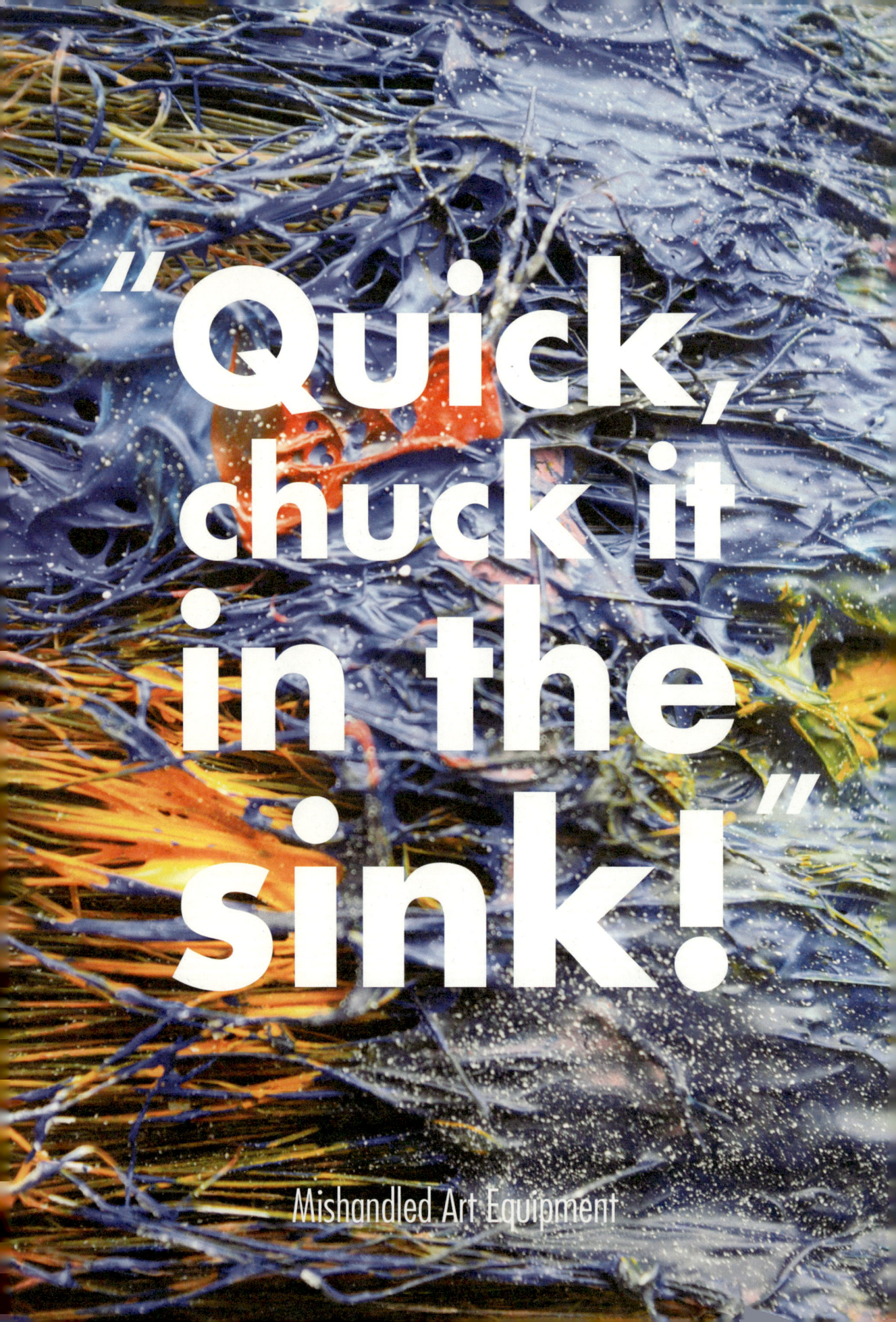

"Quick, chuck it in the sink!"

Mishandled Art Equipment

"It's not ruined, Miss! You're being so extra."

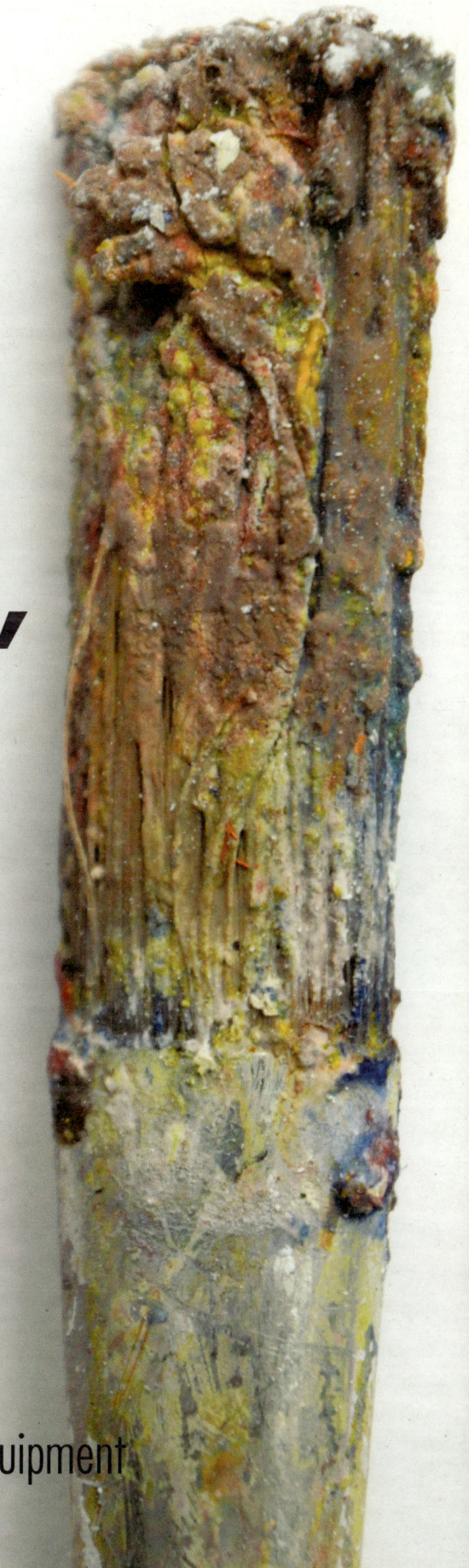

Mishandled Art Equipment

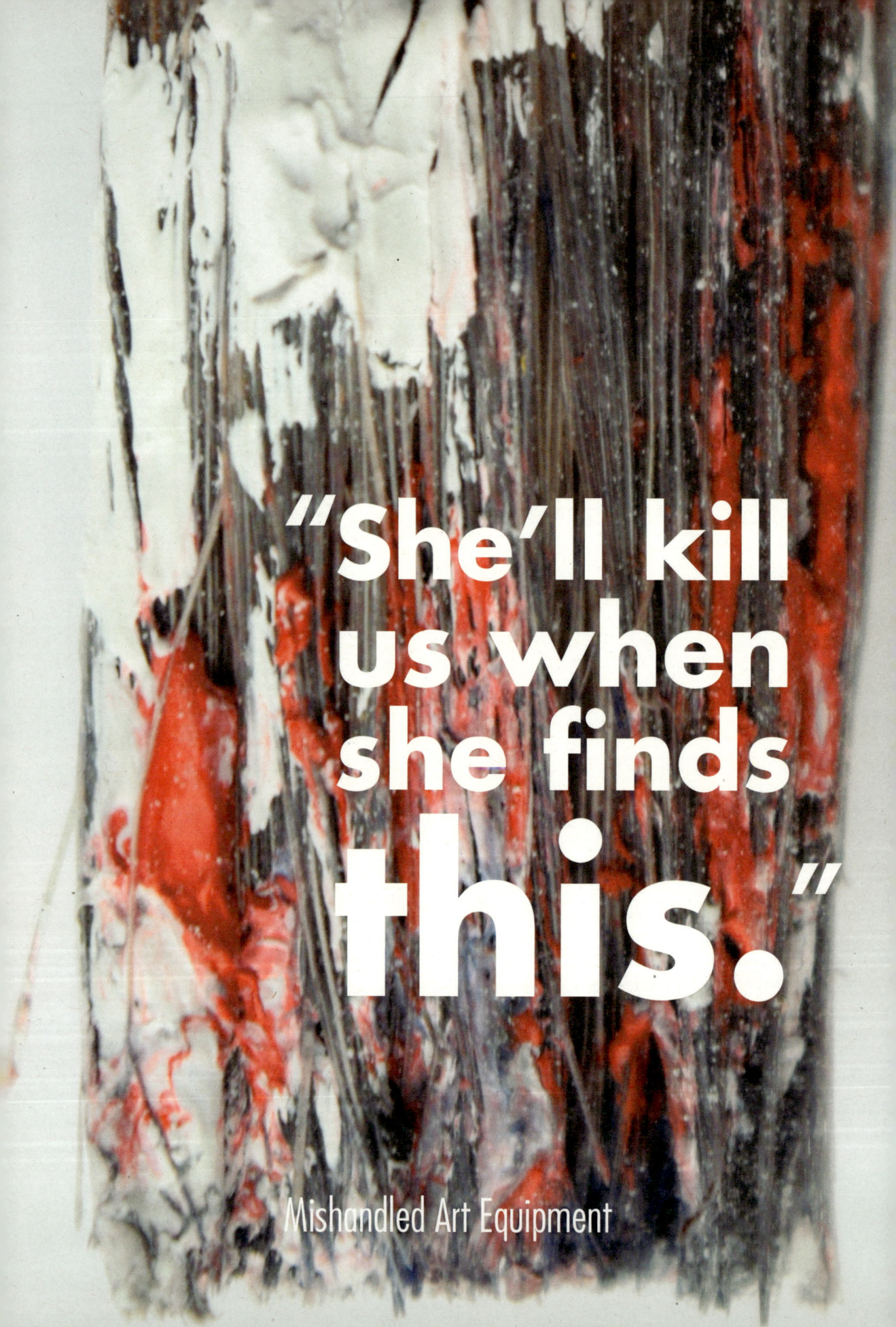

"She'll kill us when she finds this."

Mishandled Art Equipment

ALICE McVICKER & JAYEM WON

By looking through a window we are able to bottle an image confined to the structure of the frame. Looking through the frame, the bottle is no longer just a bottle and the onion is no longer just an onion. They become shapes that react against the edges of the frame, where the lines push each other to create a new space – the negative space. The set of eyes, the object and the window in between, exist in the same dimension; yet, what we see through the boxed frame becomes a staged reality that only exists within the frame, in other words the frame is able to create a simulated reality.

The school environment is like that of a simulated reality. The structure of the school determines when to have a break, when to have lunch, when to learn Maths or English, even when to go to the toilet. It resets the body clock of human anatomy and is able to operate through a completely different concept of time. Similar to how negative space is created, the pupils and staff bounce off the structure of the school, holding it together. The new policies and rules can shift the boundary that is created – as one can shift the composition of still life within the frame – yet all these changes remain confined within the given structure of the school. It is uncanny and surreal how this seemingly different planet exists within the same space of our reality, which makes me question: who is on the other side of the window? Perhaps we are all living in a simulated reality?

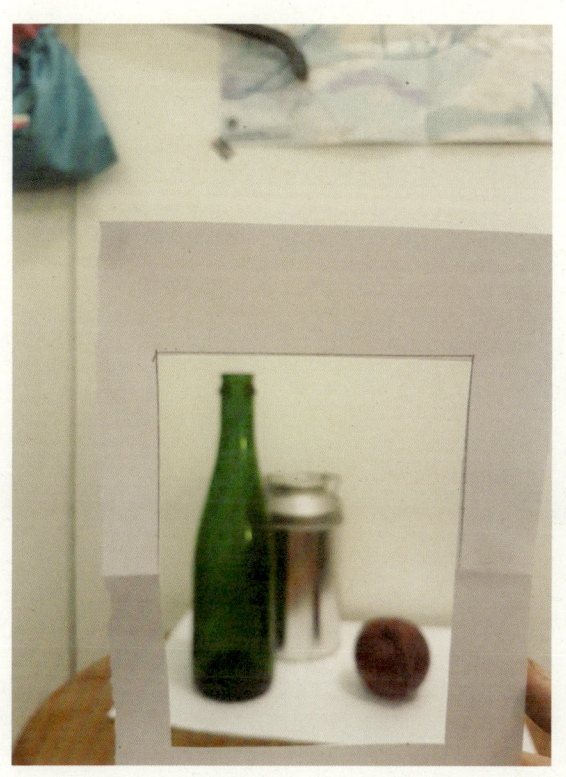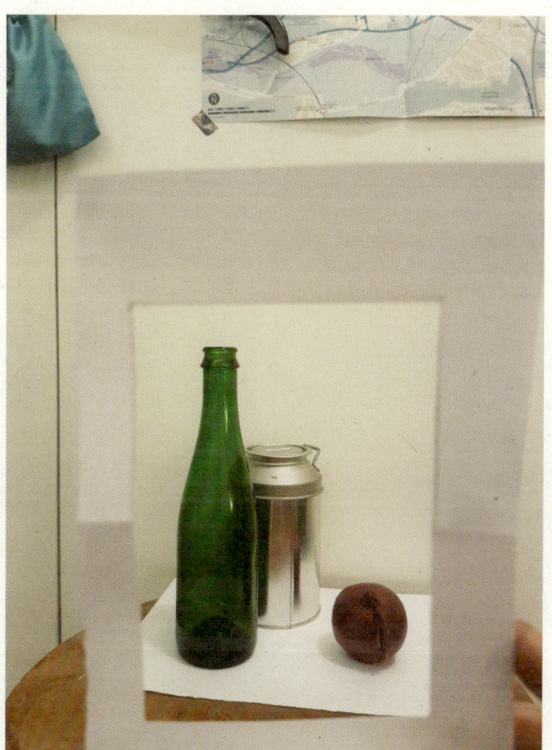

Introduction

Mind Map

Mood Board

Artist

Pastiche

Artist 2

Pastiche 2

Self Assessment
Action Point

I Reached for the new page,
I tore, I wrote, I stuck.
I googled the title, the results were syrupy.
It was excessively sweet, I waded through the substances until I found which was stickiest.
I grabbed it and pasted it in my book.

My mood was black and amber and gold,
I found God plotting routes through fragments of time.
I quartered myself in great secular adhesive .
My torso fell upon an elastic equilibrium as through shot from a sling.
My torso whizzed through the fragments of time, my legs sank into some unimaginable bog,
my head though with the weight of God did not fall.
But was suspended from strands of PVA.
It bruised, and softened but could not free:
The struggle of Eternity!

I was put back together I found my way
A name on a piece of paper
I HATE DEAD ARTISTS!
Especially those who retract ,who consult other dead artists,
who speak their youth in whispers.
The inevitable pastiche.
TWICE OVER!

I would choose my own but it weren't up to me, none of it.
No choice of two roads; if there were I doubt I would have chosen both.
Thank you Corso, you did those then, but that was then, that was then.
Where is my action!
Here's my point.

The global slippery pluralism of culture is reflected in education, where translation becomes a key factor. Students from different backgrounds, while adapting and developing, reshape their knowledge. To promote their agency, alternative pedagogies have identified approaches interested in remapping new codes to generate inclusive learning.

Besides, employment of teachers with culturally diverse backgrounds can boost hetero-geneity of teaching, and fill the gap of differences, by embracing notions of being-with to negotiate and to remap codes within educational institutions.

Nevertheless, in an Anglophone educational system that relies on English language clarity, new born shared meanings might struggle to flourish. To promote learning beyond linguistics, to produce creative responses to concepts, Art and Design, with its inclusive multimodal approach, is the ideal terrain where different backgrounds can converge in the concept of interculturality.

Translations of modes, carrying their collective knowledge, can recreate agency through aesthetics emerged from written tasks on students' experience, relaxing dialogues that recall memories, and meaning making through different techniques and materials. Communication and translations of symbolic significances, icons, in the chain of meanings, can offer variations of themes, generating new displayed responses and infinite interpretations.

Backgrounds, is the result of above implications. The unique dynamics experienced in a classroom have been characterised by cultural pluralism, generating dialogue among an heterogeneous group: Albanian, English, Farsi, German, Greek, Jamaican Glypsy, Polish, Turkish, Urdu student speakers and English and Italian teacher speakers have converged to exchange knowledge.

An assemblage of individual artworks shows how an Y9 group has employed the Collagraph technique to translate and remap new codes. Free from fixed canons, recycled materials have been translated and reshaped to assume new symbolic meanings. Following personalised aesthetics, the making of students has created unique patterns that reflect the hybridity and fluidity of contemporary urban culture.

A final anonymous survey has shown how inclusivity has aided students in feeling respected and valued:

> 'Miss helped me when needed, and it wasn't a problem because there is always a solution'.

> 'I have been supported and treated like an equal'.

> 'Whenever I needed help, Miss would be there'.

> 'I could express my own ideas'.

> 'The teacher helped and gave me challenges she knew I could achieve by putting more effort in to the work'.

> 'Miss always explained what to do and gave good ideas'.

> 'I have been helped to improve my work and not punished because of my learning pace'.

Backgrounds has provided the opportunity to consider how emerging orthodoxies can be implemented to enhance diversity within Art and design subject, where imagination allows creative connections among objects in the world, meanings as signs, and fluctuation across modes.

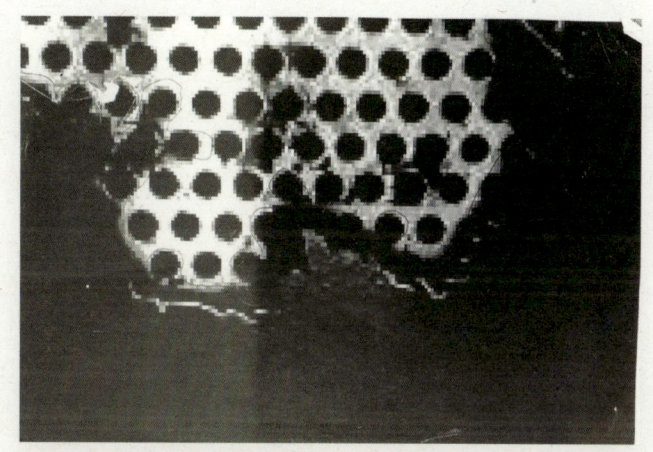

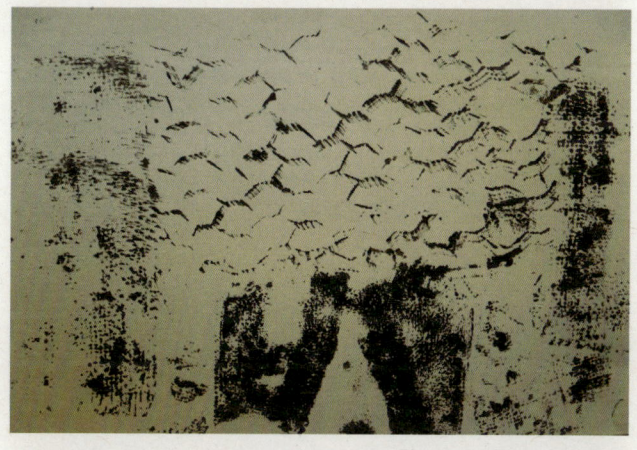

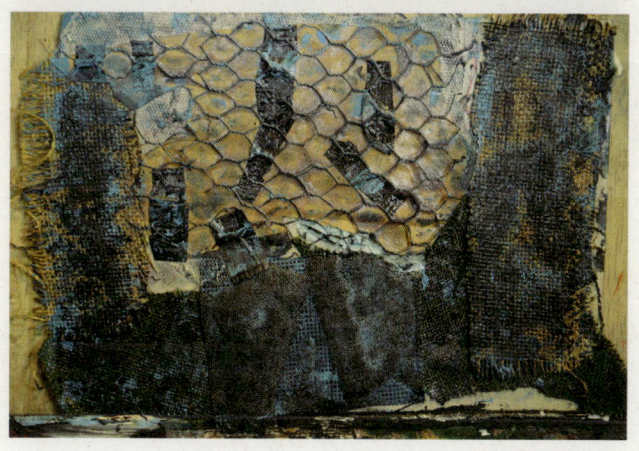

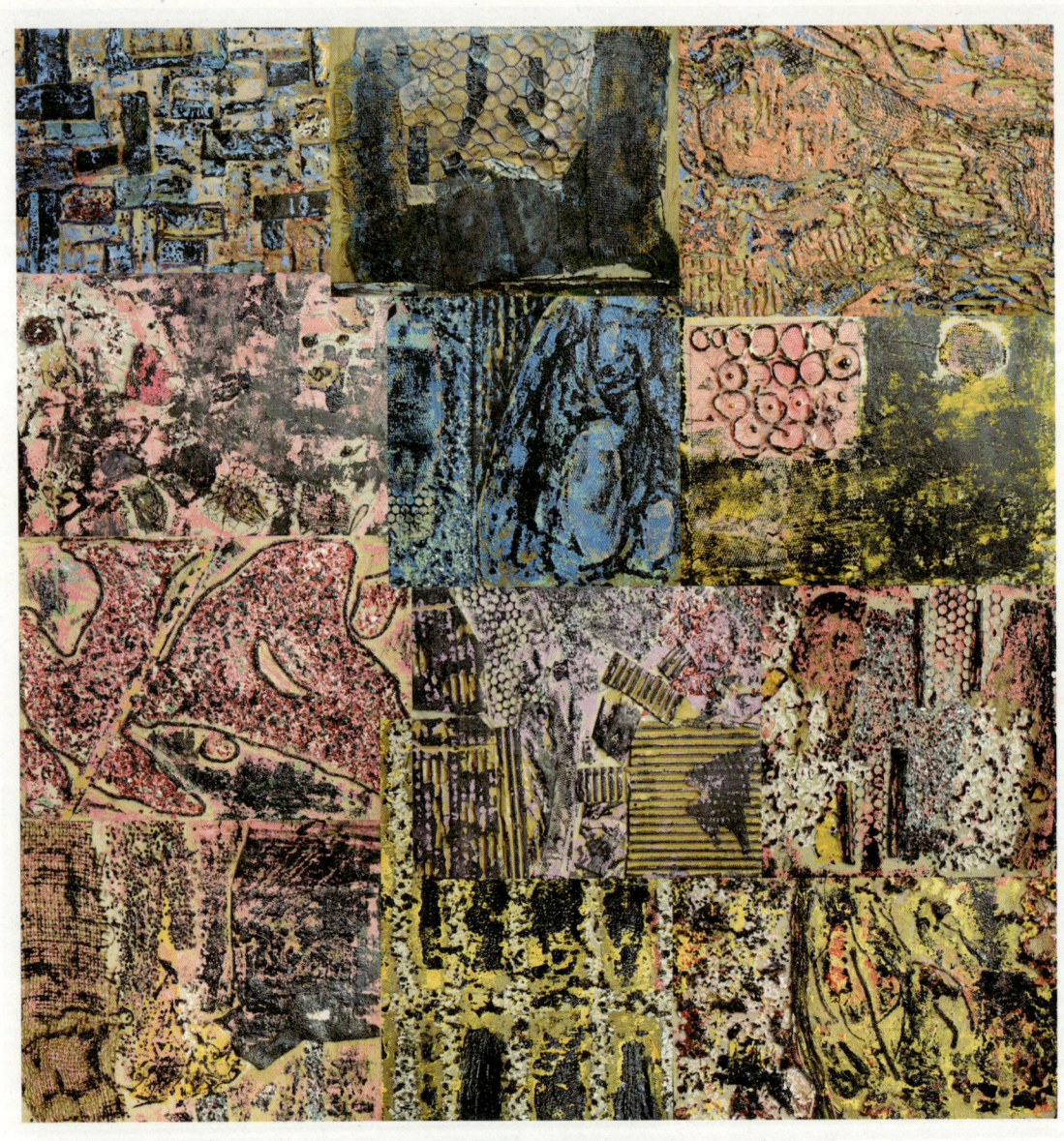

150

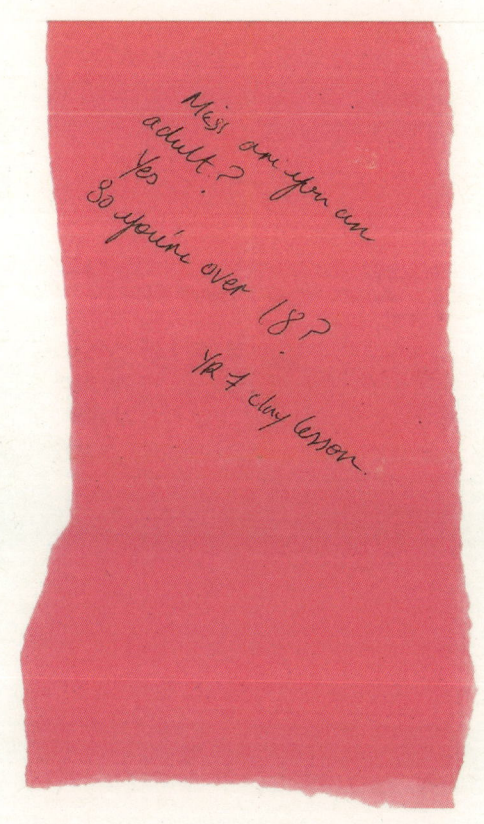

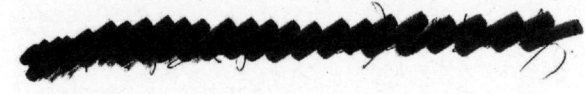

 It was so hot I had to wear
my umbrella hat.

" woah Buses then were sick !"
      Year 7 PSHE LESSON
      [60's Bus] on
                STEREOTYPES

Is a boy version of a
midwife a midhusband

Whats the difference between
a chicken & a hen?

Graphics Y17.

[CHICKEN PHOTO HW] "Can we cut off the white bits"

"Can we put it on powerpoint so it prints 4 in one go rather than 4 different word [documents]."

"I was good last week because I wanted to be good — this week I don't want to be good cus I want to sit there"

Year 8 Art.

[Referring to hat and coat in assembly]
"take it all off"

L:"All off? I'm going to walk in nudey"

Yr 7 Assembly.

'the traffic lights [green man]
don't work when you push
the button.... the
government controls them.'

Yr 7 PSHE.

I'm going to sell this
pot on ebay.

Yr 7 clay lesson.

A relationship can go from normal
to sexual in seconds

PSHE year 7.

156

Wednesday 14th June 2017

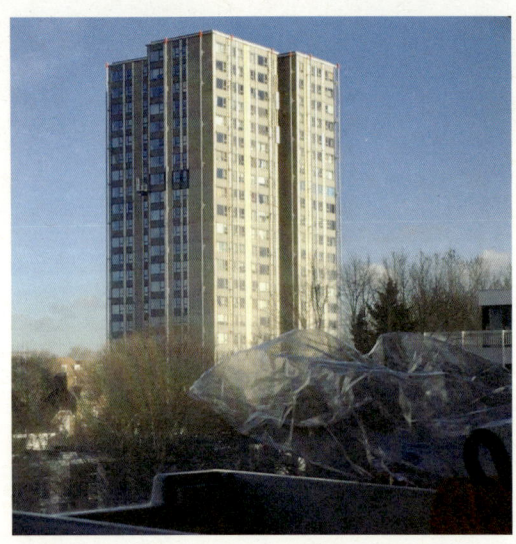

CHALCOTS ESTATE, NW3

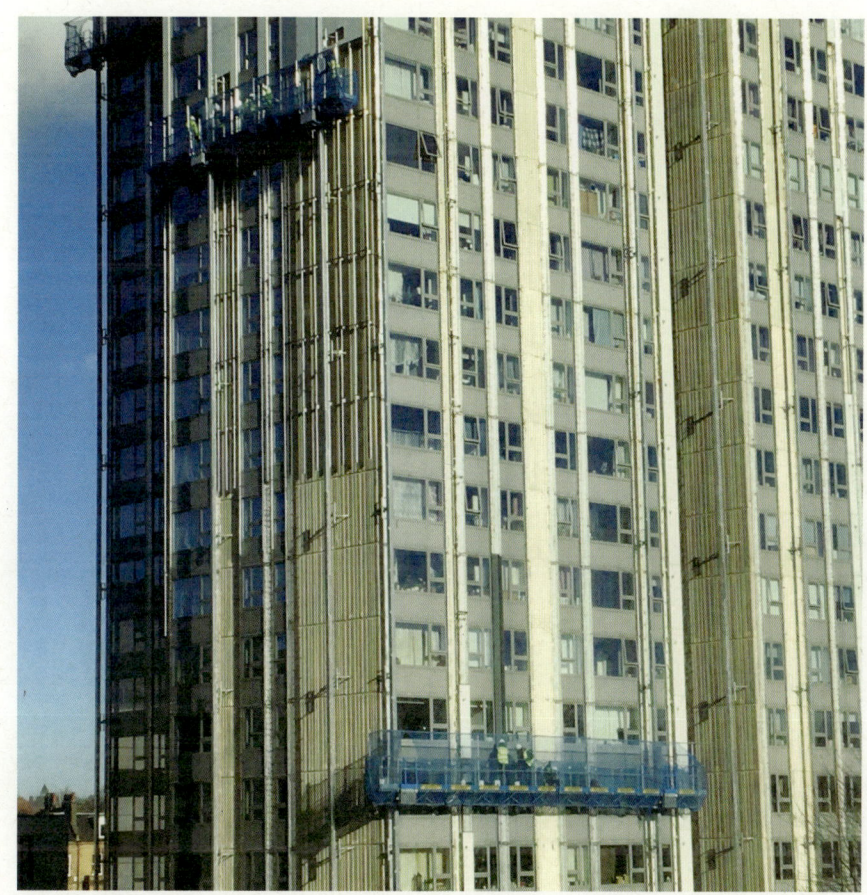

EXPOSED

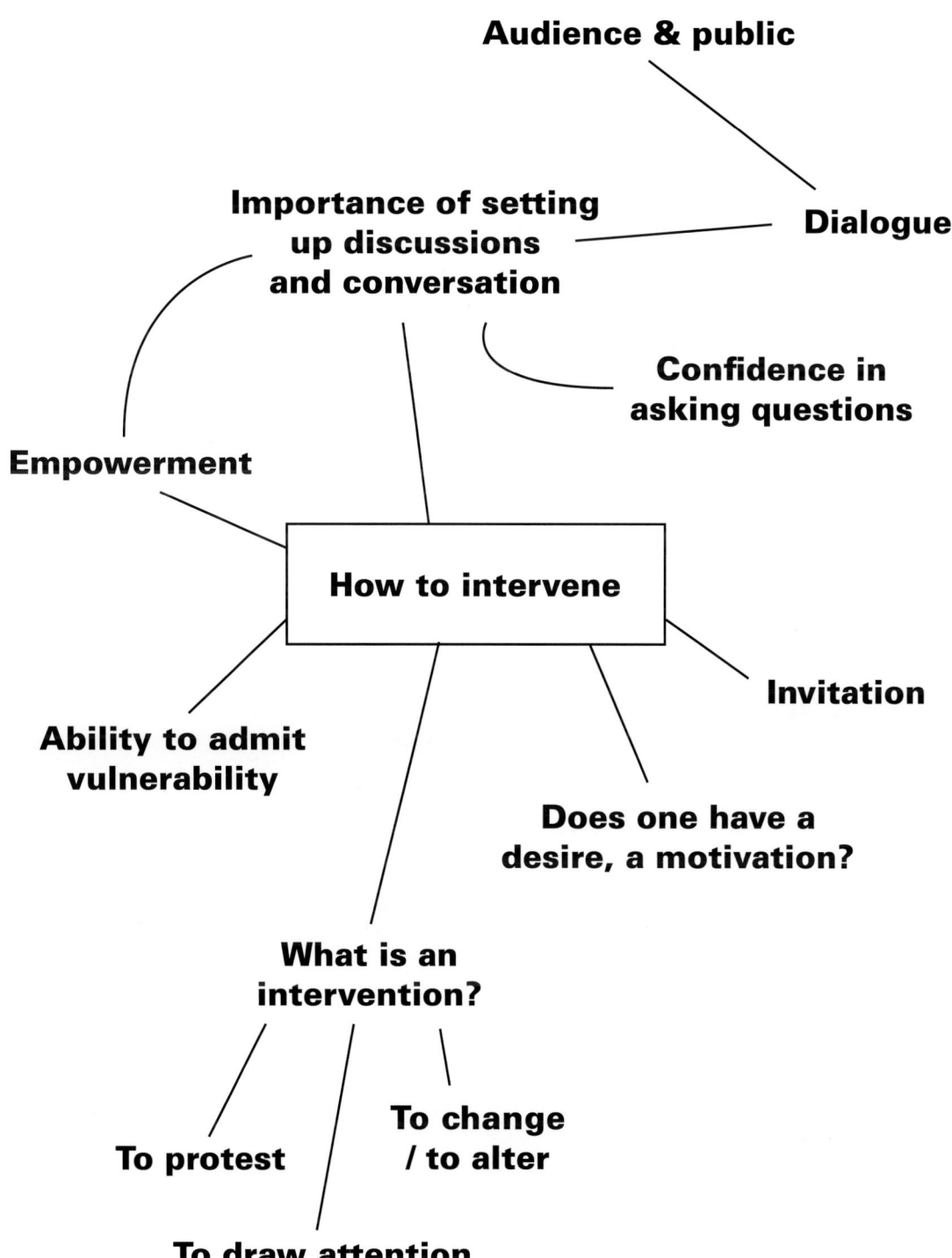

Audience & public

Dialogue

Importance of setting up discussions and conversation

Confidence in asking questions

Empowerment

How to intervene

Invitation

Ability to admit vulnerability

Does one have a desire, a motivation?

What is an intervention?

To protest

To change / to alter

To draw attention

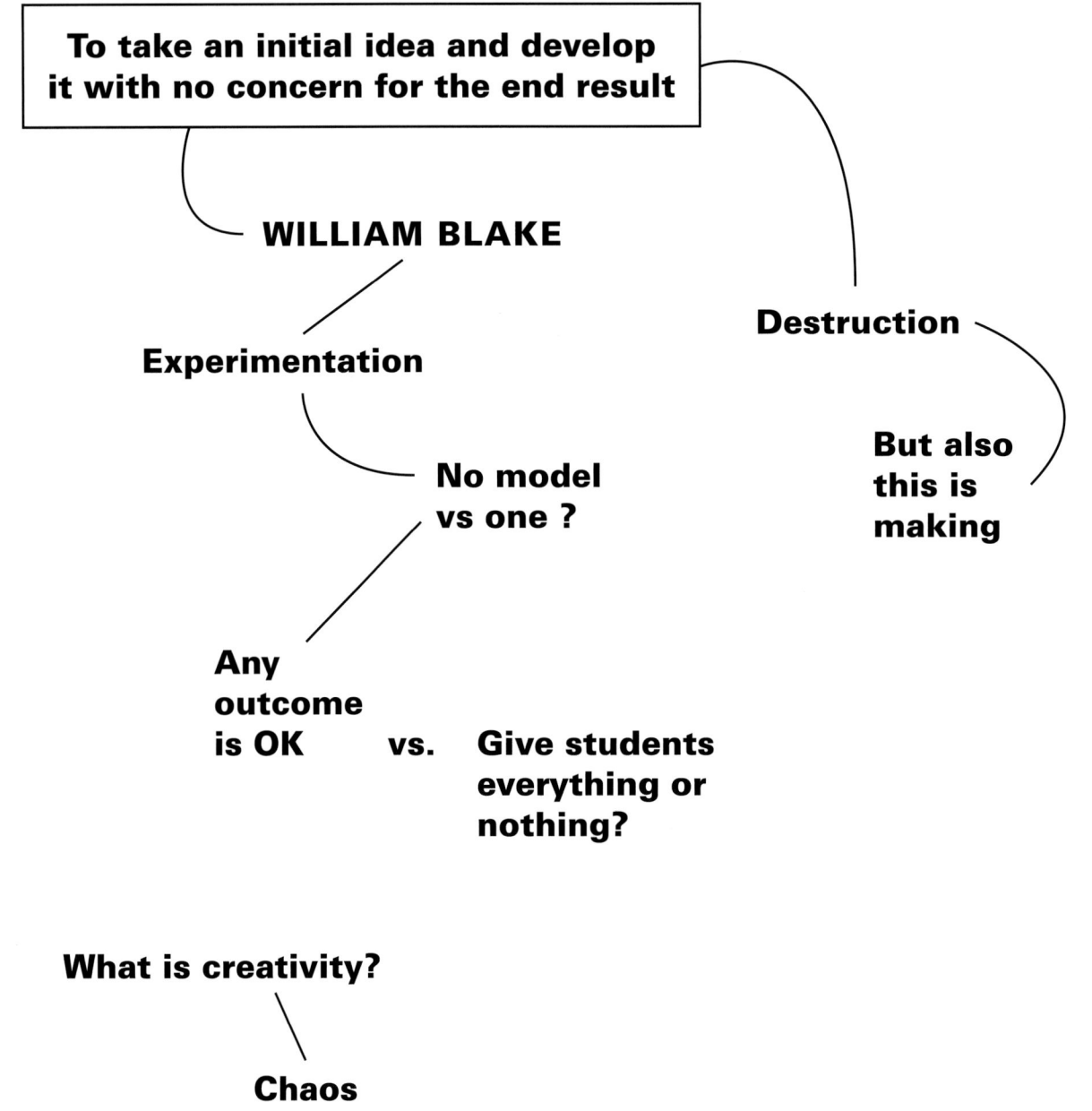

To take an initial idea and develop it with no concern for the end result

WILLIAM BLAKE

Experimentation

No model vs one ?

Destruction

But also this is making

Any outcome is OK   vs.   Give students everything or nothing?

What is creativity?

Chaos theory?

B
I
N
A
R
I
E
S

VERBS

Linguistically deny finality

Never use words like 'painting' or 'sculpture'

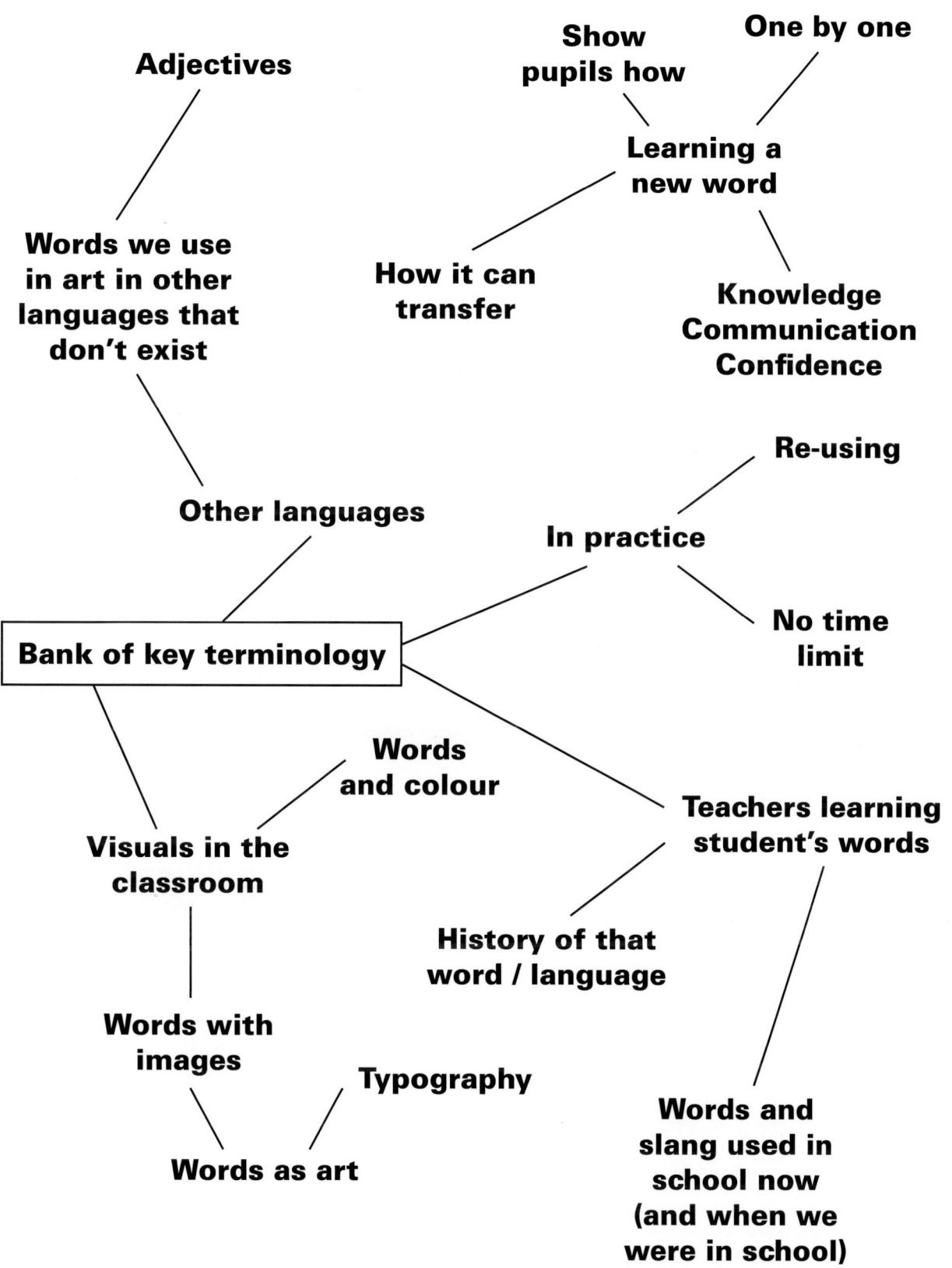

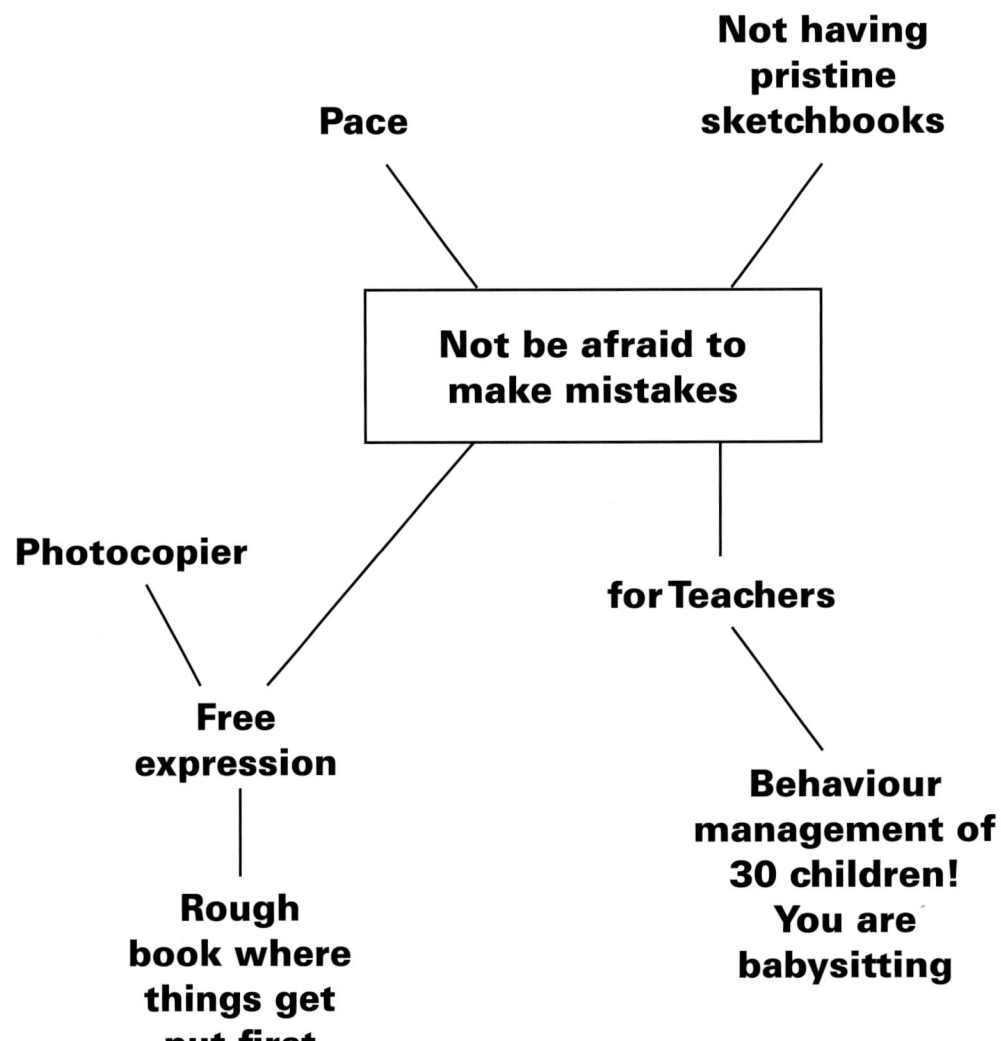

Pace

Not having
pristine
sketchbooks

Not be afraid to
make mistakes

Photocopier

for Teachers

Free
expression

Behaviour
management of
30 children!
You are
babysitting

Rough
book where
things get
put first

Index